T0354373

Also by William Pillow
*Grave Convictions*
*Love and Immortality: Long Journey of My Heart*
*Meet Yourself Again for the First Time*

# Mind, Body, & Spirit

## Challenges of Science and Faith

WILLIAM PILLOW

iUniverse, Inc.
New York   Bloomington

**Mind, Body, and Spirit**
**Challenges of Science and Faith**

*iUniverse books may be ordered through booksellers or by contacting:*

*iUniverse*
*1663 Liberty Drive*
*Bloomington, IN 47403*
*www.iuniverse.com*
*1-800-Authors (1-800-288-4677)*

*Because of the dynamic nature of the Internet, any Web addresses or links contained in this book may have changed since publication and may no longer be valid. The views expressed in this work are solely those of the author and do not necessarily reflect the views of the publisher, and the publisher hereby disclaims any responsibility for them.*

*ISBN: 978-1-4502-3663-8 (sc)*
*ISBN: 978-1-4502-3662-1 (ebook)*

*Library of Congress Control Number: 2010908424*

*Printed in the United States of America*

*iUniverse rev. date: 06/14/2010*

*For my beloved wife, Betty, whom I hope to see again when I too cross over into the spirit world*

# Contents

## PART FOUR
## IS THIS ALL THERE IS TO LIFE?

## PART FIVE
## WHY DO UNTO OTHERS?

## PART SIX
## THE FUTURE

# ACKNOWLEDGMENTS

Our Creator, my birth family, and our married family naturally come first for my gratitude in being able to write this book. I give special thanks to our son, Brad, and our daughter, Val, for their loving personal support, encouragement, and assistance in my writing.

Two other persons have served unceasingly in mentoring my writing, both from differing points of expertise. Lillian Stover Wells, PhD, retired dean of psychology at National University, has been of unparalleled assistance with regard to concepts in the book. Jack McMahan, a student of science and religion with degrees in theology and philosophy, continues to oversee grammatical and philosophical aspects of the book.

Near the close of this book, I say that I credit more than two-dozen other individuals and decisions in my life that contributed to the synchronicity I believe guided the paths I followed. Several were keystone figures. Allan Fore was my first father figure and the mentor of my following a career in pharmacy. Rob Hawkins was an ex-marine friend who helped me buy and insure my first car. Warren Weaver was a personally encouraging professor of pharmacy who later organized a group of Christian pharmacists. Eva May Scott was the pharmacist-owner for whom I first worked as a graduate pharmacist. Gary Draper was a personally supportive supervisor at Eli Lilly and Company. Also at Lilly, Robert Manning and Chuck Cavalier were instrumental in influencing a positive career for me there.

I greatly appreciate the permission extended to me by Llewellyn Worldwide, Woodbury, Minnesota, for enabling the reproduction of material from the four books by Michael Newton, Ph.D.

# INTRODUCTION

*"No amount of experimentation can ever prove me right;*
*a single experiment can prove me wrong."*
Albert Einstein

Welcome to our world! The crush of everyday life typically requires each of us to depend on beliefs we were taught or learned from experience. Don't touch the hot stove! Watch both ways before crossing the street! Mind your investments! Don't drink and drive!

Why would we ever doubt the wisdom of cherished beliefs: they are an integral part of us. But scientists are continually advancing remarkable theories that suggest a new paradigm about life itself. The fabric of our existence on earth is woven by the choices we make. Our thoughts shape our lives and wellbeing. Our minds, bodies, and spirits depend on our daily decisions and behavior. Sooner or later we may stumble across a surprising discovery that conflicts with our beliefs and genuine contemplation reveals that our discovery just may be true.

Recognizing that virtually none of us can keep informed about our changing world, this book shares my personal search for answers. The diverse topics offered here are not exhaustively discussed. For that, an extensive bibliography is provided. Rather, each chapter represents a different window on the human experience, from before birth until the time after physical death, including a perspective of our souls' existence in the spirit world. Within each chapter are unusual perspectives about our world and our selves. These offer new insights or different ways of thinking about our lives. Each revelation is built upon a strong foundation of more than two hundred reports from researchers around the world, included in the bibliography. For your convenience, an index is provided too.

Nevertheless, what you read here will stimulate within you a variety of reactions: humor, reassurance, surprise, shock, fear, doubt, or even rejection. However, this book also recognizes that you may be among the many who seem to be searching for greater meaning in their lives. You may find concepts herein that challenge your consideration despite your cherished beliefs. You may find that you need not deny your earlier thinking, just consider each idea with the serious question "What if...?" What would it mean for you and for your loved ones? The new "truth" may become more valuable to you than any dogma or cherished beliefs.

There are two consistencies that persist throughout this book. One is the skepticism that these pioneering researchers and I had shared about the metaphysical nature of their findings. They, like me, were trained and practiced as traditional scientists throughout most of their lives before they literally stumbled across their shocking discoveries. These included near-death and out-of-body experiences and past life and life-between-lives hypnotic regression. Despite their insistent searching of the medical literature at the time, these pioneers found nothing to explain their initial experiences. The other consistency involves the nearly identical results from thousands of studies, which make their reports all the more compelling (Moody; Morse; Newton; Ring; Weiss; and Whitten).

Please read this book as you would a mystery novel, allowing each twist and turn to carry you along in a swirling river of white water currents. Your mind's natural skepticism will ride shotgun to protect you from having to totally sacrifice closely held convictions. All the while just remember, "Truth often is stranger than fiction."

I was reared as a Southern Baptist and almost entered the Christian ministry early in my life. But I was encouraged by my mentor to become a pharmacist. After my retirement, my wife's lingering illnesses brought me concerns about life, death, and the hereafter, questions not clearly answered by my Christian upbringing. The more I searched, the more mind-boggling evidence I found that forced me to reconsider my lifelong skepticism about things which I couldn't prove or physically sense. This simply whetted my curiosity and challenged my natural disbelief.

All of my subsequent research over the past dozen or so years offered me the reassurance I was seeking. But it did even more. It challenged me to share with you what I discovered, as incredible as much of it appears. My previous work had involved editing two trade journals and writing texts for continuing pharmacy education. So I turned to my experience and wrote this and two previous books involving my surprising findings about life, death, and the afterlife. I wrote those books to force me to organize, clarify, and share what I had learned. This book expands upon those two publications by adding perspectives from new research.

It is important to note that the pioneers who uncovered the metaphysical concepts in this book were themselves reluctant to publish their discoveries until these were reinforced by their continuing research. They realized that their reports could jeopardize their professional standing because of the revolutionary nature of their findings. I too have noticed the jaundiced eyes and skeptical expressions from friends and acquaintances I've encountered about my books. But I'm so convinced of the importance of these new concepts that I'm compelled to share them with you.

This book does not intend to convince you about what you read here. It simply addresses your and my humanity—what makes us who we are as best I can determine from the most recent research. I ask only your willingness to contemplate topics according to their merit in your eyes.

My studies also reaffirmed my conviction about the intelligence and existence of a transcendent power that is beyond human conception and was the creative source of all nature and humankind. My research convinced me that this humanly unfathomable power always has existed in a non-physical (invisible) reality. A lack of the physical manifestation of that power in the modern world only adds to my wonder and respect for Our Creator's wisdom.

I believe there is a strong likelihood of the interconnectedness of everyone and everything in the cosmic universe. I feel that each human being was created with resourcefulness beyond our imagination to enable us to cope with adversity and to rise above our perceived limitations. In that sense this book explores how choices about our mind, body, and spirit can significantly influence our lives.

It is important to define the term "environment" as it appears in this book. It does not mean the most frequently used current application: parts of Mother Earth that are said to be threatened by emissions, oil drilling, reduction of wildlife habitat, and the like. Instead, environment encompasses the setting surrounding a person and the characteristics of that setting that may influence the person in some way. An example are the chemicals to which an expectant mother may be exposed and the potential effects of those chemicals on the mother-to-be and on the fetus.

Various terms are used in this book to refer to the Source of All, including the personal pronoun "He." This is not intended to imply that God is of a male gender. It simply is the conventional use of that pronoun in referring to the transcendent power.

Occasionally, scientific or personal details are included: the science helps reinforce the amazing nature of the subject and the personal offers a glimpse of feelings experienced by the author. Also, certain passages include references to other parts of the book pertinent to the discussion at hand.

For reference purposes, the bibliographic sources of content are cited as follows: for authors with multiple publications, each publication title or year will appear in the text with the author's name; for authors with a single publication, the author's name will appear in the text with the publication title; with the understanding that publication titles will appear in the text only the first time they are mentioned in the book. In rare instances where one or more authors' names are cited without publication titles or dates, this signifies that the text material appears in those authors' books or in their multiple books.

# PART ONE

---

# As a Man Thinketh, So is He

# CHAPTER ONE
# SOME FACTS ABOUT THINKING

---

*"The world we have created is a product of our thinking;
it cannot be changed without changing our thinking."*

Albert Einstein

---

As you read through this part of the book, you may question the value of paying so much attention to "thinking." However, I believe you'll find at least some of its dimensions worth contemplating further. After all, you might even wonder "What if...?" What would any of this mean not only for you but also for your family?

Even if this chapter sounds philosophical, it is based on sound scientific data. It provides a broad-brush look at just how significantly our thoughts can influence our health, our environment, our interpersonal relationships, and even our successes or disappointments.

The obvious advice is "just stop thinking about it!" Have you ever tried to stop thinking? Even seven-year-olds say they can't stop thinking enough to go to sleep. Mary Louise Bringle offered an excellent online article "I Just Can't Stop Thinking About It: Depression, Rumination, and Forgiveness" in *Word & World* 16/3 (1996).

So if our thinking controls our very being, what insights can we find on how to improve our thinking. Of course, there also is the matter of what objectives we have for influencing our thinking. Just as our thinking can have a negative impact on us, our thinking also can have a negative effect on others. The same is true for positive thinking.

## » Focused Thoughts

In an earlier book I described an aspect of thinking we all typically employ in performing routine tasks (2009). Examples are riding a bicycle, driving a car, and locking a door. If some skill is involved, as in driving a car, we master the skill then give little thought to it later. This is termed "procedural memory." We may even have forgotten when and from whom we learned how to perform the procedure.

Perhaps, like me, you may have driven a car, ridden a bicycle, or locked a door automatically. Later, I might question whether I did lock the door. Driving, I sometimes pass the intended highway exit if deep in thought about something else. Also like me, you even may be unable to account for what was going on around you during the previous several minutes, from a lapse in attention. This is not to criticize our action, but to acknowledge that it is a natural part of us.

As you might expect, focused thinking sometimes involves sincerity. We all participate in "rituals," from saying "Good morning" and "Thank you" to religious rituals. You will read later about evidence that subtle energy may be part of human behavior called "intention." This requires focused thinking, may involve sincerity, and is particularly applicable to intercessory prayer. This subtle energy may affect others as well as our selves. It's been shown, for example, that honest gratitude can have a beneficial effect on our bodies. Also, our feeling about caring for others can include both intention and sincerity, whether this is a personal act of helping another or an indirect act of contributing to a charity.

I have found it important to try to be more focused "in the moment" in everything I do. This seems nearly impossible with the flood of demands for my attention. But then I find that I don't have to question whether I locked the door or ignored a friend who passed by as I rushed somewhere.

## » Instinctive Ability with Numbers

One of the criticisms I have about today's store cash registers is that it deprives teen-agers manning checkout stands from counting out change. I've had experiences where cash registers were temporarily inoperable and young people had difficulty giving me the correct change. I grew up counting dollars and cents, almost without thinking. Maybe addition and subtraction is a bygone subject for early education.

But now scientists have found an innate ability in young children about counting. It is said to be "hard-wired" into the brain. A good example can be seen on television programs about mammals picking fruit. They instinctively go for the tree, bush, or limb with the most delectable. In short, some animals recognize a difference in quantity. Anthropologists found that humans in primitive cultures also have had a general grasp of quantity.

Recent brain imaging studies revealed "a sliver of the parietal cortex, on the surface of the brain about an inch above the ears, is particularly active when the brain judges quantity." Called the intraparietal sulcus, this area contains "clusters of neurons sensitive to the sight of specific quantities." They fire differently according to the number of objects seen: "Some vigorously at the sight of five … less so at the sight of four or six [or] not at all at two or nine. Others [respond according] to one, two, three, and so on."

According to Stanislas Dehaene, a cognitive neuroscientist at the Collège de France in Paris, "focused math education … sharpens the firing of these quantity neurons." He is author of the books *The Number Sense* and *Reading and the Brain*. He believes that this capability can "begin to communicate with neurons across the brain in language areas," enabling young children to put numbers into words.

Benedict Carey discussed Dehaene's work in his article "Studying Young Minds and How to Teach Them" in the online *New York Times*. According to Carey, scientists also say that "Cells in the visual cortex wired to recognize shapes specialize in recognizing letters … [can] communicate with neurons in the auditory cortex as the letters are associated with sounds," although this capability doesn't occur until about age eleven. As suggested by Dehaene, a focus on math education with young children can enhance their ability with numbers.

## » Irrational Thinking

Every one of us probably believes we always make rational choices. It may surprise you how wrong we often are. Two books provide an unusual perspective on human behavior from in-depth research. The books are Ori and Rom Brafman's book *Sway: The Irresistible Pull of Irrational Behavior* and Dan Ariely's book *Predictably Irrational: The Hidden Forces that Shape Our Decisions*.

Dan Ariely's online Weblog "Predictably Irrational" explained one factor that shapes our decisions and actions irrationally at times. Our cranial neocortex is the center of our higher mental functions not shared by other primates. But experience has shown that this does not *always* make us more rational than other animals. Apparently we humans add other considerations into making decisions from mental inputs not directly related to the decision at hand, emotions for example. Our neocortex provides our sense of right and wrong as well as empathy and the ability to reinforce societal rules. "Yet, in certain contexts, the neocortex can cause us not to maximize our self-interest," Ariely said. "Evolution then is a mixed blessing: it makes us better at some things and worse at others."

Ori and Rom Brafman's book provided illustrations from everyday life where seemingly irrational behavior resulted in outcomes ranging from the crash of a jumbo jet to auction bidding far beyond the value of an item. Their book offers suggested strategies for disarming irrational behavior by recognizing its implications.

Some illustrations of this behavior may seem humorous despite being true. They include:

- Having second helpings if it costs no more even when our stomachs are full
- Splurging on an expensive meal yet using a fifty-cent coupon on a can of soup
- Stealing office supplies but not money
- Never checking further about someone or something after our initial impression
- Willingly shelling out five dollars for a cup of coffee
- Pursuing a bad business plan rather than starting over

Examples of irrational thinking may make us chuckle. But it seems to be a fact that this is a learned behavior, a human trait that an individual likely will have difficulty changing. I believe psychologists would remind us that each of us becomes accustomed to his or her learned behavior over a lifetime and it's not readily susceptible to turning off or on like a light switch. Nevertheless, this human characteristic, like other learned behaviors, can be modified with appropriate effort.

## » Fantasies and Faux Pas

All of us at some time have had thoughts surface in our consciousness that we'd never, ever risk saying or doing. These range from the impolite to the risqué. Often, these occur at the most potentially embarrassing moments. Yet they are among the spectrum of thoughts that zip in and out of our heads.

Fortunately, we typically have enough self-control to be aware of the latent danger of succumbing to these moments. Our restraint may soften or even disappear if alcohol or drugs get involved. Tensions between individuals, at work, at home, or elsewhere may push us over the cliff, and soon it's too late to withdraw what's been said or done.

Benedict Carey provided insight into this kind of thinking in his article "When the Imp in Your Brain Gets Out" in the *New York Times* online. He quoted from Edgar Allen Poe's essay on unwanted impulses *The Imp of the Perverse*: "That single thought is enough. The impulse increases to a wish, the wish to a desire, the desire to an uncontrollable longing." Once the words have flown or the act is done, beware the consequences.

The "imp" obviously is an impulse that naturally might have appeared in our thoughts in our very early years before we learned to behave according to social norms. The *American Heritage College Dictionary* calls an imp "a mischievous child" or "demon." One cause might be the adolescent male urge that accompanies the surge of testosterone. However, as you'll read later in this book, the proverbial "hell" now is believed to be a product of our minds, just like the devil and demons.

Interestingly, Rebecca Webber had an article "The Wholesome Guide to Misbehaving" in *Psychology Today*. The kind of misbehavior she addresses includes "what time we get to work, how far over the speed limit we drive, [and] what kinds of white lies we tell." She also recognizes that being naughty makes us feel nice and allows us to sense a different life style. But Webber acknowledges that such behavior helps us realize that this conduct "might not be sustainable for the long term." No doubt some people may consider this article to be on the cusp of encouraging very risky behavior that could backfire.

## » Territoriality

This discussion applies too to the topic on "Intractable Situations" in the later chapter on evil. But it applies most directly to how people think and behave. Territoriality is natural because it arises from primitive animal instincts. You've likely watched the territoriality of wild animals in videos of African wild life parks. They mark their territories to discourage competitors. Other family members typically treat the matriarch or patriarch with respect. Often this role is hard-won and vigorously defended.

The problem with this thinking in humans is the extremes to which some people go. Even though the human habitat is drastically different from the African savannah, human self-control is too often lacking. Road rage and spousal abuse are examples. Competitive behavior in the business world sometimes reaches a similar intensity. Individuals and groups practice territoriality. It has been the cause of wars, ethnic discrimination, and ideological differences.

Serge Kahili King's online article "Territoriality" suggests that the passion humans invest in protecting their turf might be more wisely used "to focus intensely on [more worthwhile pursuits] and energize that focus with all your love, power and skill. Who knows what amazing things might result?"

## » Perceived Threats

As perceived by a group, state, nation, or world, a threat is generally viewed as something that could wreak harm on a significant number of human beings. But an individual best recognizes a personally perceived threat. The potential list is limitless, ranging from a personal insult to a confrontation by an armed person or a dangerous animal. Stress may persist in a continuing perceived threat, such as an authoritarian supervisor. The degree of threat seemed related to an individual's felt extent of control over the situation. Ronald Rapee's online abstract of his research paper "Perceived Threat and Perceived Control as Predictors of the Degree of Fear in Physical and Social Situations" addressed this variable.

Occasionally, humans might take lessons from animals. A fascinating case in point was illustrated in Olivia Judson's article "Leopard Behind You" that appeared in The Wild Side section of the

*New York Times* online. She described various animals' vocal warnings about threats of dangerous predators. The word "dangerous" is used because, for example, an eagle might be a threat to small mammals but not to adult antelopes. Various animals therefore have an assortment of different alert calls that have a particular meaning. Young ones seem to learn these from their parents. Animals other than the kind issuing the alert have learned to pay attention too, apparently able to recognize whether the warning is applicable also to them.

The illustration seems especially applicable to this part of the book in our efforts to be our "brother's keeper." Neighborhood watches seem to be expanding in our country. Parents and older siblings sometimes are successful in helping younger kids avoid the peer attraction of gang membership. Recently there even seems to be more state and national activism among the formerly "silent majority." Sadly, though, there seems to be an understood penalty on the "street" for anyone caught "ratting" to the police about the identity of the perpetrator of a crime.

## » Spiritual Threats

This topic is included in this chapter to illustrate the power of our thoughts. "Thoughts" as used here involve our mindsets: our beliefs, attitudes, convictions, insecurities, fears, uncertainties, and such other thoughts we hold about life and death.

You've heard it said that "you can't carry it with you" when you die. But noted psychic James Van Praagh disagreed. His book *Ghosts Among Us: Uncovering the Truth About the Other Side* claimed that the human mindset we have at death of the physical body can significantly influence our souls' transition to the spirit world. Van Praagh wrote that souls do carry their human state of mind with them. Such mindsets might include misperceptions of death, fear of eternal damnation, or disbelief in God or Heaven.

Van Praagh indicated that any such negative thought energy might impede souls' access to the "white light" and to the higher astral levels. Instead, souls might confine themselves to a lower plane, at least initially. Both Van Praagh and Michael Newton's book *Destiny of Souls* claim that the spirit world respects a soul's choice even if it is based on faulty information.

Van Praagh describes ghosts as earth-bound souls who refuse to leave the earth plane for a number of reasons. For example, they may believe they're not dead, some have unfinished business, or others may want to protect their loved ones. By contrast, those souls who appear to get stuck in a low astral plane seem to be locked into their earthly mindset. Only as they willingly seek freedom from that state of mind to progress spiritually do they move into higher astral planes.

If this were true, it would appear that the mindsets people acquire might account for so-called "negative" near-death experiences (NDEs). These cases exist but occur much less frequently than positive NDEs. Survivors of negative NDEs often described their experiences as confusing, disturbing, or even "hellish." Some researchers suggested that patients' reactions might be caused by their fright, bewilderment, or even religious beliefs (Chopra 2006).

Howard Storm's book *My Descent Into Death* described his negative NDE that turned positive when he eventually called upon Jesus to save him. This transitory aspect of negative NDEs seems fairly common (Sabom 1982).

You may share the skepticism I used to have about all things paranormal, especially psychics. Now I believe there are a few psychics with genuine talents and a great many more who have only marginal abilities or even are frauds. Thousands of Van Praagh's clients over the past twenty-five years have testified to his accuracy and integrity.

## » Temperament

Temperament is a human trait defined by the online *Merriam-Webster Dictionary* as the "characteristic or habitual inclination or mode of emotional response." Robin Henig provided a fascinating glimpse of researchers' studies about the causes of human anxiety. Harvard's Jerome Kagan initiated the work in 1989. Henig published the *New York Times* online article "Understanding the Anxious Mind" describing Kagan's studies and results.

Henig wrote that infants which displayed "being easily upset when exposed to new things" at four months "were more likely to grow up to be inhibited, shy, and anxious." Kagan believed that two physiological influences contributed to this, stemming from the activity of the brain's amygdala and its prefrontal cortex. The amagdala senses "perceived" threats while the prefrontal cortex dampens those signals. Using MRI brain scans, researchers detected two different levels of brain development in some of the babies: a highly reactive amygdala and/or an unusually thickened prefrontal cortex.

Kagan and his colleagues attempted to correlate the MRI findings between babies who "were in constant motion, kicking and moving their arms fitfully, furrowing their brows, arching their backs, or crying" with those "who gazed contently throughout" the studies. Longitudinal research enabled these studies to follow up the social behavioral traits of these babies during adolescence and later. Those who exhibited overly reactive behavior as babies typically professed perceived uncertainties, unease, or imagined threats as they grew older.

Interestingly, these studies did not account for the unconscious environmental influences experienced by those babies *before* four months of age. The chief source of these influences exists in the implicit memory system. The following explanation was quoted from the online presentation "The Two Pathways of Fear" (advanced level) from the Canadian Institutes of Health Research:

> "The parallel operation of our explicit [hippocampal] and implicit [amygdalic] memory systems explains why we do not remember traumas experienced very early in our lives. At that age, the hippocampus is still immature, while the [fear-sensing] amygdala is already able to record subconscious [implicit] memories. Early childhood traumas can disturb the mental and behavioral functions of adults by mechanisms that they cannot access consciously."

Implicit memory is imprinted in the subconscious mind. Emotion and event memories recorded there in early childhood are not consciously recallable but remain to influence unconscious response to stimuli throughout one's life. Note that the fear-sensing amygdala is mature at birth, while the compensating prefrontal cortex (fear-suppressing) develops later.

A possible breakthrough has been made in showing the effects of implicit memory on the brain. An online article by Deborah Brauser announced this research. Amit Etkin and colleagues at Stanford

University, Palo Alto, California, found that "patients [with generalized anxiety disorder] were completely unable to regulate emotional conflict and failed to engage the pregenual anterior cingulate [area of the brain] in ways that would dampen amygdalar activity [of the brain]." The researchers further noted that this is the "first solid demonstration that a psychiatric population has a deficit in a form of unconscious [implicit] emotion regulation." This fits in with the theory, from Freud forward, that "abnormality in unconscious [implicit] emotion regulation is one of the core deficits."

An infant's (and even a fetus's) early emotional experiences can leave unconscious emotional scars. For example, it is a documented fact that newborns focus on their mothers' faces at birth and those deprived of mothers' nurture can develop "attachment disorder."

In contrast, some mothers may feel that their children possess exceptional traits such as intelligence, athletics, competitiveness, resourcefulness, leadership, or extroversion. These parents would seem likely to praise these qualities and could instill in their children false beliefs. Such might be the case in some situations involving children who boast an Indigo status as discussed later in this book.

Temperament has been considered an inherited trait. However, the online article "Boys and Temperament" quotes the conclusion of child psychiatric researchers Stella Chess and Alexander Thomas that "temperament has nine irreducible components ... from birth [it] begins to react with the temperament of others [even parents] ... [and] with the environment."

Joseph Wyatt's online article "Is Temperament Inherited?" cites an article in *Psychology Today* which claims that "babies may indeed be born with temperamental predispositions but that is not to say those are inherited ... a fetus gets an enormous amount of hormonal 'bathing' through the mother [and she] puts out hormones in response to stress." The article emphasizes, "Highly pressured mothers-to-be tend to have more active fetuses and then more irritable infants." The fetus and baby's environment seems to have a much greater influence on temperament than once was recognized.

## » Expectations

Expectations seem to have an uncanny way of influencing outcomes of wishes, hopes, and prayers, just as discussed in later topic in this book called "The Power of Focused Intention." Excellent examples of the potential effect of negative expectations are mentioned in the next chapter in the discussion of placebo and nocebo mindsets. It obviously is uncertain what specific nature of expectations might influence outcomes. But it seems likely that anticipating the worst, perhaps because of a previous experience, would not be most conducive to success. You might imagine that young people with a string of turndowns behind them would not make particularly appealing appearances as they reluctantly further pursue job openings. Inner fear sometimes shows.

Achieving human potential is implicit if not explicit in many discussions in this book. Obviously, such achievement depends upon how we think about the life into which we were born: not just how we think at any particular time, but how we *continue* to think—our attitude—toward life itself. If you have any question about your own potential, you'll want to read Patrick Henry Hughes' story in the discussion later in this book entitled "Angels in Disguise."

*Time* magazine had an article in its Social Norms section that seems to reflect another influence of negative thinking. It is John Cloud's article "Why Your Memory May Not Be So Bad After All: New Data on How Internalizing Stereotypes Affects Boomers." Cloud asks why "some minority groups continue to perform worse than others on academic tests as well as ... income and job status." One theory is that members of these groups may internalize characteristics that stereotyping perpetuates. In other words, they may "expect to do worse." The article also cites a new study reported in the *Experimental Aging Research* journal which shows that "older people can ... become victims ... of low expectations."

## » Emotions as Thoughts

Holistic physician Bradley Nelson's book *The Emotion Code: How to Release Your Trapped Emotions for Abundant Health, Love, and Happiness* described an interesting experiment demonstrating the effects of emotion on white blood cells, a protective component of our immune system. This involved a man who remembered feeling constantly threatened by kamikaze bombers while serving on an aircraft carrier in the Pacific during World War II.

White blood cells were withdrawn from his blood and placed in a Petri dish. He was connected to electrodes that measured the electrical activity of his body. The Petri dish was placed at some distance in a special device that could record the electrical activity of the white blood cells. The subject then watched newsreel footage of kamikaze suicide pilots diving toward his carrier. His somatic (body) memory of the earlier threat to his life caused a spike in his body's electrical activity. Surprisingly, across the room, the monitor of his white blood cells' electrical activity showed the same spike. These results were replicated even when his white blood cells were in another room or in a distant laboratory! Later in this book you'll read scientific findings that even dogs, plants, and water seemed able to "read" inexplicable energy emissions from people's intentions or emotions. This phenomenon may be related to what some call the "observer effect," discussed later in this book as "Consciousness Effect on Quantum Behavior."

The American Academy of Family Physicians' Web site FamilyDoctor.org stressed the "Mind-Body Connection: How Your Emotions Can Affect Your Health." It listed nine life situations that "can disrupt your emotional health and lead to strong feelings of sadness, stress or anxiety." These included death of a loved one, job loss, having a baby, divorce, money problems, and moving to a new home. The article also emphasized that "good" changes can be just as stressful as "bad" changes. The site made the point that patients always should inform their physician even if an annoying complaint doesn't appear to be evidence of illness, but "your body tries to tell you that something isn't right."

Gary Wilson and Marnia Robinson provided a fascinating perspective about emotions in their online article "Love and Fear" that appeared in the journal *Entelechy: Mind and Culture*. They acknowledge that various spiritual teachings say fear and love are the "only two fundamental emotions." Wilson and Robinson also claim that the bodies of humans and other mammals recognize this as a true fact. Threatening sensations from fear stimulate increased levels of the stress hormones adrenaline and cortisol. By contrast, feelings associated with love have soothing and reassuring effects and cause increased levels of oxytocin.

These authors further describe the powerful effects of oxytocin on our bodies. Oxytocin:

- Reduces fear and speeds healing
- Reduces antisocial behavior
- Counteracts the effects of the stress hormone cortisol
- Calms anxiety
- May increase longevity
- Has been nicknamed the "bonding" or "cuddle" hormone

As a unique neurochemical, oxytocin perpetuates its own effects. In other words, increasing its levels improves the mind and body's response to it. It actually seems to cause nerve cells to sprout more oxytocin receptors, causing them to be more sensitive to its effects. In case you're wondering, oxytocin cannot be safely and effectively administered as a medication.

## » Concern About Body Image

Girls, in particular, may "inherit" a dangerous character trait from their mothers. It's called body dysmorphic disorder (BDD). This does not appear to be a genetic disorder but an overbearing concern about their bodies. It can relate to their self-confidence, affect their eating habits, and cause them to resort to cosmetic surgery. Research suggests that high levels of concern about body image begin in preteens. BDD is estimated to occur in about one in fifty people.

Children whose mother has an inordinate preoccupation about her body image are susceptible to this disorder. "If a girl watches her mother valuing appearance as crucial, she will come to see it as crucial to her understanding of being female." As adolescent girls are subjected to actual and perceived peer pressure, their self-confidence and self-esteem are paramount factors. This may precipitate BDD.

Susie Orbach is a thought-leader in cultural influences on women's attitudes about their body image and its impact on their behavior. She is a psychotherapist with a private practice in London. Her book *Bodies* reflects results of her research. This discussion is based on an interview with Orbach conducted by Pippa Wysong and Natalia Sloam that appeared online in *Medscape* Family Medicine, entitled "The Pursuit of Bodily Perfection."

Research by Orbach and Nancy Etcoff from Harvard University found that "only 2% of women felt able to say that they were beautiful ... half of 16- to 21-year-old girls would consider having surgery to change [their appearance, and] more than 1 in 10 girls aged 11 to 16 would consider having a gastric ... or cosmetic surgery." Eating disorders are another potential outcome of BDD. Orbach blames cultural influences too. Fashion ads, emphasis on beautiful bodies, and Broadway and Hollywood trendsetters are culpable. Society invites us to believe "that our bodies are not all right as they are."

## » Contagious Moods

Have you ever noticed that your mood may change according to the company you keep? In other words, other people's happiness or optimism may brighten your mood. Research has shown this to be true, not just imagined. People's happiness is largely influenced by the happiness of those they are connected to—whether they know them personally or not. This is the conclusion reached in a study by investigators James Fowler and Nicholas Christakis published in the *British Medical Journal*. It was part of the twenty-year Framingham Heart Study.

Likewise, "depression is contagious," said Michael Yapko in his article "Secondhand Blues" in *Psychology Today*. Yapko claims that depression is spread through social contact with family members and intimate others. Although the participants in the Framingham study were adults, Yapko's article stressed that depression may have biological roots in how a child is reared. Sturdy social relationships depend upon early bonding with parents and significant others. Apathetic and withdrawn mothers suffering from postpartum depression don't interact with their babies the way non-depressed mothers do. So the emotional region of those babies' brains may be underdeveloped and induce more depression in the children. "The notion that depression can be spread ... as a social contagion is supported by a great deal of evidence," Yapko said.

So what is the moral to this research? You can't control your parents' behavior but you can choose your friends.

## » Executive Decisions

These decisions are not choices made by corporate executives. They are decisions that seem to emanate from specific areas of our brains, as identified by electronic brain imaging. As evidence grows, it is apparent that these decisions may vary in terms of the type and extent of mental resources applied or required. One human requirement for making these decisions is focus or attention. It seems that the human capacity for this is not limitless. Its use can become so strenuous as to be exhausting.

For example, *Scientific American* carried an article "Tough Choices: How Making Decisions Tires Your Brain," by On Amir. "When you focus on a specific task for an extended period of time" even in simply choosing a meal to prepare or eat, "you are flexing your executive function muscles. When this resource is exhausted by one activity, our mental capacity may be severely hindered in another, seemingly unrelated activity." Researchers claim that this is true regardless of whether the decision is a major or minor one. Also, the amount of self-control and attention needed to decide and implement the outcome can be taxing like exercise is to a muscle. This should encourage all of us to take breaks periodically to prevent mental exhaustion.

## » Intelligence

Because you will see this term used in various parts of this book it seems appropriate to describe how it is defined as best I can determine it. It is discussed in this chapter on thinking because thinking involves more reasoning than intelligence does. In computer language, the *American Heritage College Dictionary* said intelligence is "having certain data storage and processing capabilities." In this context intelligence focuses more on the application of information. Just like computers, living organisms have the ability to acquire (or be programmed with) information. Then, innately or through experience or programming, they can use that information in survival, growth, and reproduction.

Stuart Pullen's book *Intelligent Design or Evolution? Why the Origin of Life and the Evolution of Molecular Knowledge Imply Intelligent Design* defines life as "possessing molecular knowledge and a mechanism to implement this knowledge in such a way that the system can survive long enough to replicate itself." In my book, "intelligence" is used in a minimalistic sense, i.e., having certain capabilities but not restricted to them. For example, a rock would not possess intelligence, a living cell would, and a human being would also possess other qualities such as reasoning.

In a larger sense, however, developmental psychologist Howard Gardner's book *Frames of Mind: The Theory of Multiple Intelligences* suggests that we forget thinking of intelligence as a single property of the human mind that can be tested by a standard intelligence test. Instead, consider that intelligence is represented by an assortment of competencies that are valued by society. For example, he offers groups of skills such as linguistic, musical, logical-mathematical, spatial, and bodily-kinesthetic. As such, the "intelligence" of professionals like musicians, athletes, fine artists, and scientists would be considered individual in their own right.

## » Sensing Other People's Thoughts

This discussion is humorously titled but researchers in social psychology claim that it actually occurs in our behavior in interpersonal relationships. As with much human behavior, there appears a degree of uncertainty whether we consciously carry out these actions very often. However, it is a well-known fact that spouses, twins, and some parents and their children literally can "read" each other's thoughts. This happens because their experiences are closely entwined and they find that they often think the same way. In order for you to access more details than are offered here it is necessary to introduce you to the three words under which you'll find this information in online searches: "social cognition and attribution."

"Social" obviously denotes our interpersonal relationships. Kendra Van Wagner defined "cognition" in the online reference "What is Cognitive Psychology?" as "mental processes involved in gaining knowledge and comprehension, including thinking, knowing, remembering, judging, and problem solving." Children begin to develop cognition around ages two to four. "Attribution" typically is used to credit a person or thing with certain qualities or responsibility. In the context of social psychology the term means that which we ascribe or conclude as a belief about someone or something.

The third concept, attribution, may be the least obvious but seems to be very prevalent in human behavior. In Carl Zimmer's article "Brain Trust" in *Discover* magazine, he quoted researcher Rebecca Saxe, "We feel as if we can *see* what other people are thinking [like in vision] ... we feel as if we're getting a perfect view of everything the way it really is." This may seem ridiculous, but it's based on our conviction that we understand what motivates us and therefore must motivate others too. Saxe is attempting to define the mechanism in brains that she said is "very complicated and specific ... generating these inferences and perceptions."

One example of attribution might be in competing with others. A sports team could study their opponents "thinking" to defeat the other team's strategy. A company might try to underbid its competitor by feeling it knows the competitor's approximate bid. But imagine the problematic situations this tendency could produce as we act on our assumptions about other *individuals'* thinking. The potential list seems endless unless, of course, we guard against behaving too blatantly. Otherwise we may be accused of excessive self-confidence.

The next chapter examines the influences of our thoughts on our health and wellbeing.

## CHAPTER TWO
# MIND-BODY INFLUENCES

*"If you realized how powerful your thoughts are,
you would never hold onto a negative thought."*

Peace Pilgrim

Because good health is of paramount importance, let's start by examining how significantly—even though unintentionally—our thoughts can control our body functions. If you have had any doubts, we will review later a new concept characterized in the book *The Extracellular Matrix and Ground Regulation: Basis for Holistic Biological Medicine* by pioneer researcher Alfred Pischinger. This describes the control mechanisms by which the human body attempts to sustain homeostasis or balance among its various systems.

## » From the Beginning

Perhaps mind-body influences are best introduced by starting at the beginning—the beginning of life, that is. Mothers, most dads, and some of the rest of us realize the intimate physiological relationship between mother and fetus, typically lasting for about nine months. Not only do blood and other nutrients flow through the umbilical cord, but also a wide variety of biochemicals. These biochemicals are the same ones that naturally appear in the mother's body to help regulate her wellbeing. Cellular biologist Bruce Lipton's book *The Biology of Belief: Unleashing the Power of Consciousness, Matter, and Miracles* stresses that the natural intent of the mother's body is to help prepare her newborn for living in her environment.

Yet, even a mother's thinking can unintentionally but significantly influence the fetus's growth and development through increased levels of biochemicals such as adrenaline. These can be unconsciously generated within her body and passed to the fetus. Pathik D. Wadhwa and his colleagues at the University of Kentucky College of Medicine found statistically significant results in their online report that appeared in *Science Daily*. "The magnitude of the fetal responses to challenge was greater in women with medical problems, high levels of stress hormones, high levels of psychological stress, and low levels of social support," according to the study.

The study is among the first to suggest that factors related to medical, endocrine, and psychosocial stress during human pregnancy might negatively affect fetal brain development and function. This appears in measurements of fetal reactivity and learning. The effects of early environment on development seem like those of a double-edged sword. Optimal environments may produce beneficial effects on brain development, and hostile environments may produce detrimental effects.

Lipton emphasized that hormones responsible for the instinctive "fight-or-flight" response induced by stress in the mother's body can have the same action in the fetus: divert nutrition from growth to areas of the fetal body for protection. "The hormones of a mother experiencing chronic stress will profoundly alter the distribution of blood flow in her fetus and change the character of her developing child's physiology."

In their article "Developmental Influences on Medically Unexplained Symptoms" in *Psychotherapy and Psychosomatics*, Buffington and colleagues wrote, "Maternal perception of a threatening environment may ... effectively 'program' the fetal stress response system and associated behaviors toward enhanced vigilance."

## » Early Childhood

Now jump forward to early childhood. Imagine a toddler not yet possessing cognition: the acquired ability to make sense of the world. Shift from the influence of the mother's state of mind to that of the youngster. Since birth the child's parents have been his or her idols of authority, whose judgment never can be questioned. A parental reprimand or rebuke may provoke an emotional response in the child because he or she doesn't yet understand the reason. Criticism of the child may have seemed justifiable in the eyes of the parent or other caregiver. But it is incumbent on the adult to help the child cope with such a negative, probably unexpected ultimatum.

Mental health professionals say it is vital to use such situations as learning experiences for the child. It is important to explain, in a loving manner the youngster can understand, why he or she was criticized and any particular restrictions were imposed as a result. It is equally important to reassure the child of the parents' love.

Child development researchers say that a young child's repeated storage of images of disapproval without commensurate reassurances of love and support can be detrimental. They can lead to his or her becoming overly inhibited, defensively hostile, and even clinically depressed. Shame is a possible outcome in life. Role modeling by the parent helps the child positively deal with mistaken impressions about parental censure. This should provide the child self-confidence later in life that is able to cope with life's exigencies and move forward.

Obviously, once the child is older and has developed both verbal ability and an emerging self-concept, he or she may be less likely to accept another's behavior as authoritative. But we are told that this typically does not occur until ages three to four. In the earlier stage of life, however, children can be immensely susceptible to generating excessive or insufficient levels of neurotransmitters, for example. The New Hampshire Natural Health Clinic's Web site describes the causes and impact of neurotransmitter imbalances in the young and offers testing and treatment.

## » Later Years

Fast-forward to adulthood, to your and my mind-body influences. Lipton's book has a section entitled "Homeland Defense." It deals not with the country's defense against the menace of terrorist groups, but with potential threats that our internal sensors might register. He mentions two separate ways our bodies could be affected by sensing stress. One is the hypothalamus-pituitary-adrenal axis (HPA). "When the hypothalamus perceives an environmental threat, it [sends] a signal to the pituitary gland ... which is responsible for organizing the fifty trillion cells ... to deal with the threat. When the HPA mobilizes the body for fight or flight response, the adrenal hormones directly repress the action of the immune system in order to conserve energy reserves." The other is our immune system, responsible for protecting our bodies through the antigen-antibody response to invading bacteria and viruses. Obviously, this system is not under conscious control.

Probably one of the most successful approaches ever popularized to control stress was a technique published by mind-body researcher Herbert Benson. His book *The Relaxation Response* first appeared in 1976. An updated version was released in 2000. Benson said most people react to stress as described by Lipton in the preceding paragraph. The results can adversely affect the body in many ways. Benson proposed that his "relaxation response" method be followed once or twice daily to break the "stress response" cycle.

The relaxation response method involves finding ten to twenty minutes each morning, probably shortly after arising, during which to totally relax. Sitting rather than lying down likely will prevent going back to sleep. Keeping time is OK, but don't set an alarm. Place a clock out of eyesight. You may turn to check the time when you think at least ten minutes have passed.

Close your eyes and relax your mind. Intentionally refrain from focusing on the cares of the day, the worries about tomorrow, and the afterthoughts of yesterday. One of the best ways to do this is to have something to concentrate on, such as a short prayer, breathing, or a mantra (word or phrase). This should be repeated slowly and continually throughout the period with awareness. If other thoughts intrude, just allow them to pass away without considering them.

Twenty minutes and twice daily is preferable. This daily practice over time will condition your body to diminish the intensity of your emotional or instinctive stress response. You will find that meditation has a similar approach. These topics also are discussed later in this book.

We often are distracted from consciously sensing how our bodies are reacting to environmental influences. We may have a "gut" feeling or a sense of discomfort or anxiety. But most of our emotional reactions occur unconsciously, without our stopping to ask ourselves what's happening within our body. If the tempo is especially high pitched, we likely are not "in the moment" but our thoughts are racing ahead to plan our next move.

Segerstrom, Schipper, and Greenberg at University of Kentucky Department of Psychology studied the impact of repetitious negative thinking on the results of influenza vaccination in caregivers. All caregivers are considered to be under stress. But the researchers found that repetitious *negative* thinking diminished blood responses to influence vaccine whereas simple repetitious *reflective* thinking did not.

Both Lipton's book and Harold and Daralyn Brody's book *The Placebo Response: How You Can Release the Body's Inner Pharmacy for Better Health* were cited to offer excellent examples of the placebo (positive) and nocebo (negative) effects of our thinking on our wellbeing. In a sense, both mental influences could be interpreted as examples of the effects of focused intention, the former positive and the latter negative.

At the risk of repetition for readers of my or other books, let me summarize these examples. A patient's cancer positively responded to Krebiozen (placebo). However, he died later when he heard the Food and Drug Administration announce conclusively that the drug was worthless (nocebo). A patient diagnosed with esophageal cancer who understood it to be fatal died soon afterwards (nocebo). However, an autopsy discovered insufficient cancer or any other malady that could kill him. Patients may "feel" an imagined side effect (nocebo) to a medicine.

In their book *Alternative Medicine: The Definitive Guide*, Burton Goldberg and his colleagues claim, "The immune system, like the central nervous system, has a memory and the capacity to learn. Thus, it could be said that intelligence is located in every cell of the body and that the traditional separation of mind and body no longer applies."

The National Center for Complementary and Alternative Medicine published an excellent online paper "Mind-Body Medicine: An Overview." Topics discussed there include:

- Mind-body interventions
- Mind-body influences on immunity
- Meditation and imaging

- Placebo response
- Stress and wound healing
- Preparation for surgery

Raman's book *Power of the Mind: Experiencing, Harnessing, and Utilizing the Force Within* offers a collection of mental exercises and case examples for reducing stress and improving wellbeing.

## » HIV

No diagnosis seems so wide spread throughout the world carrying a death sentence as HIV. Treatments continue to improve, adding extra years to life. But Barbara Hagerty found a researcher, Gail Ironson, who scientifically had documented the impact of patient attitude on progress of the disease. Imagine, though, how difficult it must be to have anything but negative beliefs after being found to have HIV. Hagerty's book *Fingerprints of God: The Search for the Science of Spirituality* described the findings of Gail Ironson and her fellow researchers.

For over ten years Ironson had tracked the lives of HIV patients (2006). She found many of them "alive seven, eight years past diagnosis." Psychologically these were patients who not only were less depressed but also were fighters, simply not accepting the worst. Interestingly, they also spoke of "spirituality" or "relationship with God." The latter might be expected to represent a positive attitude.

Ironson also discovered two clinical advantages these patients had. They maintained longer their levels of immune cells that typically battle cancer and viruses. Moreover, the levels of their HIV viral concentration did not increase as fast as other patients' did. Some notable survivors do live longer, such as Magic Johnson and Arthur Ashe, suggesting that "fighters" have an edge over the disease.

## » Friendly Stress

The emphasis on reducing stress always makes it seem undesirable. But that isn't true. There are two kinds of stress. Negative stress is sometimes called "distress." The opposite kind of stress that's valuable in life is known as "eustress." Elizabeth Scott's online article "Eustress" emphasized the important role it plays in daily life. It was first distinguished from distress in 1975 by endocrinologist Hans Selye. Both kinds of stress recruit body resources to deal with them, and both are emotionally based. But a key difference between distress and eustress is how the body perceives each one and then responds, as triggered by emotions.

A good example of distress is an accountant trying to balance company purchases without all the invoices. In contrast, an Olympic swimmer seeking to beat his previous record exemplifies eustress. The bookkeeper likely is frustrated, could feel a sort of threat, and even might hate his task. The swimmer, on the other hand, probably was excited about his chances, anticipated the opportunity with great enthusiasm, and has a mental image of success.

According to Scott, "Eustress is actually important for us to have in our lives. Without it, we would become depressed and perhaps feel a lack of meaning in life. Not striving for goals, not overcoming challenges, or not having a reason to wake up in the morning would be damaging to us, so eustress is considered 'good' stress. It keeps us healthy and happy." Yet both kinds of stress tax the body's reserves. This is why "down time" is so important.

A later chapter in this book is entitled "A Balancing Act." It deals more specifically with human body processes involved in maintaining physiological homeostasis or equilibrium. This also applies to how we handle stress. In a sense, the term "balance" is a key here too. The ceaseless demands of our daily lives pose a great challenge about how we deal with them. Routine is a hallmark of modern society and "multi-tasking" simply is a new effort to squeeze more out of our daily existence. Eckhart Tolle's book *A New Earth: Awakening to Your Life Purpose* focused on "acceptance, enjoyment, and enthusiasm" as portals to a new consciousness to rejuvenate tired life styles.

Notice that Tolle's three conditions all are attitudinal and build upon one another. The first requirement—acceptance—may cause some people to "turn off" Tolle's overall prescription for a life makeover. It seems only reasonable that we give ourselves permission *not* to stamp every moment of our lives as acceptable. Otherwise, how do we make progress? What motivates us to try to improve our status quo? Perhaps the key again is balance. Life is a mixture of good and bad, of eustress and distress. Identify the negative and try to improve it. But in everything try to maintain a balanced perspective.

## » Laughter  ,

Perhaps nothing else reveals a positive state of mind as much as an honest-to-goodness belly laugh. Fifty years ago medical science might have dismissed this idea as foolhardy. But then along came Norman Cousins. He was an influential writer and editor-in-chief of the *Saturday Review*. In the 1970s, he suffered a debilitating and painful bone disease that doctors couldn't diagnose or treat. Their collective judgment was that his malady was terminal.

Cousins, however, wouldn't accept their prognosis. He embarked upon a plan: immerse himself in humor. He gathered films, comic books, and anything else that provoked a hearty laugh. He reported, "Ten minutes of a belly laugh gave him twenty minutes of pain-free sleep." Gradually he recovered his health. Doctors and researchers were stunned. His experience was reported in the prestigious *New England Journal of Medicine* and earned Norman Cousins a place in medical history.

Cousins went on to become adjunct professor in the UCLA Los Angeles School of Medicine in 1978. He subsequently wrote books, was a proponent for world peace and holistic healing, and lived until 1990.

"Laughter Can Boost Heart Health" according to the *U.S. News and World Report*. Their article cited two research studies that said laughter reduces stress, improves blood flow, and helps control high blood pressure. Researchers Jun Sugawara and Takashi Tarumi presented these findings at the 2009 meeting of the American College of Sports Medicine. In other studies psychoimmunologist Lee Berk and endocrinologist Stanley Tan found that "mirthful laughter" could also reduce inflammatory response and increase good cholesterol levels. Berk and Tan's work was cited in the article "Laughter Remains Good Medicine" which appeared online in *Science Daily*. The article said that many researchers continue to work in this new field of research whose foundation was laid down by Norman Cousins.

## » Free-Flowing Thinking and Wellbeing

It is very well to learn about the impact of change but quite another to adopt change. Imagine being sent as an employee-representative of a sizeable organization to a conference on new techniques for improving production, morale, or even inventory management. Days later you enthusiastically return to "spread the word." Perhaps to your surprise and dismay, your fellow employees respond less than eagerly to your proposals for change. Before long, they—and you—continue "business as usual." This should be no surprise to anyone. Change can be threatening and our hectic pace prefers a comfortable status quo. Thomas Kelley and Steven Stack published a pertinent discussion with the title "Thought Recognition, Locus of Control, and Adolescent Wellbeing" in the journal *Adolescence*. To me, their paper seems as applicable to adults as to adolescents.

What Kelley and Stack advocate is not easy to accomplish and is much less easy to sustain. It sounds very philosophical but apparently is grounded in psychology. Nor is this an overnight or weekend transformation. The word "transformation" is justifiably used, for it requires a change, however gradual, in our process of thinking.

Those authors used the example of self-esteem. Compare Mike's way of thinking with Henry's. Mike has a comfortable feeling of self-worth that is reinforcing despite challenge. It is a product of his self-reflection that blends and benefits from lifetime experiences where he gains insights and wisdom about himself.

But Henry focuses his thinking on ways to improve the reflection of himself that he believes he sees *through others' eyes*. He is convinced that his self-worth is only a product of personal achievements, status, and material possessions.

The outcome might be as follows. Mike is intuitive and freethinking. Henry must concentrate his thinking externally. Like facing a raging river, Mike watches the current, focusing his thinking on observation and insight that enable him to rise above the turmoil. Henry, however, believes he must try to control the strong currents. Mike also seems able to be more intentionally proactive, while Henry continues to be emotionally reactive to others.

The point is that we humans do have the ability to use our thoughts to achieve beyond our wildest imagination. Yet we live in a reality-based environment, so we tend to believe only that which we can see, sense, or knowingly control. It has been demonstrated, however, that we can train our minds to overpower our ego-control and focus our intentions to achieve remarkable results.

## » Open Your Mind to Nourish Your Brain

How many of you, like me, ever have the title or actors of a beloved movie on the so-called "tip of your tongue" but your brain won't deliver? Or you remember reading a novel or important document, but you forgot their essence? Or even recall hiding something valuable, yet can't remember just where? In her online *New York Times* article "How to Train the Aging Brain," Barbara Strauch challenged readers to adopt an unusual practice to nourish their established but almost forsaken neural pathways. She seems to have studied her subject well: she has a book *The Secret Life of the Grown-Up Brain* coming out in 2010.

But before I reveal her secret, I predict you'll not like it—it requires you to do something I've suggested in this book, something you're likely unwilling to do. For the moment, however, please realize that I have science on my side.

Strauch says that "brains in middle age—which, with increased life spans, now stretches from the 40s to late 60s—get more easily distracted." This seems to agree with everything you're reading in this book about thinking: focusing and remembering becomes more difficult in the midst of thousands of daily demands for our attention.

So Strauch asks, "Can an old brain learn, and then remember what it learns?" Yes, she says, because "scientists have looked deeper into how brains age and confirmed that they continue to develop through and beyond middle age." She reminds us, nevertheless, that our typical habit patterns discourage this.

According to Deborah M. Burke, a professor of psychology at Pomona College in California, "neural connections, which receive, process, and transmit information, can weaken with disuse or age." "The brain is plastic and continues to change, not in getting bigger but allowing for greater complexity and deeper understanding," says Kathleen Taylor, a professor at St. Mary's College of California.

Educators say that one way to "nudge neurons in the right direction is to challenge the very assumptions they have worked so hard to accumulate while young." Taylor adds, "Adult learners should 'jiggle their synapses a bit' by confronting thoughts that are contrary to their own." In a few words, continued brain development can require that "you 'bump up against people and ideas' that are different [such as] reading multiple viewpoints … then reflecting on how what was learned has changed your view of the world." Information still is important.

"But we need to move beyond that and challenge our perception of the world. If you always hang around with those you agree with and read things that agree with what you already know, you're not going to wrestle with your established brain connections." Taylor should know: she is sixty-six!

Jack Mezirow, a professor emeritus at Columbia Teachers College, stresses that we adults learn best when facing what he calls a "disorienting dilemma," or those things that "help you critically reflect on the assumptions you've acquired." Or differently said, "challenge [your] ingrained perceptions.

## » A Felt Purpose for Living

All of the topics discussed in this chapter dealt with how our thinking affects our wellbeing. One aspect of our lives not yet examined is something many of us never reflect upon, especially in our younger years. Usually our days are so filled with school or job and family responsibilities that we may believe that this is what life's all about. Certainly mothers feel committed to offspring or split their allegiance between offspring and jobs. Fathers may consider themselves the breadwinners necessitating a primary concern for their work. Kids just follow the flow of activities and peers.

Yet there are times when some of these family members may wonder, even if for only a minute or two, what their personal purpose is in life. It's a philosophical "moment" that likely won't recur as they quickly get caught back up in a swirl of the present. Teenagers who have an overabundance of material possessions occasionally raise such a question as adolescent idealism emerges.

As many of us age, however, midlife crises begin to occur; the "empty nest" syndrome diminishes mothers' feeling of being needed; and spouses may leave for one reason or another. I have known company executives who were so focused on their work that they delayed retirement as long as possible, dreading "having nothing to do." I personally experienced the end of a dependency when my beloved wife passed over. For all of these situations, the question seems more likely to occur, "What is my purpose in life?"

Another way this may be phrased is "How meaningful is my life?" Obviously, something is felt to be missing. By contrast, some people seem never to doubt having meaning or purpose in their lives. They typically display what might be described as a joy for living: seldom complaining, often laughing, and carrying out daily responsibilities with enthusiasm. Some even make time for volunteering and helping neighbors or friends in need.

The idea of living with a purpose appeared in the titles of both Eckhart Tolle's book and Rick Warren's *The Purpose Driven Life: What on Earth Am I Here For?* These authors sought to raise readers' awareness of needing a purpose in life. Whereas Tolle proposed a value-added dimension by stimulating "acceptance, enjoyment, and enthusiasm" in daily living, Warren stressed preparation for the life hereafter by focusing our present lives on Christian principles.

Neuropsychologist Patricia Boyle had an online article on the Web site Health.com that stressed our need to pay close attention to our own personally felt purpose for being here. The reason she gave was captured in her article's title "Have a Purpose in Life? You Might Live Longer." Boyle and fellow professor Gary Kennedy published their findings in *Psychosomatic Medicine.* They say that our perceived purpose in life doesn't have to meet specific criteria and it doesn't matter whether the "goal is ambitious or modest."

This therefore seems to suggest that you also should allow yourself to be self-indulgent occasionally, enjoying something that *just you* want to do. You may still have some dependency relationships with family members or other loved ones. But recognize that you also have a personal right to choose some things you'd like to do for pleasure or accomplishment. This "personal time" actually might recharge you to better accept and perform routine responsibilities.

Personal time might mean bicycling, reading, gardening, spelunking, skydiving, or any other of assorted experiences, maybe even those you'd hesitated to daydream about in the past. Over a three-year follow-up period, researchers Boyle and Kennedy discovered that people who acknowledged a purpose in their lives were one-half as likely to die as those persons who were less able to do so. The researchers theorized, "Having a greater sense of purpose helps multiple systems of the body function better, conferring protection in the face of illness."

Purpose in life should not only instill meaning; it also may be accompanied by such enthusiasm that it becomes a passion. It's been shown that young people who are encouraged to develop and pursue a passion in sports, mechanics, or any other personally satisfying activity are less likely to waste their school vacations in idleness or get involved in gangs. Pleasure of achievement seems to fuel their "finding a meaning in life." This topic will be discussed later in this book in more detail.

This chapter explored how the *nature* of our thoughts can affect our bodies. In contrast, the next chapter focuses on how we can improve our *process* of thinking.

# CHAPTER THREE
# ENHANCED THINKING

---

*"To find yourself, think for yourself."*
Socrates

---

There are a number of ways to sharpen one's thinking. Some already exist and simply need to be utilized. Others require a more disciplined approach.

## » Power of Focused Intention

Obviously, our thoughts have an amazing potential to affect both our world and our selves. Our mindsets can significantly shape our wellbeing, beliefs, moods, attitudes, and behavior. It seems that our thoughts can affect other people too. Barbara Hagerty provided a persuasive first-hand account in her online article "Can Positive Thoughts Help Heal Another Person?"

Have you ever felt especially negative about another person? Maybe he or she offended you or refused to comply with your wishes. Melvin Morse provided examples of how this feeling may control some sort of energy and translate it into action. Dr. Morse is an eminent Seattle pediatrician with a private practice and a faculty appointment at the University of Washington Medical School

First, a question: are humans always aware when they possibly "send" energy somewhere? Some seemingly weird, otherwise inexplicable happenings suggest not. In at least the first of the following examples, the person was seemingly unaware of affecting her surroundings.

This following was reported in Morse's book *Where God Lives: The Science of the Paranormal and How Our Brains Are Linked to the Universe*. It involved his thirteen-year-old daughter. While eating dinner in their dining room one evening, Morse was almost hit in the head by a dish. It came flying off the kitchen counter. He eyed his daughter, since her behavior often reflected anger at him. But he saw she wasn't in a position to have thrown the dish. She noticed his suspicion and chimed in, "I didn't throw that dish at you, Dad, but you make me so mad I wish I'd thrown it."

Morse's book also detailed an especially well-explored case from a German law firm. Ever since a young teenage girl had been employed there, telephone and electrical equipment continually malfunctioned in extraordinary ways whenever she was present: "light bulbs … exploding, telephone bills … soared, calls … disrupted, photocopiers malfunctioned" and power surges blew out much of the equipment. Other strange happenings were videotaped. To the surprise of the many employees and investigating personnel, all of this ceased when the girl left the firm.

Under his chapter subhead "Energy in Action," Morse suggested that much evidence exists indicating "we may serve as conduits of energy from a source outside our body, funneling and channeling energy to influence our surroundings."

We all recognize that our heart, our brain, and our muscles exhibit electric charges that can be read with electronic diagnostic instruments. We have accumulated static electricity from walking on certain surfaces, then felt the spark discharge when we touch a grounded electric switch or another person. Chakras (energy focal points on our bodies) deal with electromagnetic forces that course through our bodies. There is empirical evidence that a mass of people with a focused intention can exhibit an energy force. This is discussed later in this book in the chapter "Power of Synchronized Intention."

The bottom line to this is that scientists have documented the existence of what might be called fields or sources of subtle electromagnetic energy. The detection and measurement of this energy or force requires specialized instruments. Little has been defined about the source, nature, or potential effects of this energy. The possible use of this energy for healing purposes will be explored later in this book. The intent of its introduction here is that it apparently is related to intense focusing of human thoughts.

An extension of this reasoning seems exemplified in Yahuda Berg's book *God Does Not Create Miracles: You Do!* Miracles naturally are the subject of many hopes and prayers, but their failure can be immensely disappointing. Berg quotes the ancient Jewish text Kabbalah as follows: "According to Kabbalah, God is an infinitely powerful and positive force. You create your own miracles when you successfully connect to this infinite force of goodness—connection being the key concept here."

According to Berg, "Making miracles is about effort, not faith. It's about doing a bit of work ... about taking action now ... harnessing your ability to control matter with your mind." He differentiates self-control from ego control. Ego control, he feels, is reactive; self-control is proactive. Only as we separate ourselves from this reactive mode and focus instead on connecting and utilizing universal forces will we succeed in achieving our goals.

In their book *Your Soul at Work: Five Steps to a More Fulfilling Career and Life,* Nicholas Weiler and Stephen Schoonover discuss "a number of concepts agreed to by some of the great spiritual giants of history in a language and context people can relate to in their daily work activities." The authors provide "tools and techniques" to enable readers to "integrate your personal, spiritual, and work activities." The thrust of their recommendations center on introspection and commitment:

- Reevaluate personal beliefs, reinforce ones that work, change those that don't
- Reexamine whether your line of work best suits your interests and attributes
- Adopt a fresh commitment to succeed, making life changes if necessary
- Restudy available opportunities and create other new ones
- Buckle down and give it your all

Weiler and Schoonover acquired this information from over fifteen years of observing and interviewing over four thousand managers and non-managers in more than sixty organizations throughout the world.

The authors' tools and techniques are presently being used successfully by large and small organizations and businesses in many different countries and cultures.

## » Empathy and Intention

Scientific support for the "power of focused intention, positive emotions, and subtle energies" appeared in *Dispute Resolution Magazine*, published by the American Bar Association. The article, seemingly unrelated to the focus of this book, had the otherwise appealing title "The Power of Intention in Mediation and Peacemaking." The article relates the potential impact of a 1995 neurophysiological discovery to the ability of "a mediator's unspoken thoughts, intentions, and emotions [to] profoundly affect the parties, the process, and the outcome."

It was discovered that certain parts of the brain facilitate empathy. Called "mirror neurons," these "allow us to experience in a very direct way the experience of another without conscious thought or rational analysis." People who are highly capable of empathy seemed to utilize these brain structures more than other people. Obviously, this also holds special meaning for any of us seeking to positively influence the outcome of our efforts in caring for others.

## » Cognitive-Behavioral Therapy

The Website Health had an article by Marianne Flagg "Anxiety: Using Positive Thinking." It too emphasized that positive thinking can improve your wellbeing. Scientific research has demonstrated this link and also has shown that we can change to "healthy thinking." Cognitive-behavioral therapy (CBT) is one way to accomplish that.

Anyone can do this alone or with the help of a counselor. First, keep track of what you're thinking about yourself. All too often, we overlook our attributes and successes by concentrating on our perceived shortcomings and failures.

Second, seriously challenge the legitimacy of what you're thinking about yourself and do so honestly. If necessary, develop two lists on paper, one with negative thoughts and one with positive. Are you leaning toward unwarranted self-criticism?

Third, take the initiative to "self-talk" your way toward a better balance in your thinking. Try it for a while, artificially if necessary.

If you're a chronic worrier or habitually depressed, you may need help from a stress center. Otherwise, you likely will find that positive thinking makes you feel better. You will notice in a later chapter my personal struggle with this.

## » Critical Thinking

Perhaps in recognition of the growth of information and the value of disciplined use of mental processes, the concept of "critical thinking" arose. It is worth noting for its misuse for self-serving purposes as well as for its intended goal of advancing knowledge for the welfare of mankind. Those persons who pursue only selfish interests sometimes refer to the latter practice as "idealistic."

Critical thinking acknowledges the varied mental capabilities of the mind and the brain. It seeks to minimize clutter, waste, and misuse of cognitive processing. It does so by adopting thoughtful and reasoned approaches based upon practice and experience. It realizes that these are simply goals; also, that all human endeavors are subject to natural limitations imposed by emotion, belief, attitude, mood, and closed-mindedness. The nature of critical thinking therefore may be affected by any underlying motivations.

Critical thinking is the product of a life-long, self-guided commitment toward self-improvement. It is not a simplistic procedure: it can suffer from misguided intent, lack of persistence, or lagging devotion. Critical thinking is the subject of entire books, such as John Chafee's book *The Thinker's Way: Eight Steps to a Richer Life: Think Critically, Live Creatively, and Choose Freely* and Karl Albrecht's book *Practical Intelligence: The Art and Science of Common Sense.*

As early as 1901, psychologist Edward Thorndike developed a concept of the "science of education" concerning which subjects students should study. After administering intelligence tests to nearly nine thousand high school students in the 1920s, Thorndike concluded, "it didn't matter what students studied because the smartest ones always learned the most anyway." This was documented in Diane Ravitch's book *Left Back: A Century of Battles Over School Reform.* Richard Epstein's *Workbook for Critical Thinking* provided a useful tool for self-study.

Standards for critical thinking have been established by such organizations as the National Council for Excellence in Critical Thinking Instruction. These standards stem from their policy statement that critical thinking is an "intellectually disciplined process [of] conceptualizing, applying, analyzing, synthesizing, and/or evaluating information ... from or generated by observation, experience, reasoning, or communication, as a guide to belief and action."

## » Self-Actualization

Another personal trait that relates how people think to how they behave or perform is called "self-actualization." The concept arose in the human resources (personnel management) field. It has been defined as "to develop or achieve one's full potential," according to the *American Heritage Dictionary*. Abraham Maslow included the following characteristics as typical of self-actualized individuals. He or she:

- Has an awareness of and is comfortable with reality yet open to new experiences
- Is honest, open, genuine, without façade
- Has respect and esteem for self and others
- Seeks self-improvement not just selfishly but for its enhanced contribution
- Is mission-oriented as a responsibility or duty, even if not a personal choice
- Has a sense of security and self-sufficiency yet resilient, may appear autonomous
- Possesses a sense of awe, pleasure, and wonder, even mystical about life itself
- Has a feeling of empathy and respect for others and their shortcomings
- Is highly ethical and clearly subordinates means to ends
- Respects diversity in others and is eager to learn from them

You might want to remember these characteristics as being notably absent in people described in the later chapter "You're *What?*" Also later in this book you will read that Maslow revised his recommendations for self-actualization near the end of his life. He then favored living for a higher purpose.

The next chapter suggests ways we might apply some basic mental exercises to our thoughts and thinking for better daily living.

CHAPTER FOUR

# MINDFULNESS, MEDITATION, LIVING IN THE NOW

---

*"We crucify ourselves between two thieves:*
*regret for yesterday and fear of tomorrow."*

Fulton Oursler

---

The concepts in the chapter title are everywhere, not just in this book. Among many other publications are Eckhart Tolle's, Bhante Henepoia Gunaratana's *Mindfulness in Plain English,* and Anne Inhen and Carolyn Flynn's *The Complete Idiot's Guide to Mindfulness.* It seems like overkill, enough to confuse and discourage anyone.

## » People's Opinions

Loss of commitment is a real pitfall for people who are sincerely interested yet have honestly tried these concepts without success. It should be sufficient to *want* to improve your life. But if you read these books you're probably thinking like I was, "This is too complicated. Forget it!"

It may seem too "complicated" because it's a mixture of Western interpretations and applications of Eastern cultural practices, often from the centuries-old teachings of Buddha. Something seems to have been lost in the translation! It's not the purpose of this book to straighten all of this out. But it is my hope to try to simplify what I believe is the underlying thesis of achieving a more peaceful and happy existence.

Several posts I read on various Weblogs on this subject criticized the whole idea as "New Age" and self-aggrandizing. That opinion relates somewhat to my objection to so-called "enlightenment," expressed later in this book. Other posts seem to believe that the topics in the chapter title pertained to improving one's "humanity" or caring for others. Still others criticized the "enlightened" for forsaking sensitivities to real problems around them and for being unwilling to honestly express true feelings, while seeming to almost feign a state of bliss.

## » Effort and Reward

Let me try to differentiate the three concepts in the chapter title and offer you a manageable approach. Tackle as much of this as you want to and can manage amidst your hectic daily life style. So far as I can tell from my personal experience, it seems to help me, yet it doesn't stifle my other interests and responsibilities.

Let's admit, up front, that there is a range of effort required and a variety of degrees of payback. Maybe it's like wanting to beautify your home with flowers. You can buy an already potted flowering plant to put outside your front entryway. If you want year-round color, you may have to care for it inside your home depending on your climate zone. Garden centers make it easy to lay down a seed-embedded mat of spring outdoor flowers, a bit more work. You can become a devoted gardener with a beautiful small flower garden. Or you can go all-out and landscape your entire property. It all depends on what you want and can manage.

I think it is like that with this overall subject. These concepts are not just a lot of hype designed to sell books or to enroll people in expensive seminars, both of which they obviously do. Underlying all of this is a body of wisdom shared by many cultures and spanning centuries of life on this planet. Any disagreement is usually found among proponents who differ in which cultural, philosophical, or pragmatic approach one should follow. Of course, there also is an abundance of naysayers who misunderstand the process as promoting self-righteousness.

## » The Mind

There is, however, a common denominator found in all of the approaches—our mind! Of course, the concept of the mind is open to interpretation. Another chapter in this book claims that each of us has a conscious mind, a subconscious mind, and a superconscious mind (Newton 2000). The mind is said to be like a three-room house. There seem to be doors between the separate divisions. For everyday purposes, the one we're continually aware of while awake is our conscious mind. It's important to acknowledge here that the subconscious and superconscious minds *may be accessible* under certain circumstances, but typically are out of bounds to our everyday conscious waking experiences.

Let's carry this one step further. Much of the time our conscious mind is a turbulent, raging river of all we see, hear, smell, taste, and feel, *and think!* The word "think" (our thoughts) is an ever-changing mixture of our conscious awareness: memories, emotions, beliefs, contemplations, imaginations, expectations, intentions, fantasies, inspirations, feelings, ideas, calculations, opinions, reasoning, wisdom, anxieties, motives—the list is endless. Obviously not all of these are present in our conscious feelings at the same time, but all of them are accessible to our thinking through our conscious mind. That's why our thinking can be so tumultuous, often shifting according to the different situations we face. No wonder that you told someone, likely your child, "Don't bother me now!" (Notice I didn't say, "screamed!")

You probably feel you've had enough about the impact of thoughts. I'm sure it seems so. But this discussion isn't about the *kind* of thoughts you're having or the direction they are going. This is about the *process* of thinking. It's the gateway to understanding mindfulness, meditation, and the power of now.

Imagine yourself getting a good night's sleep. We are told that any dreams you have are typically a product of your unconscious (subconscious) mind. Contrast that to lying in bed continually turning over in your head thoughts about yesterday or tomorrow or even replaying today. Suppose you could find a way to calm your raging river of thoughts to a peaceful stream, even for a short while.

## » Differentiation

Let's try to separate the three concepts in the chapter title and then examine each in detail.

*Mindfulness* allows you not only to monitor your individual thoughts and their impact on your wellbeing as discussed in chapter two. It also enables you to monitor the patterns or degree of turbulence in your thinking process. For now, forget considering this as a full-time effort.

*Meditation* often seems to be equated to mindfulness. But meditation builds on mindfulness by enabling you to calm your thinking in stages. Then, through graduated focusing, concentrate your attention on breathing, on relaxing, and on an increasing heaviness of your arms and legs. This will help you to form images within your subconscious mind and achieve a higher transcendence.

*Power of now* is one of the tools for focusing your conscious mind (attention) on relevant aspects of your present circumstances at any given time, rather than dwelling on the "what-ifs" of the past or future. Here again, it's discouraging to try to make this a full-time effort initially.

The rest of this chapter will discuss some times, settings, and situations regarding these concepts.

## » Private Time

Another concept I've heard many people express, and many others may think, but not admit, is "my space." Even the most gregarious people probably long for some occasional private time. There is no doubt that mothers, especially those with multiple young siblings, long for an "escape." What would you do with your private time? Among appealing uses might be relaxing in a hot tub bath, reading a favorite novel, or just resting in the cool shade.

If you're soaking in the tub, you may try to keep out any reminders of daily responsibilities. If you are reading alone and undisturbed, you're probably "wrapped up" in the story. If you're enjoying a cool breeze under a shade tree, its almost bliss to relax your mind. If you've never enjoyed these or any other pleasures of private time, you have something to look forward to. Just don't put it off to "one of these days."

For several mornings, I thought I'd try something different during my six o'clock one-mile morning walk. You will read later that this started as a chore, but it's one I gradually got used to. So I consciously agreed to kick out thoughts about almost anything except my surroundings. I found myself able to listen with appreciation to the variety of birds calling at that early hour. I didn't "think" about any particular birdcall. I simply accepted all of them with gratitude almost as if they were doing so for my enjoyment. An occasional runner or car demanded my attention, but briefly and without analysis. A robin or two would alight on the grass ahead of me, more interested in food than in me. Spring brought magnificent buds and blossoms and a new freshness everywhere.

Occasionally the hum of a home air conditioner would rise then fade, but this would not distract me for long. After my turn-around, the beauty of the eastern skies caught my eye as they began painting the horizon above the treetops. Today, they were tangerine. Yesterday, they were distinctly baby blue and pink. As I neared home and reached for my door key, the symphony of the birds reached a crescendo. I almost hated to leave them. But needs of the day returned.

If you can conceptually grasp the idea of "private time" even without experiencing it, you've made the first step toward understanding mindfulness, meditation, and the power of now. Those three concepts are built around those kinds of experiences.

## » Living in the Now

The first and third—mindfulness and the power of now—are like cousins. Meditation is a more intense or concentrated refinement of those. The power of now means what it says: avoid what Fulton Ousler described in his words at the beginning of this chapter. If you are watching a poignant movie or listening to a stirring orchestral performance, you may be enthralled without a care in the world, like the people in the three relaxed experiences mentioned earlier. Good for you! You've experienced a major component of mindfulness: focusing. Whether it was a conscious intention or not, you were "living in the now," aware only of the majesty of the performance and the intensity of the experience.

Living in the now often seems impossible to do. Personal

responsibilities stretch in all directions: past, present, and future. All three may appear at once if you are simultaneously involved: preparing lunch at home for two youngsters; on the phone asking your husband to pick up Mary from school for a piano lesson; and checking out a bill involving last month's charges for your mother's surgery. Postponing each to its own time so you can address it alone might be nonsense. Balancing responsibilities sometimes seems like walking a tightrope across the Grand Canyon.

As mentioned earlier, Tolle seems to approach a situation like the one just described by recommending acceptance, enjoyment, and enthusiasm. In other words, be fully conscious of what you're doing at any given moment and embrace it rather than wishing it away. Then, encourage yourself to discover some pleasure in what you're doing, such as finding your husband quite willing to chauffeur Mary. Finally, don't let anything you do dim your enthusiasm for living.

Daniel Siegel's book *The Mindful Brain: Reflection and Attunement in the Cultivation of Well-Being* approaches mindfulness from the standpoint of neuroscientifically-based benefits for health and interpersonal relationships. Mindfulness is considered by some people to be too difficult to understand, let alone practice. But Siegel's three books forged the link between behavior and brain plasticity, showing that mindfulness can improve brain functions in areas responsible for:

- Body regulation
- Attuned communication
- Emotional balance
- Response flexibility
- Empathy
- Insight or self-knowing awareness
- Fear modulation
- Intuition
- Morality

## » Attitude

Are all of these ideas easier to read about than to do? That may be true for many people. That seems to depend upon one's attitude. Am I interested? Should I try them? Might it be worth my effort? Sometime step outside yourself figuratively and try to see what kind of general attitude you reflect to yourself and to others. No point in trying to list all the variations or the self-proclaimed reasons (excuses?) Neither this book nor any other may be likely to change you. But just remember, "Nothing ventured, nothing gained."

I think you get the idea about living in the now. Mindfulness seems to be just an extension of that. I guess either one would be difficult without the other. Meditation, however, is more demanding, and this book can't do justice to differentiating the types, requirements, and possible benefits. Suffice it to say that many practitioners and proponents of meditation stress that it takes commitment, practice, and persistence to achieve benefits. There are other examples of achieving transcendence—an awareness of an elevated state of mind said to approach realization of the divine—through other modes of experience, sometimes unintentional.

## » Mental Imaging

This practice has many proponents, from meditation to athletics. It involves a focused application of something with which we all are familiar—imagination. Consider a high-jump athlete, a person in chronic pain, or an advertising executive making a pitch to a future client. All have certain goals in mind. It is a scientific fact that sincerely visualizing the actual achievement of a particular goal can influence bodily processes enough to facilitate reaching the goal.

This part of the book was devoted to thinking. The next part discusses some extremes that shape our lives.

# PART TWO

Going to Extremes

CHAPTER FIVE

# Into the Jaws of Desperation

---

*"I have peered into the abyss of insanity and grabbed
at any toehold or handhold to keep from tumbling in."*
William Pillow

---

The title of this part of the book may seem to be a radical change from the earlier part. But it illustrates just how far afield our thinking can carry us in different aspects of life. As with the earlier part, this one might encourage us to examine our own thinking and beliefs—to consider "What if...?" What if my thinking and beliefs, and my consequent conduct, are significantly affecting not only myself but also my family and others in a negative way?

## » A Personal View

My wife, Betty, suffered three strokes beginning before 2003. Her second one during that year left her unable to regain her mobility, so I cared for her at home. She remained in good spirits and kept well otherwise. We bought a used wheelchair van, and she continued to participate in outside activities.

In 2008 she had a devastating left-brain stroke. Harvard brain researcher Jill Bolte Taylor best described the impact of her own massive 1996 stroke in her book *My Stroke of Insight,* which required eight years for her to recover fully. Like Jill, Betty lost all her ability to read, understand, or utter any language. Her right side was paralyzed but she managed a wry smile with the left side of her mouth and a firm grip with her left hand. Betty required a tracheostomy (permanent breathing tube through neck) and a stomach tube for feeding. She was aware of family members' and friends' visits. However, I do not believe she ever knew me as her husband, the situation she was in, or when she was home.

After Betty spent nine weeks in three hospitals, I brought her home with me. I was determined to help her recover a quality of life at least as good as before her newest stroke. Visiting nurses and aides helped me keep her nourished and free of infection. After the stroke, I continued to work toward her improvement, and I prayed that I would continue to be physically and mentally able to care for her.

Then it happened, like a bolt out of the blue. I surreptitiously got a copy of the magnetic resonance imaging (MRI) report from the admitting hospital. Details did not require an explanation. If she ever regained an awareness of her condition, I realized she would know that her family did not follow her "Do Not Resuscitate" (DNR) instructions in her living will. On the several occasions when we updated our wills, Betty was adamant never to be kept alive under artificial feeding and breathing circumstances. The lightening bolt struck me dumb!

I suddenly recalled the emergency room doctor's asking whether my son and I wanted to "let her go." Because that question came only a half hour after Betty arrived at the hospital, I insisted that everything possible be done to help her. Surely she couldn't be that sick! Twice again in the next five days we had opportunities to let her go, by refusing permission for the feeding tube and the tracheostomy to be installed at separate times.

My dogged desire and unfounded persistence to help her get well apparently blinded me to the truth. Either I didn't listen carefully enough to her doctors' prognosis or they toned it down to avoid conflict with my unbounded optimism.

Now I was squarely confronted by the truth! My emotions ran wild for days, from rage to frustration, from failure to desperation, from guilt to escape, and every shade and intensity in between. I already was on Prozac for depression and Serax for anxiety. My moods ran roughshod through every waking moment. But I dared not show any of this to my beloved wife, my son or daughter, or any other caregivers or friends. It would be an admission of my weakness. This was the independence and determination that had been my hallmarks forever.

## » Rumination

Although this term is used for cows chewing their cud, it also is used to describe the vicious downward spiral characteristic of depression. I continually found myself in its vortex, unable to free myself. It is self-feeding, as each episode of "What if…" prompts other episodes.

There seemed to be no rational way to break free. With me, it wasn't accompanied by tears but by anger, most of it directed at myself. Why had I been so stupid? I even increased the dose of my anti-anxiety medicine from three to four times a day. I discovered that I couldn't tolerate bourbon, once my favorite, so I turned to three or four beers a day and dark chocolates at strategic times when I felt a rumination approaching. The more-frequent anxiety medication dulled my senses considerably. Yet I was still able to conscientiously and accurately conform to Betty's feeding times, breathing treatments, and administering assorted medicines through her feeding tube every four hours 24/7.

She remained with me for almost three months. I still weep when I recall how tightly she would grip my hand, apparently for reassurance or when she started choking. Betty had recurrent bouts with throat problems as a young child and had a mortal fear of choking. Thankfully, we were able to adjust her breathing treatments and medication to ease that threat in her last four weeks.

Even if she didn't recognize me as her husband, Bill, she had become accustomed to watching me all day every day in the hospital. She knew enough to reach out to this bald bearded man when she needed help. My most difficult times did not involve care routines but imagining what she must have felt like inside her "prison." I made myself promise that I would never reveal to anyone the radical extremes that I occasionally contemplated as possible "solutions" to free both of us.

Maintaining strict privacy about my inner turmoil, I never let anyone else in to detect my need for or to offer help. However, I eventually relented and disclosed my innermost frustrations to our family physician of twenty years. Soon, he made a three-hour house call on a Saturday afternoon to examine Betty and to help me toward making peace with myself. It was his counseling and a friend's reminder that we never can find answers to all our questions that started me on the road to personal recovery. Betty passed serenely into the spirit world four weeks after the doctor's visit from complications that had accompanied her last stroke.

## » Inner Truths

Blinded as I had been by my perceived guilt, dogged determination, and rigid independence, I desperately might have resorted to one of the escapes I mentioned earlier. I now suspect that others too have experienced the spiral of rumination. I claim no sole ownership of it. But when someone is swept down into that vortex, little else seems to matter. It is impossible to think rationally. It's like being caught up into a 747-airplane turbine engine at full thrust.

It took weeks of personal reflection after Betty's passing for me even to begin thinking straight. The full impact of the physical death of a loved one is never fully felt until it has happened, even though the likelihood is always there. The emotional scars still remain, even though their intensity eases gradually over time.

Eventually I began to recognize that I still had five wonderful loved ones alive. I, who had written a book on mind-body influences, was sharply reminded by our son and daughter that I had neglected myself for too long. It was starting to become self-evident. I was seventy-seven years of age and I felt it. I had disregarded all the factors that could sharply affect wellbeing. I had no dental or medical attention for close to three years, and I was shortcutting meals frequently. It soon became amazing to me that I had had no illnesses for almost five years, not even a cold. In that, my prayers had been answered.

Shortly after Betty passed over I developed shingles. This is a result of the herpes virus that causes chickenpox. After someone has had chickenpox, the virus apparently remains dormant in his or her nerve cells. The virus can manifest itself as eruptions on that person's body in later life. This typically lasts for four to six weeks. It can be quite uncomfortable. Stress seems to be the cause. It certainly may have been in my case.

As you'll read later in this book, the human body is amazing in its ability to maintain homeostasis or balance. I had put mine to a severe test. Perhaps my experience has better enabled me to empathize with those who are ill, especially those with mental illness. One thing I hope I've learned is that our thoughts definitely control our lives.

## » Resolve

After the passing of my beloved Betty, my doctor encouraged me to exercise more. So I began a one-mile neighborhood walk. Some mornings it rained. Skipping my morning miler may have been excusable. But an umbrella kept me mostly dry and left me without cause. The walk was one of my resolutions to pay more attention to my own wellbeing.

One night, my left knee gave way on me and I almost fell. So the next morning I searched for an elastic knee support. We did have one somewhere, but I just couldn't find it. One part of me pushed for canceling the walk. I had started this daily trek the previous week, so missing a day shouldn't hurt me.

After a bowl of oatmeal and a cup of coffee, I finally found an elastic wrap to help support my knee. A tad apprehensive, I locked the door as I left. My mind kept asking, "What would happen if I crumpled blocks away or, worse still, if I hit my head and went unconscious?" Carrying a cell-phone became the answer.

The walk is a half-mile out and a half-mile return. At first, my walk always was a case of unremitting resolve you might feel in sitting down in a dental chair. Reaching the turn-around used to be a relief. But I finally discovered for myself the true implications of my own mindset! And I've now learned to love my "milers" as my own private time.

May I close this chapter with a plea to all male readers over fifty years of age: Please have your prostate specific antigen (PSA) blood level checked soon. Prostate cancer is no longer a closet subject. I have it. I was diagnosed three years ago and received extensive radiation treatments. My current PSA level says my cancer is in remission.

The loss of a spouse is heartbreaking. But the next chapter discusses a family loss that can be even more devastating.

# CHAPTER SIX
# LOSS OF A CHILD

*"God didn't take me cause He's mad.*
*He didn't send me to make you sad.*
*But to give us both a chance to be*
*a love so precious ... don't you see?"*

*Death of a Child—Words of Sympathy*
Sandy Eakle

This book emphasizes the significance of good prenatal care and early childhood understanding and nurturing. Yet, despite all the hopes, joys, and love that prospective parents feel, something may go awry. A miscarriage, a stillbirth, or even a death of a young child seem to be the most devastating experience anyone can imagine.

Even those mothers who elect to have an abortion must sooner or later feel a personal loss. One might wonder how a mother must feel in offering her baby for adoption or in abandoning it. No doubt other birth mothers would have similar misgivings for failing to protect their babies from harm or neglect. Obviously, different circumstances motivate intentional actions. But the mother who never can carry her baby to term or loses it soon to death must stand out as the most heart-breaking scenario.

Physicians are committed to saving lives, not trained to deal with dying, as Melvin Morse points out in his book *Closer to the Light: Learning from the Near-Death Experiences of Children*. Therefore, they are skeptical of anything that seems inconsistent with their training:

parents hearing their deceased child's voice; terminally ill patients having pre-death visions of loved ones on the other side; and near-death experiences.

## » Incredible Reports

A number of very surprising, even shocking, reports have been accumulated from professional researchers. These will be discussed as they apply to the soul of the child lost or separated in the just-mentioned instances. It is crucial for you to understand that these testimonies received from parents, children, and from hypnotically regressed subjects are not offered for purposes of consolation. Grief from such losses is inconsolable. There is a consistency in these reports, however, that might encourage some parents and prospective parents to incredulously ask themselves, "What if...?"

Some research suggests that if a miscarriage or other untimely event interrupts a pregnancy, the soul who planned to be incarnated in that family has the ability to return in a baby born later to that mother and father. The same is said to possibly hold true for a child who dies early in life.

All such situations really sound unbelievable! But if you'd like a first-hand account of examples, check out Carol Bowman's book *Return from Heaven: Beloved Relatives Reincarnated Within Your Family*. Read her chilling account, if you dare, of a mother who lost her firstborn son at the age of nineteen in an automobile accident. Her second child born much later, also a boy, was preceded by and displayed what Bowman called "many elements of a family return ... a birthmark, an after-death communication, an announcing dream, telltale behaviors, and statements." This account suggests that the return of a soul in a later-born child apparently may happen even after the death of an earlier-born older child in which that same soul had previously incarnated.

Also, see Michael Newton's book (2000). In the section headed "Souls of the Young: The Loss of a Child," he says, "When a mother loses her child for whatever reason, I have found the odds are quite high that the soul of the baby will return again to the same mother with her next child." Yet, what was certainly a devastating disappointment when the first child was lost likely will never be recognized by parents as an effort to mend their broken hearts through the reappearance of the same soul in the next child.

Occasionally my friends unexpectedly offered personal testimonies that relate to incredible events discussed in this book. One occurred at lunch with a somewhat reserved man and his wife, with whom I'm better acquainted than with her husband. We were discussing the often-impromptu nature of death. The man suddenly but quietly said, "I think I'm my brother who died earlier." Apparently his brother had a "crib death" several years before my friend was born. I asked why he thought that. He simply dismissed his statement with, "I had been told that." No further discussion.

## » Angels in Disguise

Only if you consider reincarnation at least plausible may you also find this next topic at least challenging. What may seem a cruel disappointment actually might have been planned. Reincarnation planning in the spirit world seems far more involved than we humans might even imagine. Then, too, there is a lack of conscious awareness by a human being of its soul's life plans—at least once the child adopts the "reality thinking" of his or her environment. Thereafter, a "preplanned" event may be as much a surprise to the human being into which the soul incarnated as to his or her loved ones.

The idea of life planning by a soul before its earthly incarnation is incomprehensible to most people, yet the possibility of predestination is still tolerated by some persons. Both of these concepts might imply a fixed, predetermined life to be lived. But during one's life, it certainly is unknowable whether the twists and turns that occur are by one's choice or by so-called "fate." Of course, the concept of fate or predestination inevitability conflicts with the idea of free will or choice.

Our focus here therefore must be the intention of the soul's life plans rather than on the life that follows reincarnation. Some researchers have added that a soul's life plan may be designed for the spiritual growth of family members, friends, or even other people: a self-sacrifice as it were. Robert Schwartz's book *Courageous Souls: Do We Plan Our Life Challenges Before Birth?* contains case examples of life planning involving such life experiences as illness, physical handicaps, deafness, or blindness.

Apparently such human lives, even though perhaps brief, could introduce a necessary aspect of love, caring, or outreach that would facilitate others' spiritual growth. Such a sacrificial gesture by a soul could, of itself, be a measure of that soul's own spiritual growth. I would suspect that such self-sacrifice is never chosen by immature souls, i.e., souls who have experienced very few incarnations.

Given this perspective, however, you assume that parents and other loved ones naturally would never accept a disappointing loss of life, incapacitation, incurable illness, or disability as being intended: not preordained but preplanned by the soul itself. But the soul is said to take the long view, realizing that its spiritual growth comes only in steps over an eternally long time of repeated incarnations.

Yet this is one aspect of life's tragedies we naturally disregard. How could we possibly even imagine that the short life of a child was designed to help other souls achieve spiritual growth, even if spiritual maturity of those other persons' souls was found to be wanting in those virtues? It would be the farthest thing from any conceivable source of consolation.

Sometimes there appears on the world stage a suffering young life whose very being and accomplishments seem to exude presence of mind from another world. Someone therefore might question whether that individual really is just human or is inwardly aware of being a part of two worlds.

A prime example lived among us recently. People of many nations are aware of this young person who almost certainly must have been a living model of such soul benevolence. I'm naturally referring to Mattie Stepanek, who died in 2004 at age thirteen from the terminal effects of dysautonomic mitochondrial myopathy, a rare disorder. He has his own website (mattieonline.com).

Anyone who has read Mattie's poetry, owned his books, or seen his personal appearances must have felt a tug at their heartstrings for this child. He had a kindly philosophy of life, of people, of nature, and the world in general. He certainly reached far beyond the understanding not only of a child his age but also beyond that of many adults. I and probably many other people couldn't help but feel we were in the presence of a child who had remained in touch with his soul or was indeed an angel. I am convinced that Mattie helped many individuals grow spiritually.

Five years after Mattie's death, his mother, Jeni, wrote a book *Messenger: The Legacy of Mattie. J. T. Stepanek and Heartsongs.* The book is available from Mattie's Website. On the Web site, Jeni revealed that from the time he was a small child, Mattie felt that his "purpose for being on earth was to be a messenger, to make people smile despite challenges."

I personally have had the good fortune occasionally—perhaps synchronistically—to discover a person whose beliefs seem to resonate with my own soul. Such an individual is Jeni Stepanek. In response to my request for permission to use the preceding essay about Mattie, she kindly consented and added the following, which I hope will inspire all the readers of my book:

> "I personally do not believe in reincarnation. I believe that each spirit, each soul, is a unique entity, created by God, and packaged in a shell for some length of time on earth. Sometimes I am overwhelmed with pondering why some sacred shells seem so heavily weighted with burdens and challenges, while others are lifted with blessings and chances. But inevitably, I come back to the beauty of the spirit, and how the spirit is what lives eternally, and a shell is simply a sacred reminder of one's essence, and the beauty is in the eye of the beholder. God sees all of creation as beautiful. As humans, we are drawn to mortal measurements. God is not. So that is part of how I am able to cope, to survive the truth of burying all four of my children, before they really had a chance to live on earth. As a mother, I wish I did believe in reincarnation, because I would eagerly await my children's spirit in some other form. But also, as a mother, I am blessed to believe that this will not happen."

The following example seems to capture several concepts: two highly controversial and one indisputable. The first two involve reincarnation; the third echoes the human potential. My second book provided examples of young children's extraordinary talents, sometimes called "child prodigies." These youngsters have lived throughout history and elicited awe and speculation, but no scientific explanation has ever been found. The cases have been used as first-person examples of reincarnation of souls of similarly talented persons who lived earlier. But it seems rare to find cases of child prodigies who also may be what I term "angels in disguise," those souls who intentionally chose to incarnate in a body with disadvantages. This just might be the case with Patrick Henry Hughes, of Louisville, Kentucky.

If you've never heard of Patrick, you've missed a great opportunity. His accomplishments are truly exemplary, almost unimaginable, and certainly inspiring.

Patrick was born without eyes and with legs he never would be able to straighten. Even before his first birthday, Patrick had an uncanny ability with the piano. His mother said, "He could go up to a piano and ... within one or two tries he could find the exact notes." His father remembers, "By his second birthday, he was playing requests." His father's reaction was, "I was just ecstatic. Maybe we're not going to play baseball, but we're going to play music together and let's see how far we can run with this!"

Patrick's passion for music grew just as his talent did. Fitted with artificial eyes and a wheelchair, he advanced in education too. His father sits with him in every class at the University of Louisville, and the dad works the graveyard shift at UPS. His father simply says, "He's my hero." But Patrick's family and he did something that all of us likely wouldn't even attempt. Therein lies the third concept: reaching our full potential. In the words of his family, "During registration for Patrick's freshman year of college, Patrick Henry and I approached the band director, Dr. Greg Byrne, about being in the pep band—the one that plays at basketball games. Dr. Byrne, one of those angels amongst us, insisted Patrick Henry join the marching band as well. It was Dr. Byrne that launched this ship: not the university and not us."

Patrick and his father are now a permanent part of the University of Louisville marching band, his father pushing the wheelchair with Patrick on his trumpet. Patrick modestly describes his situation as "not disabilities at all, more abilities." Patrick has published a book, *I Am Potential: Eight Lessons on Living, Loving, and Reaching Your Dreams,*

and he has his own Web site (www.patrickhenryhughes.com/index.
html).

## » Premature Birth Stress

Premature births pose a significant risk for parents and infants, in
addition to preemies' obvious susceptibility to immediate and long-term
effects of shortened gestation. Neonatal intensive care units (NICUs)
naturally must emphasize premature infants' need for attention. NICU
personnel therefore have little time or training to address the trauma
parents are experiencing.

As Vicki Forman described in her book *This Lovely Life,* "What
the parent is going through is more or less dismissed [in deference to]
the health issues of [his or her] child." Laurie Tarkan's *New York Times*
article "For Parents on NICU, Trauma May Last" acknowledged the
enormity of this problem. Mothers seem more likely than fathers to
be subject to post-traumatic stress disorder (PTSD). This is because
wives typically spend more time attending to and agonizing over
their infants' NICU uncertainties. But fathers too can suffer long-
term PTSD.

In contrast to the concern for a full-term baby's injury or illness,
the NICU can be a roller-coaster nightmare for a mother. She not only
is horrified by her helplessness but also is frightened by her infant's
fragile nature. Parental PTSD therefore becomes a hazard for preemie
infants as well as their parents, because of the impact of the stress on
parents' behavior toward their child. Even a minor complaint by her
baby after going home may precipitate a gut-wrenching reaction from
the mother. Tarkan stressed that "traumatized parents may find it hard
to hold or even look at their child, and that can profoundly affect the
baby's attachment to the mother."

## » You Must Go Back

Near-death experience (NDE) survivors seem to have visualized the
spirit world, the white light, and the enticing heavenly setting. Their
reports seem consistent with their expressed desire to have remained
there. However, they said they were told by spirit entities, "You must
return. Your time is not yet."

Can we accept the validity of these testimonies? If so, doesn't this support some sort of "timing" being involved in our lives? This seems to support the idea that life planning by our souls has a significant influence on our destiny.

The next chapter confronts us with a belief that we naturally hold any time we're faced with a disappointment, whether it's a job loss, a skipped promotion, or a stock market crash.

CHAPTER SEVEN

# You Owe Me!

---

*"O would some power the gift to give us
to see ourselves as others see us."*

Robert Burns: *Ode to a Louse*, 1798

---

Despite individual potential, a great wave of personal discontent has been growing in our society for years and now is reaching epic proportions. It stretches from corporate boardrooms to welfare recipients to immigrant workers. This exists as both personal expectations and group recruitment efforts to create or justify what are called "entitlements." Recipients never question the propriety of these benefits. They simply feel "owed," sometimes for no justifiable reason. If these benefits were not granted, they feel especially deprived.

## » I'm Entitled

Beverly Smallwood addressed the situation in her on-line article "The Dangers of a Sense of Entitlement." She stressed "A dangerous cancer is eating away at the soul of modern society, causing great distress in our homes and workplaces alike."

These expectations can produce much animosity, even religious and ethical dilemmas. Top company executives receive millions while their companies go broke. Blue-collar workers are shocked when their lifetime employment disappears. Some students and workers from abroad demand special accommodations to comply with their religious rituals. Multitudes believe they have individual rights never contained in our Constitution: lifetime jobs, irrational bonuses, welfare payments, union wages, and even health care.

In their article "Dionysius's Brutal Sense of Entitlement: Plato's Contribution to Criminogenic Needs" in *Psychology, Crime, and Law,* Sophia Fisher and her colleagues paint an even more dismal picture. They said, "Criminogenic needs are now well established in the fields of psychology and criminology as factors that identify risk of criminal behavior and recidivism. We propose that an inflated sense of entitlement may also be identified as a criminogenic need." According to the *American Heritage College Dictionary,* criminogenic means, "producing or tending to produce crime."

On a smaller scale, individuals who experience hardships in life may expect better from their country or even from their God. They may lash out blindly to hold accountable any conceivable person, group, faith, or reason. When faced with the worst of calamities, everyone seems to shelter a residue of blame in their hearts. Even when faced with lesser disappointments, many of us typically complain.

## » Potential Impact

We may watch as others lose loved ones or declare bankruptcy yet we personally relish a feeling of gratitude for being spared. We may turn our eyes from televised scenes of famine, disease, or slaughter around the world. Yet, sooner or later, each of us will confront doubts about this world we all share. Then, everything becomes very personal and begs for answers.

If the present state of affairs in our society is any measure, we appear to be encouraging greedy, egocentric, and careless behavior. In his online publication "Articles of Faith: The Unfortunate Age of Entitlement in America," Anthony Robinson issued this challenge: self-esteem is important, but now self-esteem "seems to have morphed into entitlement."

There appears to be a narrow ledge of self-perception that, on one side risks self-degradation, and on the other becomes the ultimate selfishness. Some observers claim that the inward focus on conscious self-appreciation may further promote intolerance, entitlement, victimhood, and narcissism. Ironically, we may disavow for ourselves standards we set for others.

The current mood, Robinson wrote, seems to be a "culture of complaint. We have," he observes, developed a prevailing attitude of "blame, complaint, and grievance." We've totally forgotten the value of saying, "Please," "Thank you," and "I'm sorry." He concludes, "Entitlement is the handmaiden of the ego, the sign of a neglected, malnourished soul."

Robinson sees a dismal forecast for America if this persists. "In the end, it's the entitled who, however rich, are truly poor. Instead of knowing life as a gift, life turns into something that's taken for granted—or worse, begrudged. That's real poverty, and no sense of entitlement can alleviate it."

America historically has been a land of opportunity for masses of immigrants from around the world. Many second- and third-generation families have built upon their parents' and grandparents' successes as entrepreneurs, skilled tradesmen, and other esteemed occupations and professions. Despite their varied origins and ethnicities, they shared a common bond: pride of motivation and accomplishment. It was this strength that made America great.

Yet it seems that our country now encourages expectations of entitlements by special groups that may displace individuals' pride of motivation and accomplishment. If so, I must agree with the dismal forecasts for America made by others mentioned in this chapter.

Recent events around the world to deprive citizens of human rights purportedly have occurred to insure welfare for the masses, but actually happen to perpetuate tyranny. There also have been suggestions of efforts for what's termed "wealth redistribution." One extreme failed example of this was Zimbabwe. On one hand such an attempt may be a genuine move to help underprivileged masses. By contrast, it may be criticized as an attempt to sway large portions of the populace to support politicians who espouse such efforts. Both instances ignore the fact that individual pride of motivation and accomplishment rather than individual dependence on entitlements has been the source of the growth and prosperity of nations.

## » Children of Divorce

Lynne Namka introduced a new dimension to entitlement in her online article "You Owe Me! Children of Entitlement." She acknowledged that two-year-olds and teenagers could be demanding but she feels that children of divorce may "engage in more entitlement behavior." This may stem from a number of reasons. For example, children may feel shortchanged especially if left in the custody of only one of the parents, leading them to expect special favors for enduring this. Also, parents themselves may overindulge children in an effort to compensate for the divorce.

Examining divorce from children's perspective may help us understand what they feel and why. Siblings' ages and degrees of maturity may significantly influence their apparent acceptance of the split. But many children still could harbor firm beliefs or misunderstandings that may threaten their self-esteem or welfare. It seems only natural that some offspring of divorcing parents suffer a personal conviction that they were, for some undecipherable reason, the cause of the divorce. If not detected and even with efforts to resolve such children's feelings, some damage may occur.

If divorce occurs with children old enough to consciously reason, it may prompt them to undertake an intensive and excruciating self-review of anything they possibly may have done to cause their parents' divorce. In younger children, divorce may reinforce youngsters' implicit memory of criticisms they received from their parents. Any negative implicit memory these children have about themselves also may be affected by disputes between their parents, as the kids suspect that they may have been the cause.

Some divorcing parents are reluctant to try to explain fully the reasons behind the divorce, either not believing the children are mature enough to understand or not wanting to create a negative impression about the spouse. By contrast, some spouses look forward to castigating their mates without any consideration of its impact on their children.

On the other hand, a mother may intentionally shield her children from the truth about her mate, possibly leaving the kids to speculate that she herself might have unreasonably instigated the divorce. Some children, left with believing that dad could do no wrong, unfairly but silently blame their mother. The reverse also might hold true. Children have great imagination, and what they don't understand they will invent. Selfishness and a feeling of injustice may follow them into adulthood, setting up unrealistic expectations of others.

The next chapter probes the extent to which we'd stoop to express our discontent.

# CHAPTER EIGHT

# INFLUENCE OF EVIL

---

*"The belief in a supernatural source of evil is not necessary;
men alone are quite capable of every wickedness."*

Joseph Conrad

---

Religious history and art are filled with forces for good confronting forces of evil. Hell is the supposed destination of all who are evil, to suffer eternal punishment. Threats of hell and the devil have been somewhat successfully employed for centuries as deterrents to so-called sinning.

Demonic beings are claimed to roam the earth, seeking victims susceptible to their easy persuasion. This harkens back to Johann Wolfgang von Goethe's play and epic poem *Faust* and more recently to Peter Kreeft's book *Angels and Demons*. In the context of disappointment, there supposedly were individuals desperate enough to trade their souls for earthly wishes. Such a clear contrast between good and evil seems not only misleading but also unlikely to exist, even though some persons seem convinced about an independent force for evil.

Earnest Valea discussed "The Problem of Evil in World Religions" in his online article. Basically, Eastern religions consider evil as the effect of spiritual ignorance. In some religions, evil and good co-exist. Christianity believes that evil results from an improper use of God's resources by engaging in improper pursuits. It also believes in a fallen angel called Satan who tries to persuade humans to do evil or to discourage them from doing good.

The old radio mystery show "The Shadow" began with a question to which we all should pay attention, "Who knows what evil lurks in the heart of man?" I believe a consensus of people would agree that evil is a man-made attribute. Many would cite Hitler as a prime example. But the existence of evil may be a bit more complicated than it first appears.

## » Intractable Situations

People may trade safety and security for risk and disappointment. Wishes and hopes are powerful motivators. Perhaps nobody trades his soul for promises from the Devil. But some individuals, mostly women, willingly enter into relationships with others, mostly men, in hopes of realizing their dreams. I think I've finally learned, after seventy-eight years, that hardly anyone else is as he or she appears. Few people are as they seem or claim to be. Remember the adage "Never judge a book by its cover"? How true it is! Maybe I'm finally agreeing with the Dutch saying "Too soon old; too late smart!"

Now there is a different kind of need for caution: the Internet. Unfortunately a relationship may develop based only on pictures and exchanged messages. What's more, pictures may not be reliable. If one of the pair goes to meet the other, the outcome may be disappointing or even devastating. All too often it is a case of a victim being snared by a predator and escape may not be an option.

So now you're thinking I'm either paranoid or hypocritical! OK. I won't bore you with extensive examples. However, just ask yourself what you discovered about your girlfriends or boyfriends after more intimate relationships. By that time, of course, one of you may decide you want out of the relationship, but the other person may even begin stalking you, refusing to let you go. The point here is to "look before you leap!" I agree that caution doesn't accompany passion nor does it mix with long-unfulfilled hopes and expectations. There seems no easy way to avoid this situation. Some disappointments are almost impossible to resolve conveniently.

Another aspect of close relationships is the matter of dependency. One of the pair may decide to tolerate conditions of the relationship however disappointing they become. It seems almost as if that individual has decided "it's better than I had before" or "I can't survive without him or her." Again, there is no easy advice that fits all situations. Unfortunately, as one of the pair demonstrates dependency on the other, that other person may take full advantage of believing he or she "owns" the dependent individual.

It is in this extreme that we must wonder if evil of a sort exists in a person as evidenced by his or her behavior, even cruelty, toward another person. Evil may be a misnomer here, but the malevolent person seems to disregard the rights of others. Ironically, this potential exists not only in personal relationships but also in mass appeal of aspiring leaders, like Hitler.

## » Domestic Abuse

Angie Mason says that male domestic abuse "is not all about anger." She blames a long-standing "belief system rooted in male entitlement." Mason authored an article in the online York, Pennsylvania, *Daily Record/Daily News*. It was entitled "Domestic Violence: Male Entitlement Mentality a Factor."

She quotes Roger Steffy that "anger, alcohol and drug abuse, mental illness, or a bad relationship" might be contributing factors but "are not the cause of abuse." Steffy is director of the ADVANCE program, part of Lutheran Social Services of South Central Pennsylvania. "Because I'm the man in this relationship, I'm in charge," Steffy said.

"Abuse can take different forms," Steffy reported. "A man might try to control which people his partner hangs out with or whether she works. He might choose how he uses violence or where he inflicts harm on her body—whether he wants to leave a visible bruise, so she'll have to stay home."

Their program's goal is to help men change the way they think and live, Steffy said. Their counselors help men to view relationships as egalitarian, not a hierarchy. Their program serves men who have been abusive and are not actively parenting children. About 80 percent of the participants are legally mandated to attend.

Stacy Kimberly, a community education specialist and volunteer coordinator for Access-York, talks to high school students about domestic violence and healthy relationships. She's heard young boys say they're not going to let women walk all over them or they're going to treat women the way their grandfather did. "It doesn't have to be that way," Kimberly tells them. "That's not how it has to be."

According to CBS' *48 Hour Mystery* "The Secret," the Justice Department reports that "Three women a day are murdered by their husbands or boy friends" and "Only one in four incidents of domestic violence against women is reported to police."

## » Reflections of Evil

Roy Baumeister and Aaron Beck's book *Evil: Inside Human Violence and Cruelty* provides a revealing perspective about the thinking process of potential perpetrators. It should be no surprise that conceivably nearly any person could perform an act that the victim believes is evil. Does that shock you? My Methodist minister once asked me a question we all may face at some time: "When I'm confronted with a troubling decision, how do I know which force I'm dealing with: my soul or my inner demons?"

Remember, in order to accept this as possible, we must step into the roles of perpetrator and victim, separately and completely. But we must do this as a two-step process, each time distancing ourselves as we switch roles. Detach from the perpetrator's perspective, for example, as we step into the victim's perspective. Likewise, we must leave behind our emotional attachment to the victim as we imagine the mindset of the perpetrator.

This may sound repulsive at first, but it prompts us to wonder whether even our remotest inclination to fulfill a desire or a felt need might ever exceed our self-control. There obviously are many kinds of circumstances, thoughts, and emotions that might drive us to the edge, so to speak. How many of us have at least experienced a situation that virtually pushed our self-control to the limits? But there seems to be a natural difference between mindsets of perpetrators of evil; of those who are grossly inconsiderate of the welfare of others; of those whose daily existence is fraught with tribulation; and of those who live fairly "normal" lives.

In his book *The Lucifer Principle*, author Howard Bloom envisioned that "evil is woven into our most basic biological fabric." He contends that both nature and human society use destruction as a tool in the evolutionary process. Along the lines of Darwinian reasoning only the fittest survive evolutionary development over billions of years. The inefficient die out. As memes, or ideas, became a part of human cultures, competition arose for dominance of ideals, witness the conflict within Christianity and between Christianity and Islam. It would appear, however, that this application of the term "evil" is in the eye of the beholder, much as it is seen from the victim's rather than the predator's viewpoint.

Also worthwhile for its contribution to perspective is Arthur Miller's book *The Social Psychology of Good and Evil*. In his Amazon review of that book, author Mark Waldman commented, "Today there is much debate concerning the role that religion plays in developing moral behavior. This book shows how limited that role may actually be by demonstrating the biological and social forces that shape many of our ethical beliefs."

Waldman's two books *Why We Believe What We Believe: Uncovering Our Biological Need for Meaning, Spirituality* and *Born to Believe: God, Science and The Origin of Ordinary and Extraordinary Beliefs* add a fascinating glimpse of yet a different dimension of evil.

Obviously, psycho- or sociopathology also can spur a person to irrational behavior, even violence. Childhood behavior can reflect early problems that may be disregarded by parents, although the kids' conduct could be predictive of their adult behavior. Joshua Gowin took a look at this in the "Crime and Punishment" section of *Psychology Today*. His article was entitled "Rethinking the Bad Seed: Are Psychopaths Born or Made?" He quoted Richard Tremblay, a psychologist at the University of Montreal who studies violent behavior in children. "Most," Tremblay said, "grow up to become violent only if their conduct is left unchecked." But those "who are extremely callous can't simply be scared straight with punishment." Certain family factors point to high risk. Yet with proper support at a young age, "they may learn to express their temperament in a more socially appropriate fashion."

## » Criminal Intent

Over the years, violent crimes have attracted the news media. Television stations have carried programs depicting the successes of FBI criminal profilers. But one might wonder what prompts a criminal like a serial killer to get started or to continue his escapades. I said "his" because males seem to dominate these roles.

The preceding discussion about psychopaths certainly applies here. Perhaps such tendencies begin early in life or are the product of mental illness. But recall the earlier discussion about fantasies and the prohibition exerted by self-restraint. Many natural ego drives involve attempts to satisfy certain felt needs. These are not limited to, but include: control, power, lust, and envy. The first two may stem from unsatisfactory childhood development: parents, siblings, peers, or others. Lust and envy may characterize restrained fantasies. Note that these drives do not include instinctive motivations like rage, anger, jealousy, or revenge, which could prompt one-time impulsive criminal acts.

Criminals tell of experiencing adrenalin highs resulting from rape and killing or the thrill of avoiding detection and capture. These seem to be learned rewards discovered during early criminal acts, but tending to become addictive like cocaine.

## » Defense of Family Honor

Most of us would disavow killing our children for any reason. But there are cultures in which families kill their daughters for acts parents believe dishonor their family. The public became keenly aware of this in a case televised nationally involving an immigrant family. Their daughter converted from Islam to Christianity and ran away from home fearing her family would kill her. The case landed in the Federal court system. Some officials involved in the litigation expressed disbelief and were prepared to order the daughter returned to her family.

Television viewers learned that families in the Near East apparently kill their daughters for what the families perceive as infractions against family honor. This seems to occur there without criminal prosecution as an accepted religious practice. Daughters are held to severe restrictions in their social life and families decide whom their daughters will marry. Any of us not familiar with "honor killing" would find it hard to believe, let alone accept. Official figures indicate that more than two hundred "honor" killings take place each year in Turkey, almost half the annual number of murders in that country.

Evil, therefore, is yet another consideration each of us must consider—both regarding others and ourselves—in our never-ending pursuits prompted by our egos. Life is indeed a balancing act.

Harvard evolutionary biologist and cognitive neuroscientist Marc Hauser's book *Moral Minds: How Nature Designed Our Universal Sense of Right and Wrong* claims that evolution shaped a sense of moral judgment within humankind. But he acknowledges that this seems to serve only as a baseline. In actual practice, there typically are underlying psychological or cultural issues that shape real-world cases. An example would be so-called honor killings.

## » Abortion

America has been split over this subject, with advocates of free choice and pro-life proponents occasionally expressing their anger in ways that necessitate inclusion of this topic here. Experts seem to agree that the embryo becomes a fetus nine to ten weeks after conception. At least one pioneer researcher claims that souls do not join fetuses until then or later (Newton 2000).

It is worth noting that pregnancy resulting from rape, incest, or passion can be prevented with the emergency contraceptive known as the "morning after" pill. One variety of that pill is now known to be effective if taken within five days. Also, most cities and towns in this country now have designated sites such as fire stations where unwanted babies can be safely left for proper care.

The next chapter explores a very real question many of us might ask in the wake of overwhelming tragedy.

# CHAPTER NINE
# WHO KILLED GOD?

---

*"There is only one religion,*
*though there are a hundred versions of it."*

George Bernard Shaw

---

Even people of faith started wondering, "How could God allow this?" To permit loss or upheaval of life on a massive scale without divine intervention could challenge even the most devout belief in a merciful God. Examples resist a theological explanation: the Holocaust, Katrina, the World Trade Center, the Oklahoma Federal building, and a bus load of Christian worshipers killed by an eighteen-wheeler driver who fell asleep.

The shock is no less devastating if it involves only a few persons or an individual. There was Joe Smith, father of five, struck down at fifty-three by a ruptured brain aneurysm and Julianne Anderson, single mother of three with terminal breast cancer at thirty-eight. We might be waiting at the airport to learn whether our loved ones survived the plane crash or at the bedside dreading the physician's prognosis. Swamped with anxiety and fear and imagining the worst, we lash out: why, who, and how? The faithless have nowhere to turn; even the faithful become disheartened. Accusations spread like wildfire—did America turn its back on God, did God turn His back on us, or could there possibly be a more plausible explanation?

## » Death of God

The question "Is God Dead?" harkens back forty-four years to a peak of publicity with *Time* magazine featuring that question on its cover. The cover story title was a bit toned down "Theology: Toward A Hidden God." That article rolled out the names of notables down through history that predicted this conclusion, including Nietzsche, Kierkegaard, and Bonhoeffer. "The basic theological problem today," commented Langdon Gilkey of the University of Chicago Divinity School, "is the reality of God."

*Newsweek* magazine updated the controversy forty-three years later with Jon Meacham's article "The End of Christian America." It referred to the results of the American Religious Identification Survey. Included among its findings was that "Americans claiming no religious affiliation has almost doubled since 1990, rising from eight to fifteen per cent." During that same time, the number willing to admit being atheists or agnostics has increased almost fourfold, from about one million to 3.6 million.

The cover story was Christian Smith's article entitled "Is God Dead (Again)?" His online piece made reference to a study that revealed the religion of young Americans, including those who identify as Christian is, in fact, more like "moralistic therapeutic deism" than the conservative faith of evangelicalism.

That study, "Moralistic Therapeutic Deism--the New American Religion," was released four years earlier in the online *Christian Post*. Christian Smith and his fellow researchers with the National Study of Youth and Religion at the University of North Carolina at Chapel Hill conducted the study among 3,000 adolescents. As described by Smith and his team, moralistic therapeutic deism consists of beliefs like these:

- A god exists who created and ordered the world and watches over human life on   earth;
- God wants people to be good, nice, and fair to each other, as taught in the Bible and by most world religions;
- The central goal of life is to be happy and to feel good about oneself;
- God does not need to be particularly involved in one's life except when God is needed to resolve a problem;
- Good people go to heaven when they die.

The term "post-Christian" had arisen during the last century to designate the decline in the influence of traditional Christianity. According to Albert Mohler, president of the Southern Baptist Theological Seminary, "The post-Christian narrative is radically different; it offers spirituality, however defined, without binding authority."

In this book the term "religion" is defined as an organized group of believers in a divine power without confining it to any particular group, e.g., Protestant or Islam. Somewhat in contrast, the term "spirituality" is intended to mean a state of mind or behavior through which an individual feels a personal relationship with a divinity, e.g., God, Creator, or Allah. Religious institutions may claim to offer spirituality although Albert Mohler indicated that the post-Christian era distinguishes between the two concepts. Some individuals equate being "religious" with being "spiritual." Some acknowledge being one rather than the other. Still others deny they are either.

In contemporary America, proponents of religion often differ from proponents of spirituality. Austin Cline's online article "Religion vs. Spirituality: Distinguishing Between Religion and Spirituality" appeared on the Web site About.com: Agnosticism/Atheism. Cline compares different views about both concepts but he mostly criticizes groups that denigrate religion. Yet he claims that those groups are unable to precisely define the differences between religion and spirituality.

Personally, I believe that, as with art, religion and spirituality "rest in the eye of the beholder." In other words, no single paradigm will either satisfy or rally all people. Beliefs are very personal possessions, as discussed later in this book. This doesn't deny the ability to change, but acknowledges the tenacity with which beliefs may be held. This includes beliefs about evil as well as about religion and spirituality. It also involves the paradox of holding onto beliefs even after they have been shown to be without foundation.

## » To Please a Few

The early years of the present century saw a concerted effort in this country to "Kill God." This stemmed from three legal arguments: rights of other religions than Christianity, rights of atheists, and separation of church and state. But these emanated from a few people's complaints about their "rights" under the U. S. Constitution. The American Civil Liberties Union (ACLU) even championed their cause.

It is ironic that these efforts were directed toward removing God from being mentioned in schools, in the pledge of allegiance, in court buildings—in literally any public place the aforementioned "few" might be forced to encounter Him. It seems the majority of people in this country indeed have remained "silent" to allow the few to kill God in public places. Therefore, consider that our forefathers meant "separation of *specific religions* and state!" They remembered when single religions held power that competed with or even replaced the power of the state! But virtually *all* religions acknowledge the existence of the divinity that our forefathers called "God." Americans therefore have every right under our Constitution to worship our God anywhere and everywhere!

A case in point illustrated this movement in Frank Salvato's online article "The First Shot in the War on Political Correctness." Salvato cited an action by a school principal in Cupertino Union School District of California. It prevented a teacher from including the Declaration of Independence in lessons on American History because it mentions God. Salvato quoted the counsel in a suit against the principal and the school district "The district's actions conflict with American beliefs and are completely unconstitutional." The district court ruled in favor of the teacher and the school agreed to revise its policy statements to allow the teacher to continue to teach as he had.

Clifford May provides a horrific view of outcomes by certain people and governments to please a few in his online article "The War Against the Infidels: Terrorism is Only One of the Weapons" on National Review Online. In short, he shows that "the picture that emerges is not pretty: An 'Islamic world' in which terrorists are regarded often with lenience, sometimes with respect, and occasionally with reverence, while minority groups face increasing intolerance, persecution, and 'cleansing,' and where even their histories are erased. And we in the West are too polite, too 'politically correct,' and perhaps too cowardly to say much about it."

Read his article. I'm sure you too, as a member of "minority groups," will agree with his dismal forecast. Even some Muslims might. The author details the "peaceful" actions by which certain Muslims not only continue to make life intolerable for minorities in countries with Muslim majorities, they also seek to eradicate any traces of other religions.

The article documents some of those "peaceful" actions, including these two: "In 2001, the monumental 6th-century Buddhas of Bamiyan were dynamited on orders from Taliban leader Mullah Mohammed Omar. In 2010, Al-Kifl, the tomb of the Prophet Ezekiel, near Baghdad, was being desecrated. On the tomb are inscriptions in Hebrew and an ark in which a Torah was displayed centuries ago. Iraq's Antiquities and Heritage Authority, under pressure from Islamists, is erasing the Hebrew words, removing the Hebrew ornaments, and planning to build a mosque on top of the grave."

At most, Western governments may issue protests, as in 2001, but do nothing more. Since these two and some other Muslim atrocities focus on a single religion, one might wonder if the United States fails to take a stronger position in "observance" of the Constitutional interpretation of separation of church and state.

## » Doubts About God

There is no doubt that organized religion is getting hit with challenges it never faced before. You can recite many examples that appeared in the public press. One is Christopher Hitchens's book *God Is Not Great: How Religion Poisons Everything*. The title of his book implies that God and religion are the same, and therefore God is responsible for wrongs committed in the name of religion. But his target is organized religion, not God.

Similarly, Richard Dawkins book *The God Delusion* spends a substantial portion of his book criticizing religion. His preface speaks of "leaving religion" in the same breath as "to be an atheist," implying that the two have the same meaning. According to the *American Heritage College Dictionary*, however, atheism is defined as "Disbelief or denial of the existence of God." Apparently, Dawkins has never heard of being spiritual—the index to his book does not include that term.

Dawkins' book builds his denial of the existence of God in a chapter entitled "Why There Almost Certainly is No God." He attacks creationism with the same vehemence as he does irreducible complexity and intelligent design. A footnote in his book said, "Intelligent design has been described as creationism in a cheap tuxedo." He applauds

Darwin's views as the only answer to the complexity of the human body, i.e., improved very slowly over a vast time through evolution.

An online report by Martee Ortiz from Boise State University "Breaking Down the Definition: Intelligent Design" disagrees with lumping intelligent design in with creationism. The report quotes Casey Luskin of the Discovery Institute of Seattle, "The news media is notorious for defining [intelligent design] very, very badly." Luskin insists, "Intelligent design [ID] is purely scientific, based on facts and theories. ID does not offer proof or evidence of God as creator, which provides one way it differs from creationism. Instead ID is a theory that life and therefore the universe did not arise by chance: an intelligent entity designed and created it." The report also quotes biochemist Michael Behe, "Luskin makes it very clear that ID is not about proving God's existence; that is a belief."

I am beginning to suspect that some people may adopt an atheistic viewpoint because they fault organized religion for one thing or many, even though we accept that mankind created religion, not God. Likewise some people won't believe in a divinity that doesn't manifest itself. Many of these people also may be caught up in the controversy over the insistence by some scientists, like Dawkins, that nature evolved on its own without intelligent design.

Apparently there is some confusion among attitudes about God, religion, intelligent design, and spirituality. Religion assumes its role in spirituality, its kind of spirituality. Yet some trends today do appear to reflect individuals' desire for a more personal relationship with the Divine. It therefore should be possible for anyone to achieve that on his or her own initiative. Some individuals or groups believe it is possible to be spiritual with a reverence for life and respect for all humanity without a church affiliation. But well-meaning religions and churches should be recognized for their sense of community and for caring for those less fortunate.

## » Assurance

Stanley Fish's column "Think Again, Stanley Fish" in the online *New York Times,* entitled "God Talk," quotes from British critic Terry Eagleton's book *Reason, Faith, and Revolution.* Eagleton felt that certain icons other than God traditionally held out by materialists for guidance don't deliver: "science, reason, liberalism, and capitalism." He challenged such symbols as unable to "forge ... direct links between the most universal and absolute truths and the everyday practices of countless millions of men and women" as compared to the Divinity.

From a global perspective, however, this all seems to hinge on a single question: how much assurance of personal security and wellbeing do we expect from God? Asked another way, do we accept any accountability for adversity in our own lives? Just for the sake of debate, if God had prevented the Holocaust, would we have expected the same protection from Katrina? Of course, had He thwarted Hitler's evil plan, we wouldn't have known to expect another miracle with Katrina. Therefore, are we really asking, "What has God done for us?" *or* "What has God done for us *lately?*"

## » Why Doesn't God Intervene?

Could humankind be responsible for God's seeming indifference to our wellbeing? Is it willful punishment from a vengeful God? As asked earlier, "Did America turn its back on God?

Probably one of the most incisive critiques I've ever read of humankind's purported accountability arising from Adam and Eve's "original sin" appeared in *The Fourth R.* It was Patricia William's article "The Evolution of Good and Evil," adapted from her book *Doing Without Adam and Eve: Sociobiology and Original Sin.* Williams tracked the evolution of four endowed capabilities of early creatures through modern man: resources, reproduction, relatives, and reciprocity. Good resources, e.g., food, were sought out, while bad resources, e.g., harm, were avoided. Appropriate reproduction assured gene survival. Assistance to relatives further protected the gene pool. Reciprocal assistance with others supported survival of both.

Before man emerged on the scene, creatures were not cognitively equipped or inclined to depart from mutually beneficial use of their capabilities. But man introduced a departure from the past. Man decided that power, possessions, and elimination of rivals were important. Thus, evil seems to have emerged from man's own devices. Allegorically, perhaps the "original sin" was man's acquisition of knowledge that he could misappropriate his God-given talents for his own benefit, even without regard for the welfare of others.

You immediately protest, and rightly so: "Is some peoples' misuse of God-given talents the source of all our problems, including natural disasters? How could that be?" Pause for a moment and ask yourself. "If God prevented all evil and accidental events from happening and blessed everyone with a safe, successful, healthy, and happy life, how would our souls ever learn anything in the eternal scheme of things?" Free will wouldn't be necessary and our relationships with one another should never sour. Our lives would be determined for us. As you'll read elsewhere in this book, a University of Virginia psychologist even goes so far as to claim that "adversity, setbacks, and even trauma may actually be *necessary* for people to be happy, successful, and fulfilled."

## » Intercessory Prayer

This may be one of the most disputed topics in this book. Fundamentalist religions are convinced that their members' prayers are effective. Some of them even believe that only *their* prayers achieve results. At the other extreme, atheists and agnostics likely don't believe in prayer, but they may be missing out on a potential direct and indirect benefit. Health professionals and scientists have attempted to correlate prayer with patient outcomes. These studies began to be published forty years ago, a Brandeis University researcher determined. The results of many medical studies have been mixed, so intercessory prayer has received a lukewarm reception by a large segment of the general public.

An online abstract of Brandeis researcher Wendy Cadge's study "The Healing Power of Prayer" was published in the *Journal of Religion*. Cadge found that the eighteen studies she reviewed "actually say more about the scientists conducting the studies than about the power of prayer to heal." She soon will complete a book *Paging God: Religion in the Halls of Medicine*.

Although "researchers ... applied clinical scientific methodologies ... that approach was fraught with problems." Cadge cited comments in some medical literature such as "We do not need science to validate our spiritual beliefs, as we would never use faith to validate our scientific data." University of Arizona David Hodge disagrees. He found a positive effect among the seventeen studies he examined "using prayer as a treatment in a medical setting." Hodge does acknowledge, however, that his "meta-analysis indicates that prayer is effective [but is not] effective enough to meet the standards of the American Psychological Association's Division 12 for empirically validated interventions." He concludes, "Thus, we should not be treating clients suffering with depression, for example, only with prayer."

This discussion could just as well have been considered in the later chapter of this book dealing with holistic and alternative medicine, since many of the variables involved in the effectiveness of prayer also seem to apply to healing energy and to the treatment of illness in general. One of the variables, patients' beliefs, has been shown to influence health outcomes. Dana King's book *Faith, Spirituality, and Medicine* addressed this relationship. King cites several studies showing positive correlations between spirituality and health. A review of 1,086 studies in family medicine literature confirmed that seventy-five percent of studies included spiritual variables. Another citation was of a four-volume bibliography involving over three hundred studies that also acknowledged the spirituality-health relationship.

You will find references throughout this book to the potential influence of thoughts and beliefs, both negative and positive, on any human activity. This includes the impact that personal thoughts about illness and treatment have on recovery. It also involves group efforts to heal through energy transfer or prayer. A later chapter in this book entitled "The Power of Synchronized Intention" discusses focused group effort in more detail. It contains the results of a doctoral study that revealed factors that can improve the effectiveness of group efforts.

The next chapter completes this part by examining the matter of humility—or lack of it—in today's world.

# CHAPTER TEN

# You're What?

> *"Before enlightenment; chop wood, carry water.*
> *After enlightenment; chop wood, carry water."*
>
> Zen proverb

Part of the reason for this book is an acknowledgment that we all must cope with a society that is very diverse. Certain groups have demanded special privileges and accommodations. Likewise, individuals and groups may flaunt what they believe to be their special talents, achievements, and material possessions.

Obviously, this is not new. Jesus criticized the scribes and Pharisees of His day of hypocrisy, i.e., self-righteously setting themselves above others by reason of their position. To believe and portray that oneself is "better" than others for any particular reason is counterproductive. "Humility is the ground for enlightenment to grow," said Andrew Cohen in an interview. Cohen is said to be a modern pioneer in evolutionary enlightenment and is founder and editor-in-chief of the magazine *EnlightenNext*.

## » Humility

The online *Merriam-Webster Dictionary* defines humility as "not proud, haughty, arrogant, or assertive." Nancy Gibb's essay "The Age of Arrogance" in *Time* magazine chastises us all for our vanity. She appeals for a return of modesty. Gibbs points to illustrations of immodesty in female attire, professional sports figures, and politicians. She stresses, "Modesty in private life is attractive, but in public life it is essential."

## » Indigo Children

An example of the dangers of self-aggrandizement involves a group of young people referred to as "Indigo children." They were described in Tobin Hart's book *The Secret Spiritual World of Children*. This label has become associated with "a new personality classification for children who are technologically savvy, often are labeled as attention disordered and nonconforming, and have a sense of entitlement or a 'deserving to be here'."

The color indigo seems to have been used first by Nancy Ann Tappe in her book *Understanding Your Life Through Color*. Tappe claimed she saw this color of aura around certain children. Obviously, this information helped parents who have children who display these traits to realize that their kids are not alone. Hart himself decried labeling "Indigo children," as a disservice to those kids. He has had these children confront him with, "I'm Indigo. Are your children?"

P. M. H. Atwater, a leading near-death-experience researcher, faulted the movie "Indigo" for sensationalizing children labeled by that name as deserving special recognition. She felt that children born since 1982 truly seem different, not only those called Indigo. She said, "Professionals in the field of child development and education, parents, even the kids themselves, are having problems with the idea that certain character traits are the province of so-called 'Indigos' when, in fact, the majority of today's children match those traits."

## » Enlightenment

In a sense, I have a problem with kids who claim to be Indigos just as I do with those who boast their so-called achievement of enlightenment. Thankfully, an Indigo child is not something you can become, whereas becoming "enlightened" is a powerful marketing tool today. Both groups naturally will criticize me for these statements. But the truth seems best depicted in the Zen proverb at the beginning of this chapter.

Interestingly, the historical movement called "The Enlightenment" was usually associated with the 18th century but its roots go back much further, according to Paul Brians' online article with that title (2000).

"This" he said, " is one of those rare historical movements which in fact named itself. Certain thinkers and writers, primarily in London and Paris, believed that they were more enlightened than their compatriots and set out to enlighten them."

Today's striving for enlightenment appears to be more related to a search for transcendence, i.e., a state of being or existence above and beyond the limits of material experience. Buddha was quoted as saying, "To enjoy good health, to bring true happiness to one's family, to bring peace to all, one must first discipline and control one's own mind. If a man can control his mind he can find the way to Enlightenment, and all wisdom and virtue will naturally come to him." One must wonder if enlightenment in this sense carries with it the virtue of humility.

Enlightenment sometimes seems related to the acquisition of advanced knowledge not available to others. The Gnostics of Jesus' day claimed to possess special knowledge. But theirs had spiritual implications whereas enlightenment today often seems to lack spiritual aspects. To me, spiritual growth of the soul is said to emphasize empathy, selflessness, compassion, benevolence, love, and forgiveness. These don't seem like attributes of which a soul would boast about—nor would a human who genuinely seeks spiritual growth.

There remains a question in my mind whether our ego can sincerely pursue spirituality. It almost seems a quest to subjugate ego drives to soul control. This book sharply delineates between soul-centered early periods of a child's life and subsequent ego-centered later periods when he or she seeks to establish a self-identity. Near the end of this book you'll read more about the soul's continuing competition with the ego to balance earthly drives with spirituality.

Those who are susceptible to the appeal of enlightenment may simply want to escape the pressures or a lack of fulfillment in their lives. Others may be more introspective and ask the basic question "What is the purpose of life?" You'll have to wait until a later chapter to examine that question.

The next part goes beyond thinking to explore our physiological control systems, our personal development, and some amazing influences on our very existence.

## PART THREE

# Beyond Thinking: Our Control Systems

CHAPTER ELEVEN
# CONSCIOUSNESS, MIND, AND BRAIN

---

*"To understand the heart and mind of a person,*
*look not at what he has already achieved,*
*but at what he aspires to."*

Kahlil Gibran

---

We've discussed thinking and thoughts and their potential impact on ourselves, on others, and on our environment. Much of the book will examine entities and processes of human beings that mediate those impacts. Although much of these discussions will seem scientific or clinical, the idea still holds that their value for you may come from your considering "What if...?" What implications might any of this have for you and your family?

First, it may seem redundant to discuss consciousness: you are very familiar with your own. It's proof of your existence. But to further explore thoughts and thinking, it is important to examine the mechanisms that scientists believe are involved, including consciousness. The term "streaming" is sometimes used with consciousness for its continuing and changing nature.

Our minds and brains also are considered in this chapter. Scientists are working diligently to define how these three entities fit together in the grand scheme of mental activities. As you'll soon discover, however, many aspects of this still are an enigma.

One aspect of consciousness is "awareness," the perceiving inputs from our five senses. This might be considered the collecting of information from our environment. But consciousness also might include information from other sources, including the brain. This could include a memory or an emotion or even a self-created thing like an intention, imagination, or a thought.

Many scientists insist that consciousness is created in the brain. The one theory scientists seem to agree upon is that consciousness is an individual matter—each person experiences his or her own consciousness uniquely. Some scientists believe that even if we knew everything that was happening in the brain at a given time, this wouldn't explain that "inner experience" of human consciousness.

It is worth distinguishing consciousness from intelligence, as the latter applies to every cell of our bodies. As discussed earlier in this book, intelligence focuses more on the application of information. Just like computers, living organisms have the ability to acquire [or be programmed with] information. Then, innately or through experience or programming, they can use that information in survival, growth, and reproduction. Consciousness, by contrast, seems to be a unique but ineffable human characteristic of perception, cognition, decision-making, intention, feeling, and memory processed in an, as yet, indefinable location.

The growing use of brain imaging techniques to observe activity in specific areas of the brain has led some researchers to believe that areas of observed brain activity match physical or mental responses to stimuli. In other words, some members of this group are convinced that the brain is the seat of consciousness. However, you'll read later how other researchers believe that consciousness might exist outside the brain or even outside the body.

It must be acknowledged that the brain is *involved* in conscious activity. This becomes obvious when the brain receives an insult or injury. Being knocked unconscious restricts conscious activity, but there are indications that a person in coma still can perceive environmental input. Also, it has been demonstrated that surgery patients rendered unconscious by general anesthesia still may remember conversations held around them.

Damage to the brain impairs conscious activity according to the extent and nature of the injury. The Impaired Consciousness Research

Group provided a summary of its findings online. The Group is part of the Wolfson Brain Imaging Center, University of Cambridge, in the United Kingdom. The question remains whether the brain is the *sole* source of consciousness.

The word "mind" is sometimes used to mean consciousness or awareness. But, as Michael Newton detailed in his book, we also have a subconscious mind and a superconscious mind (2000). These two are storehouses of memory to which we normally don't have conscious or intentional access, such as implicit memory, mentioned in an earlier chapter. The subconscious mind also automatically controls certain physiological functions through the autonomic nervous system.

## » Search for Consciousness

Perhaps the most recent advance which some scientists claim proves that consciousness is centered in the brain is the imaging of brain responses to various stimuli. This is accomplished with advanced brain imaging technology called functional magnetic resonance imaging (fMRI). Activity can be detected in areas of the brain theorized to be involved in processing the neurological responses to specific stimuli.

Ironically, at least two publications have appeared challenging the reliability of some of these results. One of these was Edward Vul's online paper "Voodoo Correlations in Social Neuroscience." The other was headlined in the British Psychology Society Research Digest Blog: "Another shock for brain imaging research—the signal isn't always linked to neuronal activity." This was based upon Yevgeniv Sirotin and Aniruddha Da's study published in *Nature*.

Technically, fMRI works by measuring blood flow in the brain. As with muscle, brain cells need more blood when they work and less when they're inactive. It's a step beyond CT scans, or CAT scans, which can map the brain's structure but not its functions. Putting someone in an fMRI machine, a giant clanking cylinder, tells scientists which parts of the brain are working and which aren't. However, it gives no direct evidence of which neurotransmitters are coursing about. Each area that lights up should be doing something, but what isn't always clear.

The advent of fMRI brain imaging has put to rest the myth that we use only ten percent of our brains by showing we regularly use our entire brains. Some parts of our brains are less critical than those involving vital functions like breathing, speaking, or comprehending, but all are used. Electroencephalographs (EEGs) can show which areas are most active during certain activities and which could be causing problems, like seizures. But even brains scans don't provide a perfect measure of how much is being used at a given time. So it seems true that we may be able to enhance our lives by strengthening underutilized parts of our brains. Robert Shmerling, a physician at Beth Israel Deaconess Medical Center, provided this revelation in his online article "How Much of Our Brain Do We *Really* Use?" in *Aetna InteliHealth.*

The origin of the popular myth that we use only ten percent of our brains is well concealed. It has been speculated that it may have evolved as a misquote from the pioneering American psychologist William James in the late nineteenth and early twentieth centuries. It seems that James not only amassed a substantial amount of scholarly work but also authored many popular articles for the general public. In these, James was fond of stating that the average person rarely achieves but a small portion of his or her potential. In the preface to Dale Carnegie's ever popular, *How to Win Friends and Influence People*, Lowell Thomas attributed the ten-percent-of-the-brain claim to William James.

In sharp contrast to the idea of using only a small fraction of our brains, researchers now have shown that our brains seem constantly at work, even when we are at rest. This emerged from fMRI images of certain areas of the brain lighting up when it is activated to perform tasks. Simultaneously, some other areas go dark. It now is felt that these dark areas reveal a special neural network that is active when we are at rest with our minds just wandering. Supporting this are measurements comparing the brain's energy consumption. There seems to be a baseline of energy consumption by the brain, above which the energy required to light up activated areas is only a small part. This led researchers to theorize that a system called the "default neural network" exists with important functions. Defects in the network are now being implicated in certain neuropsychiatric diseases such as Alzheimer's (Raichle).

If consciousness *does* involve brain processes visualized using imaging techniques, what accounts for some people without a normal brain being able to function consciously? An example was discussed in the online Fox News report "Man with Almost No Brain Has Led Normal Life," in which Swiss researcher Hans Ricke questioned whether consciousness requires a functioning brain.

Brain imaging seems to serve a valuable purpose, but does it prove that the brain is responsible for consciousness? Some researchers say it does not. The personal uniqueness of "felt awareness" can be so fleeting and functional magnetic resonance imaging (fMRI) so slow that one wonders whether the imaged responses truly reflect an immediate state of consciousness.

## » Site of Consciousness

Some scientists seem to acknowledge that the brain is *not* the seat of *all* sensory processing. Human and other energy fields increasingly are dominating theories about how we humans interact with our world and with each other. One paragraph from my earlier book is worth paraphrasing here to illustrate this point. A finding by California researcher Valerie Hunt appeared in her book *Infinite Mind: Science of the Human Vibrations of Consciousness.* It suggests that a human energy field may sense an outside stimulus *before* the brain does. Hunt reported that, to her surprise, some stimuli elicited a response in the energy field, as registered in the aura, before it did in the brain, as measured by brain waves. These included an inadvertent sound, light flashes, and even a feather touching the aura but not the skin. This delay in brain response apparently also was observed when a change in one person's energy field vibration affected another person's field. In some inexplicable way, this "early sensing" might imply that some consciousness may be processed apart from the brain.

## » Human Consciousness Project

Scientists are becoming keenly interested in research focused upon what heretofore have been considered paranormal events: out-of-body (OBE) and near-death (NDE) experiences. An AWARE (AWAreness during REsuscitation) study was announced in collaboration with more than 25 major medical centers throughout Europe, Canada, and the United States. It is the first launched by the Human Consciousness Project and is led by Dr. Sam Parnia, a world-renowned expert on the study of the human mind and consciousness during clinical death. Dr Peter Fenwick and Professors Stephen Holgate and Robert Peveler of the University of Southampton are involved too.

This multicenter effort was launched in September 2008 at

a United Nations conference. The background to this effort was succinctly described as follows: "Prior to the age of reason, mysticism and revelation served as the primary source of knowledge and wisdom in the western world. With the advent of the Enlightenment, however, a schism would emerge between the comprehension of physical realities through religious thinking and the drive to understand the material universe through empirical reasoning. Though the tension between these contrasting approaches has taken on many different forms since then, it has essentially continued to this day."

Proceedings of the conference were Webcast and can be accessed at: http://mindbodysymposium.com/Beyond-the-Mind-Body-Problem/New-Paradigms-in-the-Science-of-Consciousness.html.

During the study, physicians will use the latest technologies to study the brain and consciousness during cardiac arrest. At the same time, they also will be testing the validity of out of body experiences and patients' claims of being able to see and hear during cardiac arrest. They will use randomly generated hidden images that are not visible unless viewed from specific vantage points above the patient.

Researchers will conduct a variety of physiological tests in cardiac arrest patients. These include cerebral monitoring techniques that aim to identify methods to improve the medical and psychological care of patients who undergo cardiac arrest.

There appears to be a mushrooming interest by neuroscientists in collaborating to better define the relationships between consciousness, mind, and brain. Special research initiatives are being instituted to promote this undertaking. A few of these are: Switzerland's Mind-Brain Institute; Horizon Research Foundation; University of Pennsylvania's Center for Spirituality and the Mind; Neurosciences Institute; Harvard Mind/Brain/Behavior Initiative; Picower Institute; Dana Foundation; and Center for Neurotechnology Studies.

## » Personal Preferences Part of Consciousness

Each person has certain foods, snacks, drinks, music, hobbies, and other things he or she prefers; also, some things he or she hates. Did you ever wonder where we register these likes and dislikes? They can't necessarily be called memories, traits, or beliefs. But they seem to help characterize the individual. Are they part of our consciousness? Are they part of our DNA?

An inexplicable and almost humorous event has been happening with organ transplant recipients. One spin on this surprising occurrence is discussed in Danny Penman's online article "Can We Really Transplant a Human Soul?" It seems that organ transplant recipients receive not only the organ but also some of the donor's personal preferences. In at least one instance, cited in that article, the recipient apparently inherited the donor's mindset about more serious matters. He committed suicide in the same manner as did the donor.

Penman's article also refers to other case studies, most not as bizarre, accumulated by Gary Schwartz of the University of Arizona. In the suicide case, a heart was the organ donated. Two other books give dramatic examples of heart transplant recipients' experiences in receiving the donor's personal preferences as well. Claire Sylvia describes her personal case in her book *A Change of Heart*. Paul Pearsall provides a number of other stories in his book *The Heart's Code: Tapping the Wisdom and Power of Our Heart Energy*.

Paul Pearsall reports on the findings of his interviews with seventy-eight heart transplant patients and sixty-seven recipients of other organs. What Pearsall discovered is that, in some patients, the new heart seems to bring with it some "memory" from the heart donor. Often these memories are experienced in the recipient as new preferences, such as food tastes or hobby interests, language choices such as use of specific words or phrases, or even memories of incidents in the donor's life.

One very moving experience Pearsall relates happened at an international meeting of psychologists and psychiatrists. Pearsall spoke there about "cellular memory" as his transplant patients had reported it to him. One psychiatrist, clearly moved by the findings came to the microphone and spoke as she struggled through her tears. She was sobbing to the point that the audience and Pearsall had difficulty understanding her. She said, "I have a patient, an eight-year-old little girl who received the heart of a murdered ten-year-old girl. Her mother brought her to me when she started screaming at night about her dreams of the man who had murdered her donor. The mother said her daughter knew who it was. The psychiatrist finally decided to call the police and, using the descriptions from the little girl, they found the murderer. He was easily convicted with evidence my patient provided.

The time, the weapon, the place, the clothes he wore, what the little girl he killed had said to him ... everything the little heart transplant recipient reported was completely accurate."

These situations might suggest that the human heart is the site of individual preferences or other significant information. After all, there is increasing evidence of the heart's involvement in other human variables, including the location of the fourth chakra (discussed later). But these preference transfers also have occurred with the transplants of other organs, according to Penman. Is it possible that our organs have cellular memories that can be transferred to recipients like DNA is?

## » Brain

The left side of the brain is often said to be dominant as the decision maker. But the prefrontal lobes are responsible for coordinating activities of the brain. This is especially well detailed in Elkhonon Goldberg's book *The Executive Brain: Frontal Lobes and the Civilized Mind*. He spent thirty years studying the manifestations of injuries or other derangements in this area of the brain. The frontal lobes are the foundations of civilization, he believes. Apparently, there is no single area of the brain assigned to each of our five senses. Rather, there is coordination between and among different areas of the brain for its complex yet sometimes subtle activity.

Dutch cardiologist and researcher Pim van Lommel's online report "About the Continuity of Our Consciousness" was a compelling account of his conviction that human consciousness survives death of the body. Citations from his comprehensive report are included in other parts of this book as are relevant to those discussions.

Van Lommel quotes researcher Bruce Greyson about lessons learned from near-death experiences: "The paradoxical occurrence of heightened, lucid awareness and logical thought processes during a period of impaired cerebral perfusion [cardiac arrest] raises particular perplexing questions for our current understanding of consciousness and its relation to brain function." This "challenges the concept that consciousness is localized exclusively in the brain."

## » Brain as a Facilitator of Consciousness

Some researchers claim that, if consciousness were centered in the brain, cardiac arrest and brain death would prevent any kind of consciousness like that manifested in near-death experiences.

In his online article "Does Consciousness Depend on the Brain," author Chris Carter quotes British psychologist Cyril Burt: "the brain [does not generate] ... consciousness but ... evolved ... to transmit and limit the processes of consciousness and of conscious attention ... to restrict them" to the specifics of the environment that are important to the person at that time. Burt goes on to say that paranormal phenomena that seem to represent an expansion of consciousness simply occur when limitations are removed. Carter feels that this concept is consistent with the effects that harm to the brain has on consciousness.

Van Lommel concluded, "Consciousness can be experienced in another dimension without our conventional body-linked concept of time and space." When an NDE survivor is resuscitated, he or she is well aware of a conscious return into his or her body and its limitations. Some NDE survivors expressed disappointment for the loss of "universal wisdom and love" they felt during the NDE.

## » Stimulating Metaphysical Experiences

Some other researchers claim they can simulate an NDE by stimulating specific areas of the brain. Down through history, certain cultures have used various means to induce personal experiences that reach beyond the everyday state of consciousness. Drug abuse often involves substances known to produce hallucinogenic states. Native American and some other native cultures use plant materials such as peyote to produce visions. Shamans or leaders may use these for guidance and insight or groups may do so ostensibly for spiritual worship.

Similar experiences have been attributed to near-death survival, to meditation, and to certain electromechanical exposure. Pilots spun in g-force accelerators for jet fighter training have told of visions bordering on blackout. Various experiments involving exposure of participants' brains to electromagnetic fields have been shown to induce unusual perceptual experiences. Some persons have claimed that this has been useful in mental health therapy.

One such experimental device is called the "God helmet," using a process called transcranial magnetic stimulation" (TMS). Its nickname derives from some participants' claims of visions of God or Jesus.

This is applied to the apparatus developed by Michael A. Persinger in the Behavioral Neurosciences Program at Laurentian University in Sudbury, Ontario, Canada.

Persinger reports that very few subjects, some twenty or so, have reported a vision of a divinity. He said most of those participants were "religious." By far, dead relatives, cosmic forces, spiritual entities, or "all-around-me" sensations are more common. The nature of these experiences varies along a scale from "devil to angel" that "appears strongly related to the affect (pleasant-terror) associated with the experience." Persinger admits that some participants are reluctant to describe their experience for fear of ridicule. A variation is the Koren helmet that reportedly has produced visions of demoniac beings, out-of-body experiences, visions of other realities, and a range of other paranormal experiences (Murphy).

These accounts have led skeptics to debunk near-death experiences (NDEs) as simply products of the brain. However, since visions induced by electromechanical means happen with a live brain, they differ remarkably from testimonies of NDE survivors who are shown to have been clinically dead—heart, lungs, and brain.

## » NDE "Consciousness"

A 2010 book that quickly became a *New York Times* bestseller seems to have touched the hearts of Americans yearning for answers to life and death. It was Jeffrey Long's *Evidence of the Afterlife*. The result of ten years and thirteen hundred case studies by Houma, Louisiana's radiation oncologist, the book was the basis of Roxanne Nelson's article "Near-Death Experiences: Evidence of Afterlife, Says Radiation Oncologist" on *Medscape Family Medicine*.

Because Long found that near-death experience (NDE) survivors "become kinder, more loving, and more accepting of others, he [Long] has begun to reflect those same effects in his own life" and feels that he can be a "better physician for his cancer patients." He said he now "faces life with more courage and confidence."

One of the characteristics Long found in NDE experiences was a "crystal-clear consciousness." Netherlands researcher Pim van Lommel agrees, "[NDE] patients experience, paradoxically, an enhanced consciousness during a cardiac arrest and during a period of a temporarily nonfunctioning brain." In his country, van Lommel explained, more and more physicians seem to be "open to the possibility of a facilitating function of our brain to experience consciousness, and our consciousness being nonlocal—not cemented in place or time." Yet he acknowledges, "there is no hard scientific proof of an afterlife, and there will never be."

Van Lommel and his colleagues conducted a thirteen-year prospective study of three hundred and forty-four cardiac patients in ten centers around the Netherlands who were successfully resuscitated after cardiac arrest. Only sixty-two of those patients (18%) reported NDEs, and only forty-one (12%) had what is referred to as core or deep NDEs. But, van Lommel argues, "If NDEs are purely physiological … then most patients who have been clinically dead should report one."

## » BCI Artificial Body Control

A new science is rapidly coming onstream. It is based upon the brain-computer interface (BCI). A sci-fi adaptation of it appeared in the hit movie *Avatar*: a paraplegic Marine finds a virtual new world through apparently surreal connections of his brain to a computer. In fact, however, this is not as seemingly far-fetched as it might appear.

Although very expensive technology at this stage, BCI is appearing in a variety of research applications to create assistance for injured, disabled, blind, deaf, or otherwise handicapped individuals. This is based on the brain's ability to generate millivolt electrical signals that the computer can interpret and translate into surrogate actions by the body. Inherent in the use of the brain-to-computer system is the likely question about the source of the stimulus from the brain: mind, consciousness, thought, intention, or what?

Wellsphere's online article "The Reality of the Brain-Computer Interface" provides a good orientation to this subject.

## » Tuning In

In his book *The Human Antennae: Reading the Language of the Universe in the Songs of Our Cells* Robin Kelly uses the term "non-material science." He quotes evolutionary biologist Rupert Sheldrake that this is "the true science of life." Kelly said that "those of us who are thin-skinned *human antennas* absorb a wide range of wavelengths and …

our systems become overloaded." He stressed that we "began to regard bodily symptoms as intuitive messages: messages to be listened to intently before any action is taken." He emphasized that "the body is primarily energy, and ... our organs ... heart, liver, kidney ... could also be linked with our emotions."

Bradley Nelson's book examines virtually every aspect of emotions as a primary source of physical and mental illnesses.

Kenneth Smith's book *Awakening the Energy Body: From Shamanism to Bioenergetics* traces a five thousand year history. This stretches back to the Toltec culture's wisdom and traditions of working "with the energy body." Smith says, "Even as modern science is establishing the uncertainty of physical matter, it is asserting the reality of our existence as interconnecting quantum energy fields."

Brian Greene's book *The Elegant Universe: Superstrings, Hidden Dimensions, and the Quest for the Ultimate Theory* takes a different approach to a similar conclusion. Amidst competing "theories of everything," nearly everybody acknowledges that such a find would not end the search for truths about psychology, biology, geology, chemistry, or even physics. It should mark the beginning, not the end. It should mean an unshakable comprehension of the coherence of our universe from which further wonders might unfold.

## » Emotion and Consciousness

Many of us likely feel that we are in control of the way our behavior expresses our emotions. This would seem to imply conscious awareness and intentional participation. But a book edited by Barret, Niedenthal, and Winkielman, *Emotion and Consciousness*, paints a different picture. It was created from contributions provided by two-dozen respected professionals in neuropsychiatry from around the world.

Insights there are related to a functional model of the mind and the brain. It acknowledges the complex levels of processing our brains perform related to our minds and personalities. Yet it refutes the likelihood that we ever could be aware of more than a fraction of the brain's activity. Instead, there is scientific evidence that we can perceive the emotions of others, but that we respond emotionally in ways of which we are *not* conscious. This is certain to be factored into the continuing consciousness-mind-brain debate.

## » Consciousness Effect on Quantum Behavior

Bruce Rosenblum and Fred Kuttner's book *Quantum Enigma: Physics Encounters Consciousness* best exemplifies the often-disregarded but documented influence of consciousness on outcomes of quantum theory experiments. Lynn McTaggart's book *The Field: The Quest of the Secret Force of the Universe* showed that thought (consciousness) statistically can alter the results of random outcome generators. It also documented that consciousness can alter experimental results in quantum mechanics.

Physicists call this the "measurement problem," although it sometimes has been referred to as the "observer effect." This occurs when a human observes the results of a quantum mechanics experiment and the action of observation actually changes the results. This is discussed in Dean Radin's book *Entangled Minds: Extrasensory Experiences in a Quantum Reality.* Physicists claim it is not within their jurisdiction to comment on this. Perhaps they are unable to explain it without resorting to a philosophical or metaphysical explanation. Is this just another example of the impact of energy of intention, as discussed elsewhere in this book?

So-called "entanglement" is said to produce similar results of experimenter observation. Entanglement refers to the property of two particles that have been joined or "entangled" to behave alike after separation, even over a great distance. If one particle exhibits a change under experimental observation, the other does so too. Radin's book discusses this.

## » Reality as an Illusion

One branch of modern science claims that reality is no more than an image in our consciousness created by our brain from sensory inputs. Naturally you disagree as you pick an apple from a tree. I disagreed too, at first. But consider the idea over a period of time. Consciousness is fleeting, at times focusing on a material object and at other times engrossed in thought. We read words from a printed page then look away to cogitate on something else. The printed words are no longer "there" in our consciousness. Did we "imagine them" or perhaps simply retain a memory of what the words meant to us? As with the apple and the tree, we remember where we picked the apple as we enjoy it.

In his online presentation "Reality and Consciousness," physicist and futurist Peter Russell—one of the leading thinkers of our time—presented a cogent argument about perceived reality. He suggested that there are *two realities* and it is important to distinguish between them. "There is the reality we experience, our [conscious] image of reality." Then, "there is the underlying reality that has given rise to this experience." He designated the underlying reality as identical for all to see. "It is an absolute reality. The fact that we create our image of reality does not mean, as some people misconstrue, that we are creating the underlying reality." That underlying reality exists apart from the image in our consciousness. In other words, a tree is a tree is a tree, regardless of my perception of it.

But the image in our consciousness is a reality we *individually* perceive. Our sensory input of underlying reality gets mixed with other inputs from our previous experiences, our point of view, other sensory inputs, and so forth. For example, three people stand at the ocean's edge. One sees it as a marvelous fishing opportunity. The second notices the expansive white sandy beach and yearns to swim and sunbathe. The third feels the gentle breeze and believes it is a great day to go sailing. But all three people *see* the ocean.

If you're interested, read Susan Blackmore's online article "The Grand Illusion: Why Consciousness Exists Only When You Look for It." Two other references on this topic are the online articles "How Consciousness Creates Reality," by Claus Janew, and "Spirituality and Science: The Holographic Universe," by Michael Talbot.

## » Duality of Humankind

Britisher Anthony Peake wrote an intriguing book *Is There Life After Death? The Extraordinary Science of What Happens After We Die*. His book is noteworthy not only because of its approach but also for its author's background. Peake is a psychometrician, one who specializes in psychological measurements of mental variables. He also is a lecturer and author. Much of his book addresses states of mind or awareness. He sets his commentary in the context of historical, religious, and scientific concepts of the "duality" of an individual.

Peake's discussion about duality focuses on beliefs that the human body is occupied by two entities, one materialistic (ego) and one transcendent (spirit), to use contemporary terms. The former has been called Eidolon ("lower self") and the latter Daemon ("higher self") down through history. (See "Who and What is Daemon or Daimon?" in my bibliography.)

Readers of my earlier book may recall Julian Jaynes' theory of primitive man's "bicameral brain." He believed that modern man developed a left brain to process inputs from his five senses. But primitive man had depended on a brain that utilized other environmental and transcendent inputs, more like our present right brain. Scientists today do acknowledge that brain functions are largely split between left and right divisions, the left often called the "executive" and the right the "emotional." The left also typically is the dominant half. From that distinction many theories have developed about humankind's current mental capabilities, particularly involving the right brain. The right brain also is referred to as the creative side and has been claimed to be responsible for intuition and extrasensory perception.

## » Time and Consciousness

For some people on various occasions, time may *seem* to slow down. For example, Michael Jordan, the basketball player seemed to react faster and better than anybody else. He once was asked, "How do you do that?" He responded, "When I'm playing well, time slows down. The other players are in slow motion." I've had friends tell me this has happened to them. Apparently, this is a common talent in athletes, who may process visual data faster.

This may seem weird and inconceivable. Obviously it's not occurring to others nearby. This experience shows how very personal consciousness is. The explanation for it seems buried in quantum mechanics as something called "time dilation," involving the frequency of events being perceived by the subject.

This is the way researcher Stuart Hameroff explained it in his online interview "Consciousness, Microtubules and The Quantum World: "Something enabled you to have perceived more conscious events during that moment. Maybe it was a second, but it seemed to you like 10 seconds. You had ten times as many conscious events as you normally would, which allowed you to react more quickly."

## » In the Shadows

I sought to have a life-between-lives (LBL) hypnotic regression with the help of an eminent hypnotherapist, a past president of the Michael Newton Institute for Life Between Lives Hypnotherapy. I apparently achieved a trance state but was unable to move back past my very early childhood. The psychologist said that the extreme heaviness of my arms and legs suggested that I achieved hypnosis, but I was carrying an unresolved burden in this life that I needed to clear. We spent the remainder of the session trying to identify that problem and to open my awareness to confronting and dealing with it. He introduced me to the term "shadow of the soul."

It appears that we humans may have somewhere within us remnants of earlier experiences that shaped our lives. We may not have given much or any thought to the impact of these events on us or, perhaps, we even may have repressed them. These experiences may have begun early enough to be part of our implicit or unconscious memory. Therefore, these life-shaping influences might metaphorically be said to lie "in the shadows" or "in the shadow of our souls." These terms appear down through history in literature related to shamanic traditions of different cultures, with varying definitions.

It may appear that I am drawing an unjustifiable conclusion. But the magnitude of my "burden" seemed such that my subconscious mind might have decided to block my regression until I address the problem in my present life. Regardless, I was very satisfied with the outcome of this regression effort.

The next chapter reveals some facts about the significant influences our hearts have on us.

# CHAPTER TWELVE

# THE HEART OF IT ALL

*Your vision will become clear only*
*when you can look into your own heart.*
*Who looks outside, dreams; who looks inside, awakens.*

Carl Jung

In his book *The Biology of Transcendence: A Blueprint of the Human Spirit,* Joseph Chilton Pearce described the human heart as containing a fifth brain, often called the "heart brain." Numerous other researchers have emphasized the interrelationship of functions between the heart and the brain. Throughout history, the heart has been characterized as the seat or source of love. The fourth chakra of spiritual energy is called the Anahata or "heart chakra." It is purported to contain the seed for the ability to feel divine: pure love for everyone and everything. Details of this are discussed in Laura Henry's online presentation "The Fourth Chakra: Anahata." Chakras also are discussed in a later chapter of this book.

## » Neurocardiology

This relatively new discipline has uncovered some amazing facts about the heart, according to Rollin McCraty, Executive VP and Research Director of the Institute of HeartMath in Boulder Creek, California (2004). The human heart:

- Has sixty percent nerve cells
- Has an energy field over five thousand times stronger than the brain's
- Has a nervous system that enables it to make decisions independent of the brain
- Can receive, process, and remember information
- Sends signals to the brain to assist the brain in aspects of consciousness
- Generates the body's most extensive rhythmic electromagnetic field, permeating every cell, to help synchronize body processes
- Communicates the person's emotional state throughout the body
- Rhythms appear to be disturbed by negative emotions
- Seems to be encouraged to function more coherently by positive emotions
- Has energy fields that can establish resonance with other individuals' energy fields and with group energy fields

## » Coherence

A concept that must be explained here is that of "coherence," different from the term "coherent" used later in this book in the discussion of narrative. Basically, coherence is the process of achieving a harmonious order and cooperation of physiological processes by individual body sub-systems. Other terms related to coherence are synchronization, entrainment, and resonance. HeartMath believes, "the rhythm of the heart ... sets the beat for the entire system," according to the Institutes online article "A Brief Look At Coherence." Emotional and mental states can influence heart rhythms, as noted earlier, and thereby can affect the functioning of physiological processes. The term "psychophysiological coherence" has been used to denote "a distinctive mode of functioning" that appears to result from "sustained positive emotions."

## » Breathing

One outcome of the Institute of HeartMath's research has been the development of special breathing exercises they call "attitude breathing." These were designed to enhance consciousness by improving heart-induced coherence. Consciousness in this context means awareness as well as thinking, feeling, and doing. An example might be to help control the impact of stressful daily events.

These breathing exercises seem to be a key recommendation from HeartMath to those people interested in taking advantage of the Institute's findings about heart health. Doc Childre and fellow researchers at HeartMath have published three books emphasizing those exercises: *Transforming Stress: The HeartMath Solution for Relieving Worry, Fatigue, and Tension*; *Transforming Anxiety: The HeartMath Solution to Overcoming Fear and Worry and Creating Serenity*; and *Transforming Depression: The HeartMath Solution to Feeling Overwhelmed, Sad, and Stressed*.

Some readers of these books criticized them as simply a form of meditation, but other readers applauded the techniques recommended there as offering a longer-term benefit than meditation. Meditation, one reader felt, provides "relaxing and blissful mind states" but it lets participants slip back afterward into "our conditioned discontent and unhappiness." HeartMath's efforts appear to prepare participants to deal with everyday pressures on a long-term basis.

The Institute also has an online HeartMath store, offering a variety of other approaches for monitoring individual stress levels and developing a more heart-coherent life.

## » Personal and Group Interaction

Robin Kelly's book cites some unusual achievements by the Institute of HeartMath in focusing its emphasis "on the link between our emotions and our heart." Kelly calls our heart our "energy center." HeartMath demonstrated that the heart waves of one person could be affected by another person's brain waves when they held hands and even up to four feet apart.

HeartMath's research also suggests that individual human energy fields may influence interpersonal relations. It often was believed that verbal and non-verbal characteristics shaped people's initial impression of and behavior with one another. However, some researchers had believed that each of us has the ability to sense one another's emotional state. HeartMath now claims that evidence reveals "a subtle yet influential electromagnetic or 'energetic' communications system [that] operates just below our conscious awareness."

HeartMath proposed too that the faculty of energy resonance between individuals could extend to group social interactions. Later in this book you will read that Renee Levi's doctoral dissertation supported HeartMath's proposal as Levi probed the existence and nature of group resonance. She felt, "as human beings become more authentic, more deeply in touch with themselves and what they believe, and display behaviors that express this, that their energy fields change." Otherwise, their fields may vibrate at their own natural frequency rather than resonate with one another. Love, a major heart-centered emotion, has been called the "cosmic consciousness" when expanded to universal dimensions.

The next chapter stresses some factors that mold our lives beginning early in life.

# CHAPTER THIRTEEN
## COMING OF AGE

*"Suffer the little children to come unto me,
for of such is the Kingdom of Heaven"*
Jesus: Luke 18:16

Perhaps some of you, like me, are trying to sort out the multiple influences that can complicate our lives today. We are subjected to hundreds of thousands of demands for our attention. We'll discuss later how some of us, particularly teenagers, are beginning to react to this. At this point in the book, however, it might help to review the "rites of passage" we each experienced growing up. Maybe this will help us reflect on our personal experiences at each juncture, so far as we can recall. Our so-called "coming of age" was characterized by an emerging ego or self-identity and a fading contact with our divine heritage.

Jesus' saying echoes what some parents and researchers have found: that very young children often display an awareness of "things" that typically is not accessible to the adult. The word "things" is used intentionally: it seems categorically impossible to describe or even list all the variations of everything children might possibly sense. Furthermore, scientists can't explain what enables young children to have what might be called "sensory" experiences different from the five physical senses.

However, scientists do have a continuing emphasis on clearly distinguishing levels of consciousness as well as interrelating the mind, the brain, and consciousness itself. Therefore we shall examine the possibilities of the unusual too.

## » Psychic and Mystical Experiences

Much wisdom has been expressed from various cultures over many years in seeking to define what may appear to be mystical or paranormal experiences and their origin. In his book *The Secret Life of Kids: An Exploration into Their Psychic Senses*, elementary school teacher James Peterson distinguishes between a seeming psychic sense and higher-level spiritual phenomena. Both apparently may be manifested in children but are said to differ in origin, expression, and age.

As used in his book, Peterson defines the term "psychic" as "the ability, through whatever means, to collect sensory information from non-physical realms." He distinguishes this from a "spiritual" experience. But he acknowledges that differentiating these two terms as well as the term "mystical experience" is imprecise and can be misleading. Levels of consciousness and sources of the experience typically are unknown.

Peterson stumbled across his first encounter with children's psychic ability at a summer camp for kids. He was as surprised as the two boys were about their revelation both to him and to each other. They apparently saw strands of color emanating from his stomach as he meditated.

He noted in his book that children characteristically do not reveal such experiences to one another, for fear of being considered weird and inviting abuse from other kids. The extent to which children mention such experiences to their parents seems to depend entirely upon their mother or father's initial reaction.

Peterson does suggest that children's psychic ability may arise as part their evolutionary background and fetal development. Supposedly, our ancestors of long ago were neurologically equipped to depend upon their so-called "sixth sense."

Some researchers believe that there is a valid basis for mystical experiences in children. One proponent mentioned earlier is Tobin Hart, professor of psychology at the State University of West Georgia and founder of the ChildSpirit Institute. His remarkable book gives credence to the existence of a residual spiritual ability among young children. The Catholic Church has documented many of the more spiritually oriented ones over the years, as examined by Kevin Knight in his online presentation "Mystical Theology."

In her Amazon e-paper "Children and Psychics Abilities: How to Respond as a Concerned Parent," Theresa Kelly seems more concerned about suppressing children's psychic experiences than with acknowledging them. As described in the Amazon ad for her e-paper, its contents list four reasons for suppression. It also discusses side effects of suppression and two suggestions for dealing with children's psychic ability. In Litany Burns's book *The Sixth Sense of Children: Nurturing Your Child's Intuitive Abilities,* its title reflects her more supportive approach. Renowned author Sylvia Browne teams up with co-author Lindsay Harrison in their book *Psychic Children: Revealing the Intuitive Gifts and Hidden Abilities of Boys and Girls* to discuss the subject broadly.

## » Kids' Reactions

It is noteworthy that young children typically accept such sensory experiences as commonplace or natural. But a parent or other adult typically may criticize kids for predicting a future event, mentioning an otherwise invisible playmate, or describing colors surrounding or emanating from a person. Only then do children suddenly discover that adults consider such experiences strange, even undesirable. As mentioned elsewhere in this book, developing our egocentric self as we mature tends to cause us to lose touch with that so-called "sixth sense."

Certainly, most of us as adults have watched as a young toddler turned toward us and pointed at something in front of him or her: a rock, a tree, a puddle, or similar ordinary items. The child's expression was one of sudden discovery and sharing. Spontaneous awe and wonder seen in a very young child is unparalleled in most adults. One might ask whether the youngster is inviting us to remember our own childhood innocence, although also seeking our acknowledgement of his or her "discovery."

There are many examples of adults who never forgot their childhood spiritual experiences and vividly remember their parents' negative reaction. Only as adults were some of them able to reflect on those events in the context of recalling their parents' reprimands. Other teens totally forget such experiences, even disavowing later that they ever happened.

This vanishing act does not seem to preclude later achievement of metaphysical states through yoga, meditation, or similar mind exercises.

Neither does it appear to detract from later opportunities for spiritual growth or experiences involving higher levels of consciousness.

Some young people do seem to exhibit a measure of altruism and spirituality that makes the world a better place. One example is Geoffrey Dilenschneider. He was a teenager when his book of poems *Between Two Junes is a Forest* was published. The thoughts he shared with readers through his poems seemed to focus on everyone's individual potential and that "we all must learn to love."

## » Pursuing a Self-Identity

The human ego is our sense of self, in the context of others and the world at large. It controls our thoughts and behavior. It has been called the "executive function of the psyche." As such, our ego can be influenced by a variety of drives, both instinctual and learned. Conceivably, these drives may have a positive or negative nature, like compassion or selfishness. Their pursuit instinctively begins in the very young.

Interestingly, the loss of soul memory begins soon after the initiation of cognition, i.e., knowing and conscious (explicit) memory. This literally appears to be ground zero for the development of self, about ages two to four. It seems as though the attraction of earthly matters overtakes spiritual memory. It is said to be gradual, not abrupt. This may account for the ability of some children to still accommodate spiritual attributes like compassion and empathy later in life. Children's psychic ability also seems less prominent as they age, although Peterson seems to believe that this fades more slowly than soul memory.

There is yet another intense influence that begins much earlier than self-awareness to shape a child's emotions and behavior and can last a lifetime. It almost might be considered potentially insidious for the child.

For example, do you have any "hot buttons," i.e., unconscious reactions to what someone else says or does? Do you become uncomfortable if conversation drifts into some particular subject or experience? Do you ever excuse yourself from a group when discussions become too sensitive for you?

What we're referring to are the nuances of human behavior and their natural causes. The word "natural" is used here to mean the impact of influences that surround each of us almost from the time of our conception. These influences are not identical for each of us; rather, they are highly individualized. Their sources are highly variable and include such influences as: our parents and significant others, the environment in which we were reared, and the conditions we encountered growing up.

The cause of our unintentional and unconscious reaction to "sensitive" situations is what is called "implicit memory," imprints in our subconscious mind that stimulate a behavioral reaction. These are accumulated before we acquire "explicit memory," the kind we usually consider to be our *only* memory. In his book *Cognitive Science and the Unconscious*, psychiatrist Dan Stein wrote that implicit memory:

- Is the cognitive science analogue of the subconscious
- Was biologically given
- Occurs in the behavior of all humans
- Expresses both pathological and non-pathological phenomena

The author is Professor and Chair of the Dept of Psychiatry and Mental Health at the University of Cape Town, South Africa.

Even unintentional actions by parents may wrongly be interpreted by young children, stored in their subconscious minds as certain misconceptions, and even instill lifelong convictions about their parents' opinion of them. The outcome may be unconscious feelings of inadequacy or even inferiority. This seems especially true among multiple siblings.

A first step toward self-identity occurred very early in our lives. It is a condition known as "object constancy." This has been defined as the perception by a very young baby that the object of its attention—such as its mother—retains its identity with all its attributes despite separation, altered appearance, or change of setting. In a sense, this provides the infant's "security blanket." As the child matures, object constancy assumes a different role, in shaping the infant's ability to separate perceptually as a "self," a secure identity or personality of its own. The term that psychologists use for this is "identity formation."

However, children who undergo severe disruptions before their development of cognition and explicit memory, such as the loss of a mother, may have less than complete emotional development. This also relates to the development of "attachment." Attachment, or emotional bonding, apparently holds some social significance for newborn. This may be mediated through his or her newfound experiences of separation, reunion, and accessibility following nine months in total attachment to the mother. This also seems to affect relationships with significant others as the child moves out into the larger world with his or her growing self-identity.

Mental health professionals say that children and adults with insecure attachment histories seem more vigilant for perceived threats of abandonment, rejection, or lack of approval. This may be manifested, probably unconsciously, by certain postures, behaviors, or mental states, including:

- Holding back or withdrawing
- Avoidance, anxiety, or hunger for acceptance
- Aversion to intimacy
- Shame

Obviously, this influences the formation of self-identity. Children need to feel that they are loved and valued. Only then can they learn to trust and love. In the absence of being loved, they may feel that they are unlovable. They cannot bear to consider that the fault lies in the mother or father, so they bury their feelings in shame, as if part of them suffocated and died. This protective mechanism for the child becomes the prison for the adult. The adult then may constantly search for validation in what he believes is his or her image in the eyes and thoughts of others.

Some of us might naturally question the preceding claim that a child or an adult "cannot bear to consider that the fault lies in the mother or father." But it makes sense. Remember that all of us consider our parents as the preeminent source of authority. We may even think of them as having certain godliness, *despite* how they treat us. Recall, too, that our very early years were enveloped in implicit memory: the subconscious imprinting of emotional events that may last a lifetime, controlling our conscious behavior without our knowing it.

Some parents or even siblings are overtly controlling, adding another layer to be dealt with as an adult. Probably one of the most compelling and popular books on transactional analysis—the science of interpersonal behavior—was *I'm OK; You're OK*, written by Thomas Harris, a Navy psychiatrist, over a quarter-century ago. It accounts for the differences between our inner "parent" and our authentic "adult," the former of which describes the lingering influence of our parents on our behavior. Unfortunately, even as adults, some of us are uncomfortable or unable to challenge the life-long parental reins as perhaps well intended at the time but long since outmoded.

The process of developing one's self-identity is composed of many stages over time. It is fraught with many trials and errors before even a reasonably secure feeling is reached. However, it seems to be tested, perhaps doubted, and even reshaped over many years, even long past adolescence. To achieve a stable and comfortable adult self-identity demands a "balancing act." Each of us is subjected to multiple and frequent potential influences on our ego formation and sustenance.

Part of establishing self-identity involves self-esteem among peers. Adolescents participate in risky behaviors to "prove themselves" to others. Today, one of the most dangerous of these is a "game" they play. Unfortunately, it has happened with no one else around. It's called the "choking game," and may become deadly. Pauline Chin, herself a physician, described the perilous consequences in her *New York Times* online article "Discovering Teenagers' Risky 'Game' Too Late." Her Health section article is a real grabber, opening with surgeons salvaging a teen's organs for transplant, not following an accident, injury, or the result of illness. But after he died with a homemade noose around his neck, discovered too late to save him.

Chin first learned about the game when she cared for a child who died that way. Adolescents are known to also try it in "thrill-seeking," an attempt to get a legal high just before they go unconscious. Even though kids from seven to twenty-one years of age are said to participate, this often occurs in groups. Publicity and counseling can caution adolescents about drugs and alcohol, but these kids seem to believe that near-strangulation is harmless.

## » Experience-Based Decisions

In her book *Brain-Based Teaching and Adolescent Learning in Mind*, Glenda Beamon Crawford paints an interesting picture of adolescent thinking. She coordinates middle-grade programs from her position as a professor of teacher education at Elon University. Crawford reminds us that adolescents still may appear to remain focused on personal and social concerns. But that period has been shown to be a time too of great intellectual change. Adolescents develop abilities for "propositional and hypothetical thinking; deductive reasoning and logic; generalizing; insight and nuance; symbolic interpretation and analysis; and futuristic planning." They also become able to "monitor and regulate their own thinking processes."

Adolescents also are intensely curious, often indulging in "science fiction, fantasy, mystery, and the macabre." Several paradoxes become evident at this age. They "seek peer acceptance yet are self-conscious about their own awkwardness and perceived shortcomings; form values yet are often judgmental; and [have] unpleasant emotions of worry and self-doubt."

Without the knowledge and experience characteristic of persons many years older, adolescents "may struggle to put emotions and concerns into perspective." This may be the primary deficit that the adolescent brain has as contrasted to a more mature adult brain: the ability to make what are becoming known as "executive decisions." These are not choices made by corporate executives but are focused decisions that incorporate the wider expanse of knowledge and experience typical of adults.

## » Seeking Independence

Teenagers today face a far different world than many of us adults did. Often, it is difficult for us as parents to remember our own adolescence or to relate to the multiple influences confronting our teen-agers. So we naturally conform to the typical parental role, expecting our teens to behave as model young adults.

Nothing could be further from their nature. Joseph Chilton Pearce reminds us that the prefrontal cortex of our kids' brains has two significant growth periods affecting adolescence: one prior to age fifteen and the second from age fifteen until about age twenty-one. This part of their and our brains governs processes occurring in other parts of the brain, processes that involve decisions and behavior. Maturity of this "governor" doesn't occur until *after* we no longer call our children adolescents.

Obviously, one major change in our children's lives occurs early in life: their exposure to the lives, thoughts, and behavior of others, particularly kids about their age. In an effort to shape their own personal identity, they can be influenced by other people in many different ways.

One major factor determining their susceptibility to the influence of others is the relationship adolescents have with their parents and significant others. In this case, "significant others" are not only teachers, coaches, ministers, and friends of the family but increasingly are also people they see as role models. Unfortunately, their role models may not exhibit lifestyles we adults would recommend, and these could include both sports and entertainment figures as well as others kids in their social network.

This is where adolescents' personal interactions with and trust of parents, counselors, or mentors becomes crucial. In his article "The Angry Adolescent" in the *Aetna InteliHealth* Healthy Lifestyle, Michael Craig Miller reminds us that the adolescent is "no longer a child—not yet an adult." But personal "problems are his [or her] own to solve ... he [or she] is in charge." Miller stresses that accepting this reality makes it easier and more effective for parents to be of help. Miller is on the psychiatric staff of Harvard Medical School.

## » Too Many Choices

In his book *The Paradox of Choice: Why More is Less*, Barry Schwartz emphasizes that all of us are faced with too many choices, as a product of technology and brand competition. Schwartz is the Dorwin Cartwright Professor of Social Theory and Social Action at Swarthmore College. He makes the point that there is an illusion of a multitude of options when few honestly different ones actually exist. An Amazon review of his book said "a bewildering array of choices floods our exhausted brains, ultimately restricting instead of freeing us" and "having all these choices actually goes so far as to erode our psychological well-being." An Amazon reviewer reported, "Schwartz tells us that constantly being asked to make choices, even about the simplest things, forces us to 'invest time, energy, and no small amount of self-doubt and dread'."

One example to which we all can relate is self-doubt after a purchase. Despite the price tag, but particularly if it is high, self-doubt is sure to creep into our minds asking whether we purchased the: best price, best features, best warranty, best durability, best looking, best fitting, best smelling, best tasting, ad infinitum! Of course, if we are a teen with wealthy parents and our own no-limit credit or debit card, who cares?

But choices don't stop there, especially for teenagers, and choices they must make! Naturally, for a teen though, the self-doubt likely revolves around him or herself—after daily decisions are made! Any reader, whether a parent of a teen or not, probably would stop counting after a hundred choices any particular day.

Young people's unrealistic appraisal of possible outcomes and their compromise of common sense seem to be major factors in the widespread use of illegal substances as well as unwed teenage pregnancies.

Temperament becomes more manifest as the child seeks to develop its own identity. Free will choices made in response to earthly stimuli govern the individual's thoughts, feelings, and actions while he or she is alive. Spiritual growth becomes possible only as the soul, through its host's choices and behavior, is able to learn human applications of feelings such as compassion, empathy, gratitude, selflessness, tolerance, benevolence, and love.

## » Great Expectations

Perhaps one of the least acknowledged phases of young people's growth from ages fifteen to twenty-one is what Joseph Chilton Pearce calls "a trinity of great expectations." These three gradually emerging characteristics of adolescence involve first, "a poignant and passionate idealism;" second, an expectation that "something tremendous is supposed to happen;" and third, "a boundless and exuberant belief" of his or her "greatness." The news media has captured vivid examples of this from this country's civil rights activists to the protesters in Beijing and Tehran.

The next chapter focuses on the importance of interpersonal relationship.

CHAPTER   FOURTEEN

# Interpersonal Relationship

---

*"The most important thing in communication*
*is to hear what isn't being said."*

Peter F. Drucker

---

Narrative literally means storytelling. Before the written word, narrative was the medium by which customs, legends, and wisdom were passed from one generation to another. But narrative also involves the expression of personal feelings and the exchange of such feelings with others.

## » Value in Child Development

For young children, narrative helps them not only make sense of their own minds but also to better understand the minds of others. Ever notice how youngsters never seem to stop talking, even to imaginary playmates if no live person is nearby? Today, we all seem to have little time for meaningful interpersonal narrative, except in group settings where we often try to best one another's experiences or achievements.

The earlier belief was that not much meaningful occurs with children in their early years. However, researchers now feel that certain opportunities missed in early years can significantly affect entire lives. Narrative is now one of the most emphasized developmental areas that is inadequately addressed by parents and significant others. This lack may be compounded by parking offspring with non-related, overburdened caregivers, despite the convenience and apparent lack

117

of harm. Fortunately, some youngsters are extroverted enough to compensate for inadequate caregiver-child attention.

One of the chief proponents for the significance of narrative is Daniel Siegel, Director of the Center for Human Development in Los Angeles and Associate Clinical Professor of Psychiatry at the UCLA School of Medicine. He is both a pediatrician and a psychiatrist. He believes that explicit memory develops between twelve and twenty-four months of age, as a result of the development of the hippocampus part of the brain. In contrast to implicit memory, narrative and explicit memory enable a child to become consciously aware of him- or herself. Siegel's ideas are presented in his book *The Developing Mind: How Relationships and the Brain Interact to Shape Who We Are.*

Around the third year of life, Siegel believes that something called "autonoetic consciousness" develops. This enables the child to correlate autobiographical recall from explicit memory with other inputs that help make sense of self, others, and the world. One of the inputs that may surreptitiously appear is emotionally charged implicit memories. In effect, narrative may blend explicit memories with certain implicit memories. This could be an attempt by the brain to "to create a coherent internal interpersonal, family, and community experience." Siegel believes that information transfer across the brain will have occurred sufficiently that, by age four, "children are well able to use words to tell others about their inner feelings and inclinations."

## » A Mother's Gaze

Implicit memory, object constancy, and attachment are just three defined influences on early child development. Others are the nature of the offspring's environment and the overall relationship between the baby and his or her parents, particularly the mother. A key element, part of attachment, is what's been called the "loving gaze." Novelist George Eliot called it "the meeting eyes of love."

In her online article describing Daniel Siegel's contributions to the emerging field of neurobiology, Mary Wylie said, "every child yearns for and must have [this gaze] literally to survive." Her online article, "Mindsight: Dan Siegel Offers Therapists a New Vision of the Brain," traced the impact that Siegel and his book *The Developing Mind:*

*Toward a Neurobiology of Interpersonal Experience* had on neuroscience and mental health therapy.

A related factor in early child development is the mother's behavior regarding both the mother's gaze and her narrative-encouraging play with the child. Extremes of her behavior might be described as apathy and empathy. Earlier in this book you read about the contagious depressant effects on a child by a mother who is herself depressed. By contrast, an empathic mother is likely to perform well with her offspring in both her gaze and play. It is worth noting that empathy is a learned skill and can be developed, according to Lillian Stover, Bernard Guerney, and Mary O'Connell's article "Measurements of Acceptance, Allowing Self-Direction, Involvement, and Empathy in Adult-Child Interaction" published in *The Journal of Psychology*.

## » Don't Blame the Kids

An unusual finding by Claire Vallotton of Michigan State University sheds some likely unexpected scientific light on child-parent interaction. Yet parents may acknowledge its truth once they have time to consider it. Vallotton's research suggests that the child may determine how involved his or her parents get in personally interacting with him or her. These findings were discussed in Sharon Begley's article "It's in Our Genes. So What?" in *Newsweek*.

"How much babies gesture, smile, make eye contact, and babble affects how adults respond to them." The manner and extent to which parents interact "shape how verbal a child will be, how emotionally secure [he or] she will feel, and thus what kind of adult relationships [he or] she will have," according to the article.

By contrast, "fussy, crying babies," "homely babies," and "fidgety, difficult babies" don't encourage parents to read, be affectionate, or respond to them as well. This seems to be true with other caregivers as well. Given the vital importance of narrative as mentioned earlier in this chapter, personal interaction with parents and others seems a significant factor in well-rounded child development. Parents might take a lesson that all children, not just the "cuties," deserve this advantage.

## » Teen Cancer Patient Networking

Teens have a rough enough time finding buddies with similar interests and ethical standards. Add the burden of cancer and it's almost overwhelming. Some resilient young patients put up a good front. But inside their minds and bodies, life without friends is rough. They are yanked out of school, confined to hospital or home, and spend endless days being weakened by necessary treatments. Parents and health care professionals do their best, but being drowned in clinical details and treatments is not much of a teen life.

Now buddy help is available. A social networking site was created just for patients with cancer ages twelve to nineteen. It is called Teen Connector and was developed by the Canadian Childhood Cancer Foundation. The Teen Connector Web site is: http://teenconnector.ca/accounts/LoginMain.aspx.

One young Canadian teen named Lauren seemed to capture the value of social networking in this way: "Teenagers are at that awkward social stage where they've lost their hair, they're struggling with their body image issues, and meeting face-to-face in a support group is something that's not always comfortable. They want to ask candid questions and embarrassing questions, so support groups are not always the most comfortable setting for that."

She probed the depth of personal problems with cancer this way: "I became completely reliant on my parents. I couldn't go out and socialize and start to do my own thing. I experienced a lot of isolation, and [for] teenagers, it's difficult for them to wrap their heads around going through a life-threatening illness."

## » A Coherent Story

Narrative played a significant role in Daniel Siegel's discoveries. He heard one of the pioneers of attachment theory, Mary Main, describe what she called a "coherent narrative" in her work. This involved surveys of parents providing "their recollections of their own childhoods." The idea was to correlate the results of these narratives with how well these parents could create secure attachments for their own children.

A significant revelation emerged: the parents who provided a positive recollection of their own childhoods were found to assure a secure attachment for their children, despite the actual nature of those parents' early years. This was true even for parents who were reared in unsatisfactory conditions, including insecure attachments and abusive relationships with their parents. It amazingly appeared that these parents had somehow "made sense of their past lives" in the stories they told surveyors.

Somehow, apparently these parents had acquired a mental and emotional ability to overcome negative early events. It seemed they must have achieved this through personal reflection and dialogue with others. Wylie said "we need ... to put our experience into words in order to fulfill our biological potential as human beings." An opportunity for this occurs "in positive, healthy relationships" with significant others later in our lives.

## » Incoherence

Daniel Siegel wondered about the neurobiological mechanisms that facilitated the impact of what was termed "coherent narrative." His studies led him into an area of therapy where he discovered a distinct difference between coherent narrative and incoherent narrative: post traumatic stress disorder (PTSD). PTSD patients were unable to make sense of or coherently describe their childhoods as positive. There seemed to be some disconnect and Siegel found it in their brains: the influence of implicit memory combined with disruption in the hippocampus' processing of explicit memory. (Read Wylie's online account if you'd like her seventeen-page details of the neurobiological factors.)

## » Power to Change

This led Siegel to insist, "You can harness the power of your mind. The way you think can change your brain." Two concepts evolved from this: mindfulness (discussed in an earlier chapter) and self-regulation. Suffice it to say that mindfulness "promotes [certain] integrative functions of [the brain] ... and brings about neural changes" to enable integration, coherence, and self-regulation. Siegel commented that our efforts involve others as much as they do us, in our ability to incorporative narrative as a significant factor in our growth and development.

Wylie and Siegel emphasized, too, the role of psychotherapists. Narrative becomes a key element here too. "You [patients] begin to see the past event in the context of other events, other times, relationships past and present, and you can weave it into an ongoing narrative of your life." In other words, we can begin to put the past in the past, recognizing that it happened in a different time and place under different circumstances. As we understand this, we find that the present and future are of more importance and that the past ceases to haunt us.

Our lives are confronted with so many choices that we literally face a balancing act. This is discussed in the next chapter.

# CHAPTER FIFTEEN

# A BALANCING ACT

*"When one door closes, another opens;*
*But we often look so long and so regretfully upon the closed door*
*that we do not see the one that has opened for us."*

Alexander Graham Bell

Life often seems like a revolving door. Round and round we go. Only as we pause to step away and take a long hard look at the merry-go-round can we hope to catch a glimpse of our place in life. Only then can we begin to assess our chances of getting squeezed between the doors by the ever-pressing crowd. I think most philosophers and psychiatrists would agree that balance wins the game of life.

In order for the total child to present a coordinated personality, he or she must learn to balance any early psychic or spiritual experiences with earthly societal demands or risk being accused of abnormal behavior. This may seem a sad commentary on the present spiritual state of our world, but it seems relevant to the evolution of humankind.

Children are fond of adoration and praise, as we all are. So, this balancing act they undertake, to develop their own identity in keeping with societal demands, is likely to defer to authority figures in early formative years—especially parents and other family members. In doing so, children are likely to adopt parental or family beliefs and attitudes. This may be good or bad, depending upon what kinds of beliefs or behaviors are modeled by those authority figures.

The maturing adolescent seems less likely to defer to others in shaping his or her beliefs about the world. As suggested earlier, this may lead to experimentation "to see for myself," often risking seemingly irrational behavior. Pearce says that the prefrontal cortex serves a vital coordinating role as it develops in parallel with later developments in three other parts of the brain. In a sense, it facilitates a more integrated functioning of these other three parts. This is to create a more "civilized" status for the whole. The prefrontal cortex eventually serves a coordinating function for all of the brain.

This chapter therefore will focus on at least two parts of our lives in which we need to maintain balance: our ego-based priorities and our physical and mental health. These discussions will be wide-ranging and will include mind-bending implications, some of which I hope you can take seriously. Our subjects also will build upon ideas presented earlier in this book, to make a cohesive whole.

## » Competition

This seems to be a primary influence on the human ego. At some point, children grow from their pure enjoyment of playing games to their serious intent of gamesmanship. It must be wondered how much this change is instilled by parents seeking to vicariously compete versus nature itself.

In recent discussions with a friend who is a devoted Little League coach, he decried the negative influence that parents literally may impose upon their children. His descriptions of parents' behavior after a loss by their kid's team or by an accidental blunder by the child are nothing short of verbal abuse. The frequency with which a parent starts a quarrel with another parent over a minor incident, women as easily as men, smacks of poor role modeling for their offspring. Speaking of role modeling, all too many professional ball players do a lousy job on and off the field or court.

Competitive impulses may be innate or learned, and these often seem to depend upon environmental influences. They may be family or situationally related. Simple survival may cause life or death struggles. Competitive strategies employed by even the most strait-laced business moguls sometimes stretch imagination and honorability. Fallouts of marginally legal practices in tax returns, driver behavior, or high finance may leave adolescents with the conviction that "anything goes."

It is into this milieu that high school and college graduates are set forth, some of them "learning the ropes" early as evidenced by the widespread student norm of cheating. Much credit is given to competition for economic, societal, technological, and personal achievements of humankind. However, as you read earlier, competition may create false assurances of "being better off" through the paradox of too many choices. Of course, choice and status may be flaunted as facades for personally perceived inadequacies or insecurities. You'll read later that being authentic can help ease such personal problems.

Of course, competition is not limited to the business world or world of sports. Road rage at times seems to be the result of a driver's perceived affront to his or her power or self-esteem, or it simply might be evidence of poor emotional self-control. As you read earlier, this also may involve territoriality.

## » Perils of Egocentricity

The earlier chapter on entitlement focused on an aspect of personal behavior that seems to pose a significant hazard in today's world. It addresses a person's worldview or attitude towards other people and society in general. That chapter focused on group entitlements. But it is equally applicable to individuals. With individuals, it risks becoming extreme egocentricity. In my last book I described this state of mind as "star power." It seems exemplified in sports, Hollywood, and political figures that have a substantial following by the public and the news media. These persons may begin to believe they are beyond accountability to anyone. Russ's Web site provides an expanded examination of "Egocentricity or Sociocentricity."

In the context of this book, competition therefore must be questioned in terms of its influence on our individual mindsets and reasoning. How much does our worldview restrict us from being aware and concerned about the welfare of other people? How far does our belief in only one life drive any of us to extreme views and behavior that may threaten the wellbeing of others? Perhaps personal self-control or a balance of priorities is a key to a satisfying and successful life while respecting and observing others' rights and welfare.

Diane Zimberoff and David Hartman's online article "The Ego in Heart-Centered Therapies: Ego Strengthening and Ego Surrender" published in the *Journal of Heart-Centered Therapies* provided an interesting perspective in its introduction. Traditionally, certain cultures consider life to consist of two parts. The authors cite that Jung believed the dividing line was middle adulthood, which he felt initiated a midlife crisis and an inward search for meaning. Zimberoff and Hartman expressed this goal: "creating meaning in one's life beyond what we can do and based instead on who we are." Their article is lengthy but worth reading for any persons interested in examining the authors' proposed strategies.

## » Alternative and Holistic Health Care

You read earlier about the impact of our thoughts on our health and wellbeing. This is being incorporated into several new health care practices and scientific theories. Two unconventional approaches to health care practices are called "holistic" and "alternative." They are based upon different but related concepts.

Alternative therapy is viewed as complementary to traditional health care, witness the establishment by the National Institutes of Health of a National Center for Complementary and Alternative Medicine (NCCAM). Their Web site says, "Complementary and alternative medicine is a group of diverse medical and health care systems, practices, and products that are not generally considered part of conventional medicine."

Two of the concepts included in alternative medicine are acupuncture and acupressure. The basis for these originated in Eastern cultures but they rapidly are being caught up in Western cultures. They involve pressure or needles being placed in carefully chosen sites on the body. The underlying theme is that the human body depends upon balancing certain energy that permeates the body. The main stream of this energy is said to follow a meridian along the axis of the body and is manifested in seven points or chakras along that line. It seems that imbalance of this energy at specific chakras is responsible for illnesses in specific groups of organs or areas.

To help dispel the notion that conventional health care institutions shy away from energy healing as being voodoo or witchcraft, the eminent Cleveland Clinic established a Web site about energy healing. Both they and Indianapolis hospitals offer energy healing. It is called "therapeutic touch" and is administered primarily by nurses who have had specialized training. The Methodist Church also has a similar program called "Healing Touch Ministries."

Concepts involving energy in the detection and treatment of human illnesses go by different names, including Laying On of Hands, Reiki, and Therapeutic Touch. Prayer is claimed to be a form of spiritual energy. In his book *The Great Field: Soul at Play in a Conscious Universe*, John James emphasized that energy "healing is most effective when there is surrender to both the belief and the intention." If the healing effort comes from an "egoistic feeling that 'we have to do something'," it doesn't work. James' book grew out of a thesis for a graduate diploma in transpersonal psychology at the Crucible Centre, located in Hartley Valley, Australia.

One of the most comprehensive perspectives on energy healing was provided in Daniel Benor's book *Consciousness, Bioenergy and Healing: Self-Healing and Energy Medicine for the 21st Century*. He took both a contemporary and a historical look at the subject. His book is the culmination of twenty years of his research. Benor is a holistic psychiatrist. He is coordinator for the Council on Healing, a non-profit organization that promotes awareness of spiritual healing. He also is editor and producer of the International Journal on Healing and Caring. His book examines ways in which people can heal themselves and ways in which they can be helped to heal through complementary alternative medicine (CAM). CAM includes many self-healing approaches, such as relaxation, meditation, imagery, journaling, fitness, and proper diet. Caregiver or therapist modalities include acupuncture, homeopathy, laying-on of hands, and mental intent/meditation/prayer. Benor comments, "Many healers suggest that it is a biological energy interaction between the healer and the healee which produces the healing results."

The Web site of the Global College of Natural Medicine (GCNM) says, "Holistic medicine treats the whole person, using holistic healing, holistic nutrition and herbs to stimulate the body's ability to heal itself." GCNM offers online home study programs leading to a certificate, a diploma, and a degree in several specialties.

Holistic care is best understood as total body care. Its main thrust is to maintain homeostasis or balance within the body. This contrasts to focusing on and treating individual body parts and symptoms.

Once understood in its complex entirety, the holistic approach actually should be considered supplemental or confirmative, not a replacement, for traditional health care.

The holistic approach also involves self-care. It emphasizes such things as the misuse of tobacco, liquor, or illegal drugs; the proper use of diet and supplements; and the dangers of environmental contaminants from foods, fumes, and heavy metals. Holistic care believes that homeostasis or biological system balance is critical to proper health. The Mayo Clinic, Johns Hopkins, and Harvard Medical School are just three of the recognized health care institutions that have published guides to self-care.

## » Mind-Body Medicine

Novelist Sylvia Engdahl deplores that the research finding "physical health is strongly influenced by the mind ... has yet to be accepted by the majority of medical practitioners." In her online article "The Mind's Influence on Health," she predicts that incorporation of this research advancement into medical practice will be resisted. This becomes the premise upon which she based her book *Stewards of the Flame.*

Anne Harrington, chair of Harvard's history of science department, offers a somewhat different view. In her book *The Cure Within: The History of Mind-Body Medicine,* she explains that the belief in mind-body medicine is not new (2008). She emphasizes how deeply embedded the idea of positive mental health is in regard to good physical health. She also illustrates the ways that contemporary medicine has incorporated a focus on mind-body healing into its practice.

In support of Harrington's view, hypnotherapist Bruce Kaloski provided yet another perspective in his online post "The Mind-Body Connection and Its Influence on Health." He said that this concept existed in ancient Greece, where physicians recognized and explored the complementary links between the two. "This philosophy was never completely abandoned," he claims, "but it had been largely ignored for most of the 20th century as medical science made its tremendous strides."

Cacioppo, Tassinary, and Berntson's *Handbook of Psychophysiology* seems to nail the point precisely that mind-body medicine is an old idea but a new science. Their seminal textbook runs almost a thousand pages and likely will become a standard academic reference. As the editors acknowledge, the first edition of this handbook was published over three decades ago. Since then the science of psychophysiology has changed significantly in keeping with dramatic advances in technology. The field is diverse and includes a significant understanding about the applications of mind-body medicine.

As mentioned earlier in this book, a good example of one impact of psychological stress is a skin condition called "shingles."

## » Balancing Our Health

It seems indisputable that scientists worldwide have made great strides toward unraveling the complexity of the cellular foundations of the human body and the body's intricate internal communications network. It seems only reasonable that a next step was to define operational bases for cells and messengers and to learn the homeostasis or balance that the human body needs to maintain between systems. Interruption of this balance now is felt to be the cause of the pathology and symptomatology that eventually become manifest as acute or chronic illnesses. You read in an earlier chapter how I allowed my health get out of balance over the past five years.

Our bodies are in constant flux: tissues die and are replaced. There are special processes, special organs, and biological agents that facilitate this. For example, cells lining the surface of our stomachs are replaced every five days, red blood cells every four months, the epidermis of our skin every two weeks, and even the entire bony skeleton of adults every ten years. But this is a non-stop makeover, obviously not a timely total exchange.

To visualize this process, imagine the roof of your home as a tissue and the shingles as individual cells. Of course, your roof might have hundreds of shingles while the tissue, although much smaller, might have many thousands of cells. Using the roof as an example, however, think of watching your roof each time you are outdoors. As you watch over a very long time, you notice various shingles changing very gradually: getting thinner and older, and eventually being replaced with new shingles.

The ability of scientists to measure the age of tissues in the human body was discovered at the Karolinska Institute in Stockholm.

Researchers recalled that nuclear weapons were tested above ground prior to 1963, emitting carbon 14 into the atmosphere.

This was absorbed by plants worldwide, which were subsequently eaten by animals and people. That carbon 14 became incorporated into new tissues as cells divide and their DNA is duplicated. The DNA is not "new," simply copied, and carries a dated carbon-14 tag.

Therefore, your birth age may be different from your body's age, a lot older in fact. So says Nicholas Wade in his *New York Times* online article "Your Body is Younger Than You Think." Another example in a different part of this book discusses how walking encourages the bone-building process. It seems only reasonable that we do everything in our power to keep our "parts" healthy. But it's beyond our power to live forever. Scientists disagree on the exact reason, but the replacement process eventually comes to an end.

Although energy emissions from the human body have been recognized for many years, energy healing remains controversial. Three well-known electronic instruments continue to be essential in detecting and tracking electrical impulses from the heart, brain, and muscles: the electrocardiograph, the electroencephalograph, and electromyography respectively. Today, laser energy is used in surgery and dermatological applications. Scientific advances now are blazing the way for better understanding and acceptance of other kinds of energy as therapeutic tools.

At least three factors appear to be involved in the external application of other yet undefined energies in healing. First, a variety of human variables seem to be determinants in both the transmitting and the receiving of healing energy. These include the human nature of intention and expectation discussed earlier in this book. Second, there is the question of possible mechanisms by which this energy mediates a biological response in the recipient, still uncertain. Third, such healing energy must have some heretofore largely unexplored technical characteristics as well as a relatively undefined medium of transmission and source. Nevertheless, empirical data do show clinically significant healing in certain cases following the application of externally supplied "healing energy."

In internist Larry Dossey's online article "The Unsolved Mystery of Healing: Distant Healing, Healing Mediated By Nonlocal Mind," he quotes physicist Nick Herbert. Herbert says non-local healing is "(1) unmediated by any known form of energy in physics; (2) unmitigated or undiminished by increasing distance; and (3) immediate." "Non-local" healing refers to the phenomenon of the energy transmission being at a distance from the patient. This could be a synonym for the healing effects of intercessory prayer.

Dossey further quotes Sir Arthur Eddington's remark about "complementarity" in physics: "Something unknown is doing we don't know what." Dossey is a visiting lecturer and prolific author. He is the former executive editor of the peer-reviewed journal *Alternative Therapies in Health and Medicine* and currently is the executive editor of *EXPLORE: The Journal of Science and Healing*.

Clinical psychologists George Pratt and Peter Lambrou's book *Instant Emotional Healing: Acupressure for the Emotions* addresses electromagnetic influences on emotional states. They seem to have found that healing of anxiety, phobias, and other emotional traumas may be delayed because of energy blockages from polarity reversals in a person's electromagnetic field. Pratt and Lambrou have offices at the Scripps Memorial Hospital, La Jolla, California.

Their book describes a concept called "emotional self-management" (ESM). It relates to another concept named "thought field management" (TFM). They say TFM is an "umbrella term for a number of hybrid technologies based on what Albert Einstein originally called the 'subtle energy' systems of the body." Emotions, they say, involve the interaction of thought energy fields with changes in the human body. They are therefore susceptible to treatment through the electromagnetic meridians that connect the chakras. Their book is designed to be a self-help manual.

The next chapter examines some of the mechanisms our bodies use to maintain homeostasis.

CHAPTER SIXTEEN
# CENTERS OF BALANCE

---

*"Our own physical body possesses a wisdom*
*which we who inhabit the body lack."*

Henry Miller

---

Scientists continue to uncover secrets that help explain how our bodies survive our mistreatment of them. Some of these discoveries are awe-inspiring in their complexity. Others are so basic that we must wonder how they evaded scientists for so long. Pim van Lommel reminded us that some fifty billion cells in our body are replaced every day, or a new body every year. Basically each of us "is in an unstable balance of two opposing processes of continual disintegration and integration."

## » Human Matrix

One of the most interesting advances in scientific theory has been the idea that our entire body is composed of a "matrix" or interconnecting information system. The extracellular matrix and ground regulation is believed to be the key to understanding both acute and chronic illness. Extracellular is the surroundings—environment—of the fifty to seventy-five trillion cells that compose the human body.

Formerly known simply as connective tissue, the full biological role of the extracellular matrix had not been recognized. It seems so intricately involved in regulation of physiological processes that its differential functioning throughout the body was difficult to identify or study. This seems to have been the major reason that scientists may have been baffled. How could the many different biological functions that the matrix performs be interrelated? What possible purposes might this interrelationship have? Yet, the matrix is so central to human life that it might be considered a biological entity in and of itself.

Imagine the virtually limitless potential that such a unified communications network could have in maintaining biological homeostasis, or balance, of the human body. The magnitude of this challenge seems incomprehensible when we realize that this balancing involves each of the trillions of individual cells in our body. But realize, too, the greater potential for component maladjustment. This concept was addressed in Alfred Pischinger's book that was mentioned in an earlier chapter.

Consider for a moment the services felt necessary for a home today: energy, communications, sewerage, food, and water. Isn't it reasonable to expect that individual human cells would require similar services? Hence, this provides an elementary illustration of the massive responsibility of the matrix in managing the extracellular environment.

This barely scratches the surface of the multifaceted contributions of the matrix to biological homeostasis. This book doesn't explore the many highly specific ways in which the proper operation of elements of this environment can become maladjusted. The purpose here simply is to lay the groundwork for the conceivability of some ways that influences from outside the body might affect the matrix's balancing efforts.

An example from Alfred Pischinger's book involves continued exposure to an environmental situation or substance that may produce a physiological imbalance but a healthy appearance through adaptation. His book refers to this as "increased resistance." "If a sensitivity is created by an overabundance of a man-made substance, e.g., alcohol, that an individual previously tolerated, this sensitivity can quickly spread to other substances." This might incur an increased sensitivity to even minimal amounts of the substance. Removal of exposure may be followed by rapid recovery, but being reintroduced to the agent can causes a reemergence of the symptoms. "Often, in a person around the age of fifty, an established maladaptation becomes apparent as multiple medical conditions or chronic illness."

Linda Antinoro explained how acute illness could become chronic in her *Aetna InteliHealth* online article "Defending Against Disease With an Anti-Inflammation Lifestyle." Antinoro is a senior nutritionist at Brigham and Women's Hospital in Boston. Her emphasis is on how acute inflammation can become chronic if inadequately handled. She says that the "inflammatory response" has long been linked to arthritis, but "it is also taking center stage in heart disease, cancer, diabetes, asthma, and Alzheimer's. Equally exciting is preliminary research showing a probable association of inflammation with diet, activity and other lifestyle choices."

Antinoro explains, "Problems occur, however, when the inflammatory response does not shut off and goes from being temporary, localized, and protective to being chronic and harmful." Clinically speaking, persistent inflammation can affect cells permanently, leading to "premature cell death and disease."

The author suggests that smoking and obesity are two influences that can be controlled. "Obese individuals tend to have higher blood levels of C-reactive protein (CRP)," a test that confirms inflammation. Its blood level generally drops with the loss of excess weight. Some scientists believe that the body considers fat cells to be "foreign invaders," thus stimulating its immune response.

Trans fats and saturated fats contribute to chronic inflammation, whereas omega-3 fats have an anti-inflammatory effect, as do antioxidants. Green tea and certain seasonings—turmeric (found in curry) and ginger—are rich in antioxidants. Lastly, Antinoro recommends controlling blood pressure and getting adequate sleep to help combat chronic inflammation.

Probably the most intriguing aspect of this subject is just how thoroughly and totally, yet very specifically, the extracellular matrix or connective tissue is differentiated yet interrelated. To whet your appetite for discovering the immensity of the pervasive influence of the matrix, here are a few topical aspects addressed in the online "Connective Tissue Study Guide" and "Connective Tissue Overview:"

- Connective tissues contain more extracellular matrix than do cells;
- Connective tissues support epithelial tissue and connect it to other tissues;

- Connective tissues form tendons, ligaments, and cartilage;
- Connective tissues provide coverings that support and protect muscle and nervous tissue;
- Bone is the hardest connective tissue;
- Adipose tissue (fat) insulates body tissues and stores lipids;
- Blood transports nutrients and chemical messengers to all body tissues and transports wastes from tissues to excretory organs;
- Extracellular matrix consists of fibers and ground substance that are synthesized and secreted by connective tissue cells;
- Ground substance may be fluid, semifluid, gelatinous, or hard;
- Ground substance secures connective tissue cells and fibers in the extracellular matrix and is the medium through which interstitial fluid diffuses between blood and cells and through which macrophages and white blood cells move;
- Connective tissue functions include transport, immunological defense, mechanical support, growth and repair, energy economics, and haemopoiesis.

## » Human Liquid Crystal Conductors

Another significant scientific finding was the electrically conductive property of cell membranes. For example, the results of an experiment reported from Australia offered a glimpse of the electrical nature of human cells. This involved a cell membrane. The experiment had a commercial purpose. It was to develop a marketable biological test product. But its results clearly demonstrated the ability of electromotive force to influence the action of body cells (Cornell, Lipton).

Bruce Lipton described the experiment as consisting of "an isolated cell membrane" with "an attached piece of gold foil under it." A special electrolyte solution then flooded "the space between the gold foil and the attached membrane." The membrane's receptors were stimulated by a (electric) signal from the gold foil. This caused the membrane to open "channels" and to allow the electrolyte solution to flow through it. Lipton commented that these researchers "successfully turned a biological cell membrane into a digital-readout computer chip."

James Oschman's book *Energy Medicine: The Scientific Basis for Bioenergy Therapies* said, "The body's connective tissue system is a giant liquid crystal semiconductor." Scientists now have shown that various biological substances are liquid crystal in nature. Although the multitude of such substances is different in structure and function, they share a common property: information flow.

## » Information Transfer

Certainly one of the key aspects of human physiology is the transfer of information. The significance of proper information flow is either specified or implied in many chapters of this book. Good physical and mental health depends on it, as does the birth and proper growth and development of offspring. One of the prime examples of the impact of information flow is the extracellular matrix.

It may surprise you to learn that one of the simplest, most basic, and yet most extensive mediums for information exchange in the human body is water. The key aspect of water as a means of information transfer is the extent of its prevalence in the human body. Up to 60 percent of the human body is water, the brain is composed of 70 percent water, and the lungs are nearly 90 percent water. About 83 percent of our blood is water, which helps digest our food, transport waste, and control body temperature. Each day humans must replace 2.4 liters of water, some through drinking and the rest taken by the body from the foods eaten. In some organisms, up to 90 percent of their body weight comes from water. Several experiments have demonstrated the effect of intention energy to modify characteristics of water.

Igor Jerman and his colleagues' article "Electrical Transfer of Molecule Information into Water, Its Storage, and Bioeffects on Plants and Bacteria" was published in *Electromagnetic Biology and Medicine*. It documented the potential that "phonons' polarization waves originating from a strong pulsed electric field ... would transmit molecule information into water."

Jingong Pan and colleagues at the Center for Bio-Signaling and System Research at the New Jersey Institute for Technology studied the capability of water for information transfer. "Water, being dipolar, can be partly aligned by an electric field … may be levitated in magnetic fields … and supports resonant intermolecular transfer of vibrational energy. Our studies have further confirmed that structured clustered water can hold low frequency information." Two additional online references are "Water's Memory" and "Electromagnetic Effects and Functional Water."

## » Aging Gene

Scientists have discovered a gene that could double our chances for living to one hundred and diminish our chances for Alzheimer's. They call it "The Golden Oldie Gene." Apparently genes can come in pairs, and if you have a pair of this gene—scientifically name CETP—you're one of these favored ones. One out of five of us seems to have this.

Researchers at the Albert Einstein College of Medicine in New York watched the health of more than five hundred men and women for four-and-a-half years. Only forty of them developed dementia by the end of that time. The online report from *Aetna InteliHealth* News said that this gene (CETP) could treble the odds of reaching one hundred and cut the odds of having Alzheimer's by seventy per cent. The CETP gene affects levels of artery-clogging cholesterol, and the twin version also raises levels of good cholesterol. This not only reduces the risk of heart disease but also apparently lowers chances for developing dementia.

## » Gene Dilemma

It may have been thought that identifying genes for given illnesses was the way to prevent those diseases. A Reykjavik, Iceland, research firm actually did identify genes linked with a number of major diseases. But it turns out that single genes are not the *only* ones responsible for those diseases. Sharon Begley's article "It's in Our Genes. So What?" in *Newsweek* points out that "those gene variants … account for only a small fraction of the risk for developing these diseases."

## » Genetics: Micro RNA

Almost a dozen years of dogged research were unsuccessful on a certain strand of DNA that was felt certain to hold the gene causing lymphocytic leukemia. But a totally unexpected finding in a mutant worm saved the day. Ribonucleic acid (RNA) is chemically similar to and is produced by genes as a short-lived helpmate to the genes for producing proteins for various purposes. Scientists discovered that a gene in the mutant worm did not make protein as genes traditionally do but produced a new kind of genetic material. This is now called micro RNA. That material stuck to the RNA produced by the gene like a strip of Velcro, blocking that gene from producing proteins.

Scientists found they had to rethink their traditional dogma that cancer-causing genes produced protein. Here were cases where genes were prevented from producing protein by a different kind of genetic material, according to Sylvia Westphal's report "High Hopes for a New Kind of Gene" in the *Smithsonian*. Westphal suggested that the serendipitous discovery of this totally unpredictable mechanism for influencing gene activity might leads researchers to find other unusual ways genes might be influenced to cause other diseases.

## » Epigenetics: Other Influences

Most of us were taught or have heard that we inherited genes from our parents that determined our "inherited" characteristics. This was according to Darwinian and Mendelian theories. Inherited "bad genes" can be responsible for thousands of rare diseases. But almost ninety-eight per cent of the time humans are born with a genetic makeup capable of supporting a long, relatively disease-free, life (Strohman). For cardiovascular diseases, most cancers, some diabetes, and most mental diseases, there seems no evidence of a single gene causing them. By contrast, bipolar disorder and schizophrenia are believed to be largely hereditary.

This has led to the genesis of a new science, called epigenetics, to study and help implement advances in health care. Epigenetics literally means, "Control above the level of the gene." We had assumed that genes themselves control developmental traits, but it's been found that genes simply facilitate the cell's synthesis of key proteins needed by cells and organisms to develop properly. In other words, genes apparently supply the blueprints necessary for the cellular production of required proteins (Strohman).

It takes over one hundred thousand different proteins to run our bodies, so scientists assumed that it required us to have more that that number of genes. In other words, there was thought to be a gene-protein specific relationship. But the entire human genome was found to consist of only about twenty-five thousand genes.

What science eventually discovered was that the cell is a complex information system, able to modify its functions without changing the DNA blueprint itself. "DNA blueprints passed down through genes are not set in concrete at birth. Environmental influences, including nutrition, stress, emotions, and the force of human will seem able to modify genes without changing their basic blueprint ... and those modifications can be passed on to future generations" (Lipton).

The complexity of this system is illustrated by the discovery that an organism reportedly can survive without what were thought to be crucial genes. When a gene is missing, the organism finds other genes or finds new ways to use existing genes to produce the same or highly similar phenotypes (Strohman).

Scientists also found that one of the major health problems—obesity—can be caused by an expectant mother's exposure to hormone-mimicking pollutants commonly found in our environment. This was highlighted in Sharon Begley's article "Born to be Big: Early Exposure to Common Chemicals May Be Programming Kids to be Fat" in the online *Newsweek*. The mechanism for this was found to be the action of the pollutants on a DNA gene.

Scientists continue to uncover a variety of mechanisms by which our genes can be influenced to alter their activity. The micro-RNA described earlier is only one of these. Others include a basic kind of response that is characteristic of genes and involves "switching" gene activity on or off. The causes and effects seem highly specific to individuals rather than groups. Environments appear to be influential in some instances, yet science obviously has not catalogued the causes, mechanisms, and effects of all possible combinations in this rapidly expanding field.

Many forces operating within our bodies as well as influencing them externally consist of subtle energies. These are examined in the next chapter.

# CHAPTER SEVENTEEN
## SUBTLE ENERGY

---

*"Everything in the universe has a purpose.*
*Indeed, the invisible intelligence that flows through*
*everything*
*in a purposeful fashion is also flowing through you."*
Wayne Dyer

---

Energy is now known to be involved in and around the human body and between humans. This human energy may also interact with other local or universal energy fields. In much the same way that electromagnetism manifested itself but could not be measured more than two centuries ago, this human energy seems not yet fully understood. Also it is not as precisely measurable as is some other electrodynamic forces. Yet some researchers have made progress in detecting and approximating some forms of this energy. Although this kind of energy may have a common basis, it may exist in a variety of manifestations and/or fields. Most of us have seen a basic field exhibited by the gathering of iron filings on a paper held above the poles of a horseshoe magnet.

Probably the reason scientists have not been able to better define this "new" energy and its effects is that it seems to be characterized as what Einstein called "subtle." In that sense, this energy might well be a clue to understanding even such concepts as consciousness and related mental constructs.

The *American Heritage College Dictionary* defines the word subtle as "so slight as to be difficult to detect or analyze; difficult to understand."

It meant the same in Einstein's day as it means today. Only those researchers or practitioners involved with the manifestations of this subtle energy or with its relationship to the human body can begin to appreciate both its existence and its potential for humankind. Naysayers either refuse to accept or they publicly deny any possibility of its existence. Why would there be such opposition? It seems not to emanate from ignorance but from their views of traditional scientific materialism—not tangible enough to be understood and evaluated by objective experimentation.

## » Emotional Energy

Humans often have been described as behaving "reactively," letting their emotions or others' behavior control their response. Gia Combs-Ramirez's online article "Emotions as Energetic Messengers" captured this concept. She calls emotions "messengers in our energetic anatomy." Understanding the "messages of [our] emotions" tells us what's happening "within and around you." She says we must acknowledge or "own" each emotion we feel; we need to identify where we feel it, in our head, gut, etc.; and we should gauge our response according to how overwhelming the feeling is. Ignoring it likely will force it to move into a bodily response—an effect on our physiology. Combs-Ramirez cites six examples of emotions that we need to recognize and address to prevent their overwhelming effects on our body:

- Depression
- Anger
- Fear
- Grief
- Joy
- Love

## » At the Infinitesimal Level

In their recent book *Everything You Need to Know to Feel Go(o)d*, Candace Pert and Nancy Marriott take readers to realms of the infinitesimal never accessible to researchers before her and other scientists' discoveries. So skeptics won't reject this as a spiritual/religious book, the authors' reference to God in their book's title is because Pert's work convinced her that the intricacy of her findings required the existence of a divine planner.

My book will attempt a broad-brush description of Pert's key discoveries and the electromotive and chemical forces that enable cellular interactions to affect the whole body. Anyone interested in digging further would do well to read Pert and Marriott's book.

The other promise in their book's title—feel good—comes from the cascade of research efforts and results that apparently stemmed from her discovery as a young graduate student. She called it "one of the most influential discoveries of the 20th century in my field and in the emerging studies of neuroscience."

Pert proved the existence of an opiate receptor on the surface of the cell where opiate drugs have an effect. For many years felt to exist, such a receptor nevertheless remained elusive. This may seem insignificant to laypersons. But it enabled Pert to develop her theory of emotions and their role in "the mind-body connection as a widely distributed psychosomatic network of communicating molecules." This resulted in her earlier book *Molecules of Emotion: The Science Behind Mind-Body Medicine* and literally made her a superstar in mind-body research.

Pert's discovery of opiate receptors was important because it suggested that opiate drugs work by mimicking natural opiate-like molecules made and used in the brain. It quickly led scientists to identify the endorphins, the brain's natural "feel-good" substances. Researchers now believe that opiate receptors may also be important for the release of the luteinizing hormone. That is an important reproductive peptide and is even involved in regulation of the immune system.

Receptors had been theorized to exist for a great many years. Much of the impetus for research was from scientists' experiences with therapeutic drugs. Early researchers noted that some sort of mechanism seemed to exist in the human body whereby an "affinity" occurred between a drug and the site of its action. A number of experimental reports of drug action were surfacing that clearly indicated drug molecules must be concentrating on small specific areas of cells in order to produce their effects. Before 1973, specifics of drug action largely were unknown. Research showed that opiates acted on specific neurons, but few receptor molecules of any kind had been found. Today we realize that drug-binding sites may be part of any cellular constituent.

A receptor is a protein molecule, embedded in either the plasma membrane or cell nucleus to which a "signaling" molecule may attach. The molecule that binds to a receptor is called a "ligand." It may be a peptide such as a neurotransmitter, a hormone, a pharmaceutical drug, or a toxin. When this binding occurs, the receptor ordinarily stimulates a cellular response. Receptors are critical to the life of all cells. Every function, response, interaction, pathway, process, and any other term you might think of that concerns the moment-to-moment existence of a cell, is controlled by various receptor/ligand-induced systems.

Pert's conviction that "the mind and body are one [was based upon] … that all systems of our physiology are connected and coordinated by emotion-laden, information-carrying molecules engaged in constant cross-talk, such as between the nervous and immune systems." Pert later wrote the foreword to Jim Oschman's book in which she said "different emotional states, by triggering the release of various peptides, can cause sudden, even quantum shifts, not only in consciousness but in behavior … [and] … memory."

Indeed, Pert's accomplishments heralded the significance of infinitesimal subtle energies in mind-body relationships, emphasizing the roles of hormones, other peptides, neurotransmitters, vibrations, and electrical currents.

## » Nanotechnology

The subtlety of biochemical and electromagnetic forces in, and interacting with, the human body seems obvious from the above research. Probably one of the greatest advances to enable a better detection, characterization, measurement, and acceptance of these forces rests in the fast-emerging bioenergetic nanotechnology. Nanotechnology deals with measurements on an almost unimaginably small scale. For example, consider a common yardstick, three feet long. A meter is about ten per cent longer than a yardstick. One nanometer is one-billionth of a meter. A human hair measures approximately 50,000 to 100,000 nanometers in diameter.

The dawn of nanoscale science can be traced to a now classic talk that Richard Feynman gave in December 1959 at the annual meeting of the American Physical Society at the California Institute of Technology. Later founded in 1986, Foresight Nanotech Institute was the first organization to educate society about the benefits and risks of nanotechnology. At that time, nanotechnology apparently still was a little-known concept.

Today, it's been said that nanotechnology accounts for as much as one-third of our economy. Opportunities still abound, however, for nanotechnology to uncover the very subtle biological interactions, forces, and imbalances involved with the human body. In that regard, biological and bioenergetic nanotechnology seem in their infancy. There are a few promising reports, however, including the following.

An example of this was presented in Al Fin's online article "Pin-Point Precision: Nano Technology." He said, "The new gold-plated boron nitride nanotube-nanoneedles from the University of Illinois are a good example of technology convergence. The ability to discover the intimate workings between cell and molecular biology has never been as strong." With a diameter of approximately 50 nanometers, the nanoneedle introduces minimal intrusion in penetrating cell membranes and accessing the interiors of live cells. It facilitates a better understanding of the biological processes at the functional level, within the cell itself.

The University of Michigan News Service announcement, "Nano-sized voltmeter measures electric fields deep within cells," heralded a significant advance in measuring *intracellular* electric potential. U-M professor Raoul Kopelman discussed the device during a special session, "Creating Next Generation Nano Tools for Cell Biology," at the annual meeting of the American Society for Cell Biology in Washington, D.C. This wireless diminutive voltmeter is overturning conventional wisdom about the physical environment inside cells. Scientists earlier had measured electric fields in the membranes that surround cells, but not in the interior of the cell.

The instrument has a diameter of only 30 nanometers, and it measures photons of light rather than electrons. This allows deploying thousands of single nano-particles, each with voltage-sensitive dyes, throughout the cell. Superimposed blue light causes the particles to emit red and green light, and the ratio between the two indicates the strength of the electric field.

Results surprised everyone, revealing high electric fields in cytosol, while conventional wisdom said there were zero electric fields there. Cytosol is the jellylike material that makes up most of a cell's interior.

Changes in electrical fields associated with membranes were known to play a role in diseases such as Alzheimer's. Also, researchers already were exploring the use of externally applied electric fields to stimulate wound healing and nerve growth and regeneration. The latter is discussed in the online article from Scotland "Electrical Fields, Nerve Growth, and Nerve Regeneration" by McCaig and Rajnicek.

The abstract of an article by Tetsuya Haruyama and colleagues in *Current Applied Physics* appeared online. The article, entitled "Bio-, Nano-Technology for Cellular Biosensing," noted that cells and tissues transmit chemical and physical signals that respond to extracellular stimuli. This involves information transfer for intracellular biological processes. The authors stress, however, that these signals often are very weak and not easily detected with conventional analytical methods. The article describes two tactics they found successful. One was the molecular designing of "polymer metal polymer complex" as a molecular transducer for a cellular nitric oxide sensor. The other was a genetic construction of a postsynapse model cell for an evaluation of an extracellular neural transmitter.

According to TheWhyFiles online article "Small is Beautiful: Nanotech Meets Biology," one of the marvelous revelations from nanotechnology has advanced biological research. If you ever saw the glass or plastic containers used in biology labs, you know that the insides of those containers were flat. Nanotechnology now recognizes that living cells never see "flat." So nanotech borrowed some tricks from the electronic chip-making industry to "create a simple, ridged pattern on a plastic surface used for growing cells in the lab." This mimics natural surfaces to which cells are accustomed, and it promotes "a realistic picture of cell behavior [when used] in the lab." Wound healing and glaucoma are just two of the unfolding opportunities for studying new approaches to better health care. A major stumbling block could be the necessity for repeating previous cell studies that involved the use of flat surfaces, since the use of ridged surfaces could produce different, perhaps improved, results.

## » Cellular Use of Energy

Cell biologist Bruce Lipton's book is an excellent primer on cell biology. Some fascinating discoveries have emerged regarding the effect of subtle energies at the cellular level of the human body. For example, cell membranes contain "integral membrane proteins" (IMPs). They serve different fuctions, some as receptors and others as effectors. Receptors obviously sense cells' environments and effectors carry out necessary activities.

Jule Klotter's online article "Exercise and Osteoporosis: Townsend Letter for Doctors and Patients" illustrated how physical exercise such as walking is felt to strengthen bones by increasing bone density. Such mechanical stress "causes calcium phosphate crystals in the bone to produce *tiny electric currents*. This piezoelectric effect stimulates bone-building cells to deposit more mineral salts to strengthen bones in the stressed areas."

In the absence of this exercise "for a prolonged period, bone-resorbing cells will tear down unnecessary bone." This exercise also stimulates "secretion of calcitonin, a thyroid hormone that inhibits the bone resorption." The Mayo Clinic recommends walking at least a mile a day. The research behind this finding seems to have been done by C. Halperin, et al, in Israel and reported in Nano Letters under the title "Piezoelectric Effect in Human Bones Studied in Nanometer Scale."

Bhanu Jena's book *Methods in Nano Cell Biology* suggested "Understanding live cells at the single molecular level is the most important and single major challenge facing biology and medicine today."

A Nikon online article "Electro Physiology" said, "All living cells and tissues have electrical properties resulting from the movement of ions such as K+, Na+, Ca++, and Cl–." The article reported, "Cellular electrical activity can be studied using microelectrodes." Also, it commented that microelectrodes could stimulate and record changes in voltage or electrical current across cell membranes. Investigations may involve calculating the electrical activity of entire organs or single ion channels in a cell membrane. Changes in electrical activity can be related to functional activity, signaling, or firing of neurons. Recording may be made extracellularly or intracellularly.

Adenosine triphosphate (ATP) is considered by biologists to be the energy currency of life. It is the high-energy molecule that stores the energy we need to do just about everything we do. It is present in the cytoplasm and nucleoplasm of every cell. Essentially all the physiological mechanisms that require energy for operation obtain it directly from the stored ATP. As food in the cells is gradually oxidized, the released energy is used to re-form the ATP so that the cell always maintains a supply of this essential molecule. In animal systems, the ATP is synthesized in the tiny energy factories called mitochondria.

Russian researchers A. L. Buchachenko, D. A. Kuznetsov, and V. L. Berdinsky's article "New mechanisms of biological effects of electromagnetic fields" appeared in the journal *Biophysics*. These researchers said, "ATP production in mitochondria depends on the nuclear spin and magnetic moment of $Mg^{++}$ ion in creatine kinase and ATPase. Consequently, the enzymatic synthesis of ATP is an ion-radical process and depends on the external magnetic field and microwave fields that control the spin states of ion-radical pairs and influence the ATP synthesis."

An intriguing article appeared in the IEEE journal *Power Engineering Review*, entitled "Biological magnets in the human brain—could magnetite mediate health effects of electromagnetic fields?" The article said that microscopic crystals of the magnetic mineral magnetite have been isolated from samples of human brain tissue. The magnetite crystals could be moved around by magnetic fields only slightly stronger than the earth's natural magnetic field. Seventy crystals of two types were examined, having diameters ranging from ten to two hundred nanometers. "SQUID magnetometer readings showed that the samples of human brain tissue had the unmistakable signature of the ferromagnetic mineral magnetite."

## » Universal Field

The purpose of this academic discussion is as a background for examining recent theoretical advances in Ervin Laszlo's book *Science and the Akashic Field: An Integral Theory of Everything*. Readers of my previous book may recall that he "asked whether the universe itself might have some sort of consciousness from which ours emerged and with which ours might remain connected in some way." In her book *The Field: The Quest for the Secret Force of the Universe*, Lynn McTaggart offered a sixteen-page bibliography with an exhaustive listing of hundreds of scientists in multiple disciplines.

Several more recent books from other authors have been more fervent about their theories of a universal consciousness. In his book,

John James reasoned that the "Great Field," as he calls it, is a single, all-inclusive "essence" that encompasses all that exists. He speculated too that multiple other fields exist, interacting among themselves and with life itself. Predictably, it appears that the electromagnetic fields shown to surround and permeate us also link with the universal fields.

James described fields as being involved with information exchange, flow, and storage. They do not possess human traits such as judgment, compassion, or forgiveness. Fields therefore are responsible for the coherence among natural constants and variables, not in responding to "our daily needs and cares." In so doing, they serve our deeper needs of which we typically are not aware. In a few words, "fields are why strawberries are strawberries and beech trees are beech trees," he illustrates.

Quantum mechanics deals with particles and waves as components of information fields. Van Lommel suggests, "Consciousness could be based on fields of information." Although "electromagnetic fields of our neurons and other cells disappear" upon cardiac arrest "consciousness will continue to be experienced in another dimension ... an invisible and immaterial world."

In his book, New Zealand physician Robin Kelly tries to connect the dots, so to speak. Trained in Great Britain and a general practitioner for many years, his book describes his move into full-time acupuncture. He recounts many "powerful healing stories." He acknowledges that these are "experiences I would have regarded years ago as supernatural."

## » Thought Energy

This book has dealt with many aspects of thoughts as energetic influences on our behavior, our wellbeing, and even on other people. In his online article "Thought Energy: the Basis of a Quantum Leap in Psychotherapy," Gregory Nicosea correlates elements of quantum mechanics with the transmission of thoughts and accompanying intentions. He uses the particle-wave theory to justify that thoughts can be considered "information waves" accompanying energy particles in our natural world.

Using this approach, Nicosea believes that therapy for mental disturbances could benefit from quantum-level intervention. He links his theory to the existence of energy meridians or chakras that have been proved instrumental in health care. He speaks of "thought energy fields" as an intervention access. As such, he sees thought and emotional disturbances as susceptible to correction of energy balance much as physical ailments are.

In physicist William Tiller's online commentary "Exploring the Effects of Human Intention and Thought Energy," he describes three controlled experiments he conducted. He and his colleagues at Stanford University developed a subtle energy detector—an ultra-sensitive Geiger counter-type device—with which they demonstrated the existence of an energy field that is not recognizable in the electromagnetic spectrum. With this special detector, Dr. Tiller demonstrated that this subtle energy field responds to intentional human focus.

Results of his experiments appeared to prove the effectiveness of thought-intention in altering biological values: "increase or decrease the pH of pure water ... increase a chemical ratio [ATP/ADP] in developing fruit fly larva [and] ... increase the in-vitro thermodynamic activity of the liver enzyme alkaline phosphatase (ALP) by a significant amount."

In his online article, Tiller also detailed his theory how quantum mechanics explains the electromagnetic forces operating in the human body with regard to thought-intention. The explanation is most suitable reading for persons familiar with the quantum mechanics theory. Nevertheless, most readers would appreciate the break-through experiments that prove thought-intention actually can affect physical or biological objects whether or not they understand the scientific basis of quantum mechanics.

## » DNA Phantom Effect

Vladimir Poponin and Peter Gariaev first observed this effect in Moscow at the Russian Academy of Sciences. The experiment that produced this result was duplicated many times and the equipment was checked in every conceivable way. The experiment produced two surprising results.

The experiment was conducted using a sophisticated and expensive Malvern laser photon correlation spectrometer (LPCS). The intent was to measure the vibration modes of DNA in solution. The experiment involved a three-step process. First, the experiment confirmed that the light (photons) in the scattering chamber of the LPCS was randomly distributed. Second, when the DNA was added to the chamber, the distribution of photons assumed an oscillatory function related to the double helix of the DNA. Third, when the DNA was removed, the distribution of photons retained their oscillatory function. If the scattering chamber was not moved, this effect lingered for up to a month.

Two conditions are necessary to observe the DNA phantom effect: the presence of a DNA molecule and the exposure of the DNA to weak coherent laser radiation. The latter will suffice in two different frequencies of laser radiation. The phantom effect might also be considered a new physical vacuum substructure that was previously overlooked.

Poponin and Gariaev suggested that this effect might help explain the mechanisms underlying subtle energy, including the many observed alternative-healing phenomena. Also, this effect might illustrate a subtle energy effect in which direct human influence is not involved. Further, the field of the DNA phantom effect has the ability to be coupled with conventional electromagnetic fields of laser radiation.

## » Subtle Energy Research

One of the leaders in subtle energy research is the HeartMath Institute of Boulder Creek, Colorado, discussed earlier with regard to heart research. William A. Tiller, Professor Emeritus of Stanford University and a pioneering researcher of subtle energy, and Vladimir Poponin, formerly of the Institute of Biochemical Physics of the Russian Academy of Sciences, a co-discoverer of the DNA phantom effect, have joined the HeartMath team studying the cutting-edge human energy research.

Valerie Hunt was mentioned earlier in this book. She was a pioneer in research of human energy fields in her laboratory at the University of California at Los Angeles. Other researchers had studied extremely low biological frequency electromagnetic currents in relation to healing, tissue, and disease. But Hunt was reported to be the first to study extremely high frequency biological electric currents involving mind phenomena and human consciousness.

Hunt conclusively demonstrated the existence of more subtle energy forces, or fields, operating in and around the human body. She was able to demonstrate the existence of what are labeled chakras and auras; to show variation in both magnitude and frequency of such energy; and to document correlations of electromagnetic measurements at chakras with aura observations. Hunt's studies also suggested that detectable changes in these energy fields might help reveal health disorders.

Existing electromagnetic monitoring devices that depend on skin contact are unable to detect and measure the more subtle electromagnetic processes in the body. It is important to develop detectors that also can define electromagnetic fields surrounding the body. Research has been able to show that humans emit photons, whose flux and frequency are expected to change with variations in a person's thoughts and emotions.

One notable advance, as mentioned earlier in this book, is the demonstrated ability of thought and intention to change the structure of water. Since water is a major element distributed throughout the human body, it seems reasonable that subtle changes in water might be one mechanism by which human energy influences the flow of biological information.

Cyndi Dale's book *The Subtle Energy Body: An Encyclopedia of Your Energetic Anatomy* provides a roadmap to subtle energy theory, as far as traditional science is concerned. Traditional physical forces are discernible as electromagnetic, gravity, weak nuclear, and strong nuclear. Subtle energies, by contrast, are not measurable by contemporary instruments but are detectable by their effects. Dale quotes Tiller, "There is not just one type of subtle energy," hence the term "subtle energies."

Our world is characterized by some marvelous natural occurrences that lend themselves to interpretation as part of intelligent design. The next chapter discusses this.

# CHAPTER EIGHTEEN
# MARVELOUS COINCIDENCES OR DIVINE HANDIWORK?

*"Adopt the pace of nature: her secret is patience."*
Ralph Waldo Emerson

Most of us can rattle off the names of people who introduced us to scientific facts we respect, observe, and depend upon in our daily lives. But how many of you recognize the name of Leonardo Fibonacci born 1170 in Pisa, Italy? Having a natural talent for numbers, perhaps his chief contribution to mathematics and natural science seems to have been the result of what's become known as "Fibonacci's rabbits."

## » Golden Ratio

Fibonacci's calculations involved the breeding pattern of rabbits: how fast a rabbit population would grow in ideal circumstances. Using conventional assumptions, he found that the number of pairs per month was best described by the following series of numbers: 1, 1, 2, 3, 5, 8, 13, 21, 34, 55, 89, 144, 233, 377, 610, 987, 1597, etc. Notice that each number is the sum of the two preceding it. Eventually, the ratio of a number to the one preceding it approaches 1.618. This has been called the Golden Ratio and is replicated throughout nature. It also has served artists, architects, furniture makers, and scientists over the centuries as almost a revered piece of sacred geometry to guide their work. The list of examples is endless, so an essential one might suffice.

Robin Kelly discusses the origin and significance of this ratio in his book. The double helix DNA spiral measures 34 angstroms long by 21 angstroms wide. The ratio of these two numbers is 1.619!

## » Geometry of Nature

In my earlier book, I mentioned the work of another mathematician, Frenchman Benoit Mandelbrot, who introduced a new geometry based on fractal mathematics. In contrast to Euclidian geometry that dealt with regular shaped objects like cones and spheres, fractal mathematics deals with the irregular patterns that occur in nature: the relationships between seemingly random patterns in a whole structure and the patterns among its parts. Even though the basic formulas are simple, they require iterations, or repetition of instructions, millions of times to make sense. So the theory fell into disrepute at the time. But, with the advent of powerful computers, scientists have come to recognize its significance.

In his book, John James explained fractals as "'self-similar' patterns [of nature] are nested within one another." He used the example that twigs grow arranged on a branch in a pattern like the branches growing on the trunk of a tree. Interestingly, fractals also can be used to describe turbulence, "as in wind and water." Thus, both the coherence and the chaos of nature are reflected in fractals.

Parts of the electronic textbook "Exploring Fractals and Chaos" are accessible online. This helps give structural meaning to natural events that once were considered chaotic. A faucet drip, the weather, the formation of clouds, and human heart fibrillation were just a few of many occurrences that seem on first glance to follow no pattern. They appeared to be chaotic, unpredictable, and random until subjected to fractal studies. This seems to extend to even cataclysmic geophysical happenings like earthquakes, tsunamis, and rogue waves. Still, the value of fractals hasn't seemed to translate into providing early predictions of such events. But its use in studying patterns of natural behavior appears to have some predictive value when incorporated with continual monitoring information about earth, ocean, and weather factors. John Briggs' book *Fractals: The Patterns of Chaos: Discovering a New Aesthetic of Art, Science, and Nature* provides an excellent examination of the use of fractals in multiple fields.

The opposite of chaos is coherence, defined in the *Merriam-Webster Dictionary* online as the "systematic or logical connection or consistency." The value of fractals in coherence also extends into many fields, most notably art and architecture. Danielle Capo's article "The Fractal Nature of Architectural Orders" in the *Nexus Network Journal* examines "concepts that are proper to fractal geometry with regards to architectural elements." She shows how fractals can be used to design architectural orders to assure that small elements are inserted in a continuous and coherent whole. "If we interpret this structure fractally, we do not distinguish between the essential and the inessential. Everything is essential and so creates in this way a greater (fractal) coherence. It could be said, in this light, that the general form is not what counts the most, but rather, what is really important is the way in which parts hold together."

## » Natural Electromagnetic Frequencies

Robin Kelly's book also cites certain environmental factors that nature depends upon. Certain electromagnetic frequencies in our atmosphere are necessary for growth and repair of plant life and, thus, for animal life as well. These are called Schumann resonances (7-10 Hz). Lightning strikes over equatorial rain forests fill our atmosphere with just the right frequencies. In the 1930s, Schumann discovered a magnetic field that thrust upwards from the earth rather than down like gravity. Valerie Hunt elaborated on this in her book. She noted that this field is found in Stonehenge, England; the pyramids; and Delphi, in Greece. Hunt said that electromagnetic frequency measured there and the brain waves of proven mystics both were the equivalent of the Schumann resonances.

Estimated at an average of 7.83 Hz, the Schumann resonance is the "basic frequency of the earth." Some people believe it has natural healing properties. It also is purported to be the "fundamental flow of one's being" according to Mary Desaulniers in her online article "Schumann Resonance: Healing through Alpha Brain Waves, Meditation and Dolphin Contact."

Dr. Herbert König, Schumann's successor, demonstrated a connection between Schumann resonance and natural brain waves. Alpha brain rhythms show Schumann resonance: the brain frequency of the relaxed and creative mind. During deep meditation alpha and theta waves provide resonance between the human mind and the planet earth.

## » Global Guidance Systems

Birds, salmon, and sea turtles are among nature's creatures with an innate global guidance system that enable them to return to their birthplace to reproduce offspring. *Nature* posted an online article "Extraordinary Cats: Homing Instincts" that discussed this innate ability of cats. The article gave examples of cats that found their way home in extraordinary circumstances. Although many of them crossed long distances and some repeated the trip, the honors go to Tigger and Ninja. Tigger was "a three-legged cat who has made the three-mile return to his old home more than seventy-five times." Ninja was the tomcat that showed up at his old home a year later, 850 miles away. Salmon, the article claims, are suspected of using smell; birds and bees of depending on astrological signposts; and sea turtles of following ocean sounds.

Molly McElroy's online article "Model Systems in Neuroethology: Magnetic Information in Animal Orientation" discusses the earth's magnetic orientation as the possible "homing" mechanism for animals. Her article also related that the magnetic mineral magnetite has been found in the brains of some animals as it was in the human brain. Eventually magnetite was found in the brain linings of bees, termites, rhinoceros, and pigeons. Christopher Ibotrain wrote also that these magnetic crystals are manufactured by the living cells and arranged in such a way that the maximum magnetic effect is achieved. The significance of finding magnetic properties in human brain tissue has not been conclusively shown.

In Olivia Judson's "The Wild Side" in the *New York Times*, guest columnist Leon Kreitzman provided a unique perspective of nature in "Let's Hear It for the Bees." It seems that "plants have carefully timed routines, called 'circadian rhythms,' internally generated to open and close their flowers at set times of day. Flowers of a given species also produce nectar at about the same time each day, as this increases the chances of cross-pollination." Fortunately, "honeybees concentrate foraging on a particular species in a narrow time-window [and] have ...

a daily diary that can include as many as nine appointments ... the bees' time-keeping is accurate to about 20 minutes." The bee, like other living creatures, "has a circadian clock that is reset daily to run in time with the solar cycle."

## » Even the Mundane

The lowly paramecium, the amoeba-like single-celled mobile organism most of us studied in biology, now are believed to have the same type of microtubules we have in our cells. Some scientists are beginning to believe these represent on-board computers, helping to make decisions. In the paramecium's case, this means where to go and what to do to insure survival and nutrition.

The continuing search for answers to these amazing phenomena even led to the establishment of the journal *Mathematical Modelling of Natural Phenomena*. This is an international research journal, which publishes top-level original and review papers and short communications and proceedings on mathematical modelling in biology, medicine, chemistry, physics, and other areas. The journal is essentially functioning on the basis of topical issues representing active areas of research. The journal publishes research articles and reviews within the whole field of mathematical modelling, and it will continue to provide information on the latest trends and developments in this ever-expanding subject.

Certain slime mold organisms exhibit a remarkable capability to organize for the good of all. When food is exhausted for an amoeba called Dictyostelium discoideum, millions coalesce into a single, slug-like creature that forages until it finds a new source. Afterwards, it assumes a mushroom-like formation, scatters as spores, and the cycle starts again. There seem to be built-in mechanisms that insure altruism.

The other slime mold, Physarum polycephalum, is a single cell containing multiple nuclei. Researchers had thought that specialized cells controlled its group-forming behavior, but they found that this occurred as a result of networking: linked interactions between its individual cells. Scientists claim that this mold not only has memory but also has computer-like capabilities.

In a remarkable experiment, scientists found that this mold could construct "networks of nutrient-channeling tubes that are strikingly similar to the layout of the Japanese rail system," called one of the most-efficiently designed transportation systems in the world. (Keim, Sanders)

## » Natural Forces

The strength of electromagnetic, gravitational, and nuclear forces of nature are precisely hospitable to life. If any of them had varied in the slightest amount, the earth could not have supported life. No known physical constraints require this. Leading physicists and cosmologists insist that the Big Bang had to be amazingly fine-tuned to create an inhabitable planet. Random choice of conditions would reduce the chance of earth being hospitable to $10^{123}$ (ten with 123 zeros after it) (Rosenblum and Kuttner).

## » Magnetic Field Protected Early Life

Another piece of the puzzle about early life on earth has been found. It involves the approximate date that a magnetic field first covered the earth. The timing is important because it falls during life's earliest stages of development, between the periods when the Earth was bombarded by interplanetary debris and when the atmosphere filled with oxygen. Several earlier studies had suggested that a magnetic field is a necessary shield against deadly solar radiation that can strip away a planet's atmosphere, evaporate water, and snuff out life on its surface.

The University of Rochester's John Tarduno reported the results of the study in *Science*. The researchers detected a magnetic signal in 3.45-billion-year-old rocks that was between 50 and 70 percent the strength of the present-day field. Lisa Grossman's online article "Earth's Magnetic Field Is 3.5 Billion Years Old" appeared on *Wired Science*. The rocks were discovered in the Greenstone Belt in South Africa.

## » Significance to Human Existence

The Anthropic Cosmological Principle concludes that the stability of structures essential for life, from atomic nuclei to the whole universe, depends on delicate balances between different fundamental forces. These balances are believed to occur only in a tiny fraction of possible universes—so that this universe appears fine-tuned for life. The universe needs to be as big as it is and as old (15 billion years) as it in order to evolve carbon-based life forms. This is because carbon is produced in stars and this process takes over 10 billion years. Glenn McDavid provided a number of excellent commentaries and references in his online presentation "The Anthropic Cosmological Principle and Related Issues."

The purpose of this chapter was not to take a position in any debate. It was just to help us realize that, if certain physicochemical aspects of our world varied even slightly, life on earth might not exist.

You likely will agree that humankind is particularly fortunate to live in a world that is so exquisitely designed. The innate intelligence with which all living creatures are endowed enable control elements like DNA and the brain to adapt and improve in keeping with environmental influences. Combined with other remarkable environmental constants described in this chapter, we should be especially grateful.

The next chapter begins a part that addresses the doubts some people express about feeling unfulfilled in their lives..

PART FOUR

Is This All There Is to Life?

CHAPTER NINETEEN
# WHAT ARE WE SEARCHING FOR?

---

*"You are a child of the universe*
*no less than the trees and the stars;*
*you have a right to be here.*
*And whether or not it is clear to you,*
*no doubt the universe is unfolding as it should."*

*Desiderata*, Max Ehrmann

---

The title of this part of the book is a question that many of us might ask ourselves at both extremes of ambition: resounding success or dismal failure. We may become so jaded after spectacular material accomplishments and possessions that we wonder, in moments of self-reflection, "Is this all there is to life?" By contrast, in the throes of self-doubt after a string of failures, we naturally might arrive at the same question. So this seems another good time to contemplate "What if…?" What if these discussions hold a special meaning not only for you but also for your loved ones?

For more than two millennia, churches increasingly held sway over people's beliefs about life and death. As you found in an earlier chapter, however, people's attitude toward religious assurances have begun shifting. This seems not just a matter of church participation but a question about the lack of providential intervention in mass calamities and a reformed set of beliefs about God. Despite this, or perhaps because of this, many people seem to have arrived at new concerns about life itself, questions more piercing than any they have heard answered in church.

Eminent physicist Richard Feynman addressed this topic in his book *The Meaning of It All: Thoughts of a Citizen-Scientist.* "I think we frankly do not know ... the meaning of it all," he admitted in his remarks to the students and faculty at the University of Washington in Seattle as part of the John Danz Lecture Series. This admission by mankind would be a step in the right direction. It avoids preconceptions that we have arrived and restores the potential of the individual. Feynman is a Nobel Laureate and his 1959 talk describing the precise science of manipulating matter at the molecular and atomic levels brought him the title of the "father of nanotechnology."

Feynman illustrates his admission with the purported disparity between religion and science. He feels that there is none. But he illustrates with the gradual shift of attitude by a young college student from a religious family as he advances in his study of science. Whether from sensing the enormity that science knows about everything, he starts to doubt as his studies encourage it. Eventually he may disbelieve God, perhaps influenced by professors who also disbelieve. An old expression seems to capture this "To put the cart before the horse."

Feynman reemphasizes the danger of individual, societal, national, or cultural preconceptions concerning the use of scientific advances, especially for applications involving moral law. He stresses the need to respect uncertainty for what it is or as he says, "Humility of the intellect."

Psychologist Charles Tart reinforced Feynman's cautions in Tart's foreword to Kenneth Ring and Sharon Cooper's book *Mindsight: Near-Death and Out-of-Body Experiences in the Blind.* Perhaps the near-unbelievable topic of that book warranted Tart's commentary. He described the often-observed reluctance of even scientists to be open to the unknown; instead, they seem "too satisfied with answers we have." Unfortunately, he observes, this is "a dominant philosophy of modern culture." Apparently sociologists have long termed this "scientism." We seem to become "too emotionally invested" in what we think are satisfactory explanations. Charles T. Tart himself is well known for his expertise and his publications in the field of consciousness, spirituality, and transpersonal psychology. His Weblog is http://blog.paradigm-sys.com/ and his many books are featured in his Amazon Author's page.

"Done with the proper attitude of curiosity and humility," Tart asserts, "I find essential science quite compatible with spirituality." But scientism often seems to believe that "all ideas of any inherent meaning or spirituality to the universe have been declared invalid." As a psychologist Tart was convinced that "without a sense of meaning bigger than your life of personal and social gratification, human beings not only do not thrive, they sicken, and they die."

## » Self-Help Efforts

The news media reported three fatalities and eighteen hospitalizations resulting from a sweat-lodge ritual in Sedona, AZ. Steve Salerno's article "Self-Help Doesn't Help—And Often Hurts" emphasized the human costs we may incur by our felt need for self-improvement. This appeared in the *Wall Street Journal* online.

An incredulous reader of that article naturally might ask the question in the chapter title "What Are [They] Searching For?" This Arizona event was only one of many self-help programs for which people spend eleven billion dollars annually. Salerno then poses the challenge, "But really, what's the harm?' He then writes, "This is not the first time that self-help tactics have gone awry." The remainder of his article captures mortality statistics from these activities that should discourage anyone. It seems that some who enroll in live self-help events would do better seeing a psychologist. Suicides are just one of the reported outcomes.

The inclusion of this article is not intended to dissuade people from an earnest desire to improve the quality of their and their families' lives. Before total commitment of mind and body to self-improvement, however, it seems wise to carefully examine what will be involved: risks as well as benefits.

Whatever the individual reasons, more people seem to be searching for something. Even though it may be elusive, the popular media apparently believes it is worth their attention. Even *O The Oprah Magazine* carried a cover feature "Who Are You Meant to Be?" It is extensive with personal commentaries and a self-evaluation questionnaire. The overall tenor of the presentation seems to discourage an attitude of helplessness.

Rather, it encourages a personal introspection that likely will offer a manageable plan for improvement, if any seems desirable.

## » Transcendence and Postmodern World

Dutchman Rogier Bos called this a "postmodern world" and looked at the increasing interest in transcendence in his Weblog presentation "The Meaning of Transcendence in the Postmodern World." Transcendence and enlightenment have attracted increasing attention as perhaps alternative approaches to religion and spirituality, seemingly related to helping answer burning doubts about life itself.

Transcendence is used many times in discussions about metaphysical experiences, such as meditation. The term seems to have originated to describe the nature of God. The *American Heritage College Dictionary* defined transcendence as "beyond the limits of experience and hence unknowable" and according to Kant "preeminent and supreme" and "above and independent of the material universe." It also is used to imply rising above one's perceived limitations and achieving beyond expectations. You can understand how, thru metaphysical experiences, it also implies being able to catch a glimpse of, or even reach, the state of the divine. As such, transcendence might facilitate spiritual growth.

It's understandable that church members might expect to have their institutions either dispute or explain things like transcendence and enlightenment as related to faith, life, and death. Churches, for the most part, seem reluctant to become entangled with the metaphysical, just as science does. This might behoove the religious establishment, however, to try to mediate such debates that strike at the heart of life itself.

## » The Search

Interestingly, Rogier Bos dug deeper than transcendence into the more pervasive question about people's attitudes, beliefs, and behavior that became this chapter's title, "What Are We Searching For?" He concluded, "our world displays a quest for transcendence ... but what are the questions the world is asking ... what lies behind this quest?

This felt need for a transcending experience may sound reasonable when we consider that much of our life is concerned with survival, routine, chores, frustration, and anxiety. Bos said, "In this way, the yearning for transcendent experiences could be interpreted as mere escapism, but I believe it is much more than that: it is the desire for life as we feel it *should have been.*" It's almost as if "within the human heart there lies an awareness that life as we experience it is not the life that we were created for." Some have expressed this as "a longing for home." The term "home" also was mentioned by many subjects hypnotically regressed by Michael Newton to their life between lives, meaning the spirit world (2000).

Earlier, you read that some very young children exhibit unusual abilities. Seemingly related to this, we also discussed that memories of the spirit world fade as children adapt to societal and environmental influences of growing up. We are told that such memories are stored in our subconscious and superconscious minds (Newton 2000). If that is true and knowing that those memories may fade because our sense of reality emerges as we consciously begin to confront life, could that memory be what we are searching for?

There is a true story about an elderly lady who was seen by a psychoanalyst after being examined by traditional physicians without success. No medicines had helped. Even with family around her, she constantly complained, "I miss my friends so much!" The psychoanalyst was trained in life-between-lives hypnotic regression and the patient consented to try it. During the trance, her face brightly lit up and she exclaimed, "Oh! There they are! I miss them so much!" Upon further clarification, it became clear that she had been longing to see members of her soul group (Newton 2009). (Soul groups are discussed in a later chapter.)

This yearning for meaning in our lives is exemplified in different ways, as follows.

## » Unspoken Fear

It may seem odd to include death in this chapter. After all, our effort is to find a satisfying, worthwhile meaning for our lives on earth. However, the inevitability of death never completely disappears from our mind and may unintentionally influence our search for a better life on earth. We grow up with beliefs about death learned from our parents and grandparents, just as each generation of our ancestors taught one another. Over the ages, religion has had a strong hand in shaping those beliefs. An example is by instilling a fear of punishment for sinning. Realistically, this likely has significantly subdued humankind's primitive instincts and behavior.

Nevertheless, these beliefs also must account for the prevailing attitude of the finality of death. It seems impossible to ignore this unwillingness on the part of both religion and the faithful to accept the soul survival of death of the physical body. Including the awareness of soul survival then makes our search for a meaningful life on earth more productive, in that we begin to consider our earthly sojourn in the eternal scheme of things.

For anyone open to inquiring further about soul survival after bodily death, I enthusiastically recommend Elizabeth Kubler-Ross's book *on LIFE after DEATH*. It is a brief but compelling personal account. She has listened to thousands of nearing-death patients, studied the testimonies of thousands of near-death-experience (NDE) survivors, and even has had a profound spiritual epiphany herself. The vision she offers is of a loving, forgiving divinity and spiritual growth of each soul over multiple incarnations through self-assessment rather than punishment. She reminds us, however, that ending one's own life prematurely is considered a wasted opportunity. If she doesn't convince you that life continues and only the dimension changes, nothing will.

## » Enrapture

Perhaps many people have experienced the sort of transcendence provided by an overwhelming sensation of being lifted out of the ordinary, freed from any cares, and infused with delight. This can occur, for example, when we are enthralled by a majestic symphony or renowned choir performance. It brings with it an unparalleled sense of tranquility; the joy of being whisked out of the ordinary and carried along with the sensation; and an unrestricted feeling of surrendering to the flow. In this respect a longing for such experiences is often explained as the search for "a reality that is more real than the one we live in". Enrapture is different from the theological term "rapture."

Somehow there seems to reside in the human heart an awareness that reality as we experience it is but a drab reflection of what it should be. Native Americans and others have resorted to psychedelic substances to achieve this state of mind, the former having incorporated this into their religious rituals.

Apparently we may approach states of transcendence in the worst of times (Scribd). Linda Chamberlain's online slide presentation "Crisis and Transcendence: When the Worst that Can Happen Becomes the Path to Growth" makes a compelling case. Two quotes from her presentation seem worth noting: "Openness doesn't come from resisting our fears, but from getting to know them well" and "The path of acceptance: don't just do something, sit there."

Chamberlain encourages those faced with extreme crises to use the energy generated by fear to push forward rather than to retreat. Understand your mental and physical tendencies and learn from them. "Think outside the box" instead of repeating previous failures. Practice pausing, then acting, rather than reacting.

## » Rationalism versus Mystery

In his presentation mentioned earlier, Rogier Bos believed "the rationalism of enlightenment ... rejected any sense of mystery, choosing instead to break any whole down into subparts so that it could be controlled and tweaked logically and without emotion ... [and] has been rejected for its materialism by focusing 'our attention on that which we can explain and categorize and predict'."

In the same way, materialism seems to discourage us from embracing the mysterious. Anything beyond the bounds of physical existence may seem not only incredible but also threatening. We may consider it demeaning to display the wonder and awe we felt as young children.

## » The Church

Bos continued, "The church is uncomfortable with transcendent experiences for fear that reason should loose its governing influence on our behavior; the church presents a concept of a God that it claims to be transcendent; but the concept leaves little room for mystery, wonder, and the unknown. Postmodern people reason much the way Einstein did. Their observation is that 'if indeed there is a God behind reality, responsible for it all, and upholding it all, He must be so awesome and so *other* that there must be a great deal of wonder and mystery involved in his worship'."

Bos stressed, "the Anthropic Cosmological Principle brings to us an idea perhaps as old as humanity itself: that we are not at all just an accidental anomaly, the microscopic caprice of a tiny particle whirling in the endless depth of the universe. Instead, we are mysteriously connected to the entire universe; we are mirrored in it, just as the entire evolution of the universe is mirrored in us."

It has been said that a new spiritual movement is underway. One of the catalysts seems to be some members of the clergy. It should not surprise anyone that members of the cloth often face personal questions about life, death, and the meaning of being spiritual, not just religious. Perhaps the greater surprise is when some of them share their uncertainties with the rest of us. This then risks putting them on a collision course with other more conservative theologians.

How is this any different from the many health professionals who risked losing their professional reputations after alerting us to a "new reality" revealed through near-death experiences and hypnotic regression to past lives and life-between lives? The rest of us may start to question our beliefs—at least privately—even though we dare not admit this to others. For those of us who yearn for a deeper meaning in our lives, do we turn our backs on the emerging new paradigm of life after death? Do we ever dare contemplate its potential impact on our earthly lives and the lives of our loved ones?

Most religions acknowledge the existence of a heaven and an afterlife but may make certain requirements for admission. But the "new" theologians mentioned here and in one of my previous books share with us visions of something more: an eternal existence. Neither they nor we can scientifically prove the existence of this non-physical reality. This may never be possible. Yet, they willingly confront criticism from their brothers and sisters of the cloth to share with us the gems of truth they mined from their searches.

One of the more recent of these is Bishop John Shelby Spong, retired Episcopal Bishop of Newark. He is the author of several books about Jesus and Christianity. His most recent book is *Eternal Life: A New Vision*. Notably it is subtitled *Beyond Religion, Beyond Theism, Beyond Heaven and Hell*. Perhaps his beliefs are best captured in his own words from his book: "I believe deeply that this life that I love so passionately is not all there is. This life is not the end of life."

The search for meaning begun in this chapter continues in the next chapter, shifting to more individualized concerns.

CHAPTER TWENTY

# WHO AM I?

---

*"We are not human beings having a spiritual experience.*
*We are spiritual beings having a human experience."*

Teilhard de Chardin

---

If the title of the preceding chapter had been "What Am I Searching For," could you answer the question honestly, even to yourself? This is not intended to criticize you. Rather, it is to wonder how well we each know ourselves. From the moment we arrived in this world, influencers shaped our lives. In our early years it was our family. Soon it became other kids. Then came significant others, such as teachers, preachers, bosses, and co-workers. Almost without end, others molded us by how we responded to their influences. For most of our lives, our *authentic* versions risks getting buried.

## » Our Mental Control Centers

The term we seem to hear more often today than "conscience" is "ego." Perhaps this is a dismal commentary on our society's moral health. Of course the word "ego" is used with both negative and positive implications. Perhaps its worthwhile to examine just what Sigmund Freud meant by the terms "ego, id, [and] superego," since he believed that we humans possess all three dimensions of our psyche.

Freud's ego is the mediator of our perception of and adaptation to the real world. It is virtually inseparable from our id, the unconscious energy that fuels our instinctual needs and drives for pleasure. Riding shotgun is the semiconscious policeman, our superego.

Other mammals possibly might be considered to have a type of id but neither an ego nor a superego. Because the superego is our internal censor, it seems to consist of a learned prohibition of certain behavior, perhaps even of certain thoughts or contemplations. Some such prohibited actions are cultural, such as killing, rape, or theft. Probably more are learned from parents, family, and significant others.

Our ego therefore appears to develop amidst these two strong influences. It often is referred to as our identity or self. It easily becomes obvious that each of us differs in our superego or conscience as well as in our ego, and that early childhood through adolescence shapes these two dimensions of our psyche. Shame and guilt seem to be internal reflections of repression of our instinctive drive and passions as believed to be required by our superego. The other extreme is some people's apparent lack of a responsible superego or conscience.

## » Innocence

Peter Vajda explained the pitfalls in his online article "Why Being Authentic Is So Difficult." But beware! He depicts scenarios that most of us would rather not acknowledge or just as soon forget. The same holds true for much of this chapter.

Few of us will remember the impact of early family influences before age three. We flourished on love and attention. To get that, for the most part, we behaved as we thought our parents wanted. But we often got mixed messages and signals we weren't capable of getting clarified. So we got reprimanded. This was the beginning of our insecurity. Unfortunately, much of this could have been imprinted in our implicit (subconscious) memory and continue to affect us the rest of our lives.

## » Learning to Act

Before long, other children came into the picture, possibly siblings and certainly playmates. We began trying to establish our own identity. If we had siblings, we may have been introduced to competition for parental love and attention. It may have seemed that our behavior always was improper and our efforts never were enough. So we eventually found artificial ways to behave to get what we wanted. We literally began to wear "masks" suited to the situation. We became actors learning roles.

Things got more complicated when we mixed with peers and in-groups. Now we found ourselves paying close attention to the image of ourselves that we saw in reflections from others. Sometimes we had to sacrifice loyalties to parents and friends to gain acceptance from the in-group. Soon we had collected a variety of new behaviors and masks. Add this to our felt inadequacies about physical attractiveness, clothing, and possessions. Compound this with risky behavior for acceptance.

Some of us become accustomed to making excuses for almost any way we fall short of others' expectations of us. Over time we may acquire a whole assortment of excuses. When we score poorly on an exam, skip an appointment, or fail to perform in some other way, we just shrug it off with a customary complaint. "'Customary' means that the excuse or the practice sooner or later becomes predictable to others," said Benedict Carey in his article "Some Protect the Ego by Working on Their Excuses Early" in the Health section of the online *New York Times*. Psychologists even came up with a title for the practice: "self-handicapping." They believe its motivation lies in avoiding embarrassment, another risk to authenticity.

## » Actors on the Stage of Life

Parental influences never ceased, or so it seemed. Manners; school grades; home runs or touchdowns; best colleges, professions, and marriages; and so forth, the image they wanted us to portray. As we became parents, the cycle was repeated with our children. We wanted the best, for them and for us. Not outright subterfuge, mind you, but just enough to keep up our façade. Sooner or later, the performance became the reality. We became the actors whose roles we developed and we lived.

## » Avoidance

The last decade or so introduced a new restriction on authenticity, the so-called "political correctness." It was considered socially proper to avoid language or actions that could be perceived to exclude, marginalize, or insult people who are socially disadvantaged or discriminated against. Using the adjective "political" seems to reflect governmental and academic efforts to accommodate the needs of the country's increasingly diverse population.

## » Untruths

Anyone faced with revealing a truth that might risk insulting or injuring another person's feelings probably has stooped to tell a so-called "white lie." The intent of a white lie usually is believed to be to avoid hurting another person's feelings. But research has shown that men and women lied with equal frequency. However, women were more likely to lie to make the stranger feel good, whereas men lied most often to make themselves look better.

People who tell white lies may feel perfectly justified in doing so. Unfortunately, like any lie, the other person may eventually learn the truth and fault the first person as untrustworthy. As Mark Twain wrote: "None of us could live with a habitual truth-teller; but, thank goodness, none of us has to." For more on this subject, see the online article "Can Love Survive Without the Little White Lies," by Lucy Taylor.

## » A Play With No End

Later in life, after spending much time, effort, and money, we may begin to feel lost. We even may start our own personal search for our true identity. Mental health professionals welcome us. But it may be too late. We built ourselves up in our own eyes too. Our self-esteem is all too often hinged on how we want others to see us. Shame and humility are too high a price to back out now. Ironically, our lack of authenticity sooner or later becomes obvious in one circumstance or another, to one person or another. Our ego may win out, but our soul may lose. Remember the perils of "star power," mentioned earlier?

Underscoring doubts about humankind's existence is a natural skepticism, as is expressed in the next chapter.

# CHAPTER TWENTY-ONE

# WHY DON'T WE BELIEVE?

> *"For those who believe, no proof is necessary.*
> *For those who don't believe, no proof is possible."*
> Stuart Chase: *The Tragedy of Waste*, 1925

People's beliefs seem to be of two basic types. First, those that are dependent on what might be termed "known" evidence, accepted by believers because they personally can sense the existence of something or they feel confident in scientific proof. Second, there are beliefs that are based upon the term "faith," as best exemplified among the world's religions.

For centuries, people generally held one of these two types of belief. Religions held sway and science felt it had determined everything that physically, chemically, and biologically could be known about mankind, the earth, and the universe.

Today, religion is being challenged and science is being revolutionized. Technology has provided advances that could not have been imagined a century ago. Science and religion are recognizing that their outer limits now may border on the metaphysical, although believers in both camps disavow this.

Why don't we believe? Is it because of earlier disappointments? Or do we harbor learned disbeliefs that are difficult, maybe impossible, to shake off? Would we feel threatened by the existence of something that we were convinced does not exist? Or do we question with a mindset that seeks the truth?

## » Larger than Life

This book confronts a disbelieving public. It attempts to offer some semblance of credibility that each life on earth is intimately tied in with a "larger than life" set of influences, often beyond our personal control. Perhaps this approach will help us at least contemplate that our lives are interwoven with one another as part of a grand design, one which exceeds even our most optimistic fantasies.

As a starter, what is the extent of your convictions about life itself? We know that we are alive (pinch yourself!) and that there are billions of us around the globe. But some scientists are trying to tell us that we simply see illusions.

With the Hubble telescope's fantastic revelations, we may grant that the (our?) universe is a bit larger that we thought. But it still is difficult to imagine putting a man on Mars. But why should we? Would that tell us anything we don't already know? Of course, that's what scientists do: some insist on existing paradigms; others seem to question the reality of almost everything.

## » Origin of Beliefs

There are many intriguing theories about why and how we acquire our personal beliefs. Naturally, it's impossible to be any human other than a hermit without a few cherished beliefs that we delight in pitting against another individual's beliefs. It's almost as enjoyable as a game of tennis, golf, or racquetball. But sometimes there's no winner, yet maybe some hurt feelings.

This book examines some theories about beliefs. It probably isn't necessary to spend time trying to convince you how much our supposedly rock solid scientific convictions have changed over the years. It's said that the volume of scientific literature *doubles* every three to five years. So we'll just try to get you to expand your imagination. Little kids do it easily. Why can't we? Imagining doesn't make you give up your present beliefs. It just asks you to honestly consider the question, "What if…?"

## » Human Nature

Andrew Newberg and Mark Waldman's book *Born to Believe: God,*

*Science and the Origin of Ordinary and Extraordinary Beliefs* claims that humans come biologically equipped to believe. Early in life we adopt others' beliefs. First parents, then trusted others, and eventually teachers. Depending on the religious nature of our family, our beliefs may be influenced by religious leaders.

A child starts out accepting as fact the existence of Santa Claus, the Tooth Fairy, and other mythical sources of pleasure. Only later does he or she learn to question some adopted beliefs. Otherwise, our brains find it difficult to accept opposing beliefs.

Dean Radin's book *The Conscious Universe* provides a fascinating examination of how human experience creates mindsets about anything and human nature influences willingness to alter that mindset. The varieties of individual circumstances that reinforce or alter our beliefs are many and truly individualized in most cases. There are some group effects. But it seems that resistance to change beliefs is much easier to rationalize than it is to change.

This is especially true for certain beliefs *about our selves* as discussed elsewhere in this book. Newberg and Waldman stress that, "although we are designed to have beliefs, all beliefs have limitations, and every one of them contains assumptions and inaccuracies concerning the true nature of the world."

Those authors do note, however, that biologically we are prone to periodically search for deeper, more profound aspects of existing beliefs about our world and ourselves. Spiritual experiences can change beliefs, often dramatically. A good example is the impact on the lives of survivors of near-death experiences. Deep meditation is another.

## » Do You Believe in You?

Let's get personal for a moment. Do you believe in yourself? Likely you will answer this question with a resounding positive answer. None of us likes to admit to others, let alone to ourselves, our innermost feelings. You've heard the ideas, "Is the glass half full or half empty?" and "Which do you notice most: the donut or the hole?" Psychologists tell us that we frequently may replay our failures and deficiencies, but likewise we seldom stop to think about our successes and attributes. Earlier in this book we examined how our thoughts significantly affect our behavior, our moods, and even our wellbeing itself.

Despite the fact that this section could be the most important part of this book for you, nothing I say here will make you a winner automatically. I could have listed several steps that I might have guaranteed (falsely) would work magic. But learning alone doesn't work. If you already hold yourself in high esteem and your positive self-image propels you in everything you pursue, more power to you. But if that's true, you already realize that what I'm saying is realistic.

Self-esteem is composed of an accumulation of all the experiences, emotions, and memories you've encountered from *before* you were born and up until the present. You aren't even aware of some of them—implicit (subconscious) memories are involved in creating your *implicit* self-esteem. Yes, there are two self-esteems, one explicit and one implicit. You'll read elsewhere in this book how present-day experiences can shape a person's outlook despite past experiences. Just don't judge yourself too harshly and do keep your eyes on the donut.

Tara Brach's book *Radical Acceptance: Embracing Your Life With the Heart of a Buddha* recommends a somewhat different approach than plain optimism. She advocates that we try to achieve a better understanding of ourselves and of our reality. In other words, try to recognize our human tendencies to judge ourselves unfairly. Stop mentally racing ahead to predict a negative outcome. Instead, focus on the present. Do a sort of physical and mental assessment about how you are reacting to what's happening at any moment. If the situation is uncomfortable, acknowledge to yourself that it is. Don't sugarcoat it. Don't try to rationalize excuses. Instead, remember who you are, your past successes, and your positive attributes. Accept momentary hardships and adversities; try to be as calm and as peaceful as possible; and work through your feelings to better times ahead.

Linked with this is our recognition of our behavior toward others. Inevitably, someone will irritate us or hit our "hot buttons." It could be a good friend who does so inadvertently or someone trying to "best" us—trying to improve his or her own self-esteem by degrading ours. If you've always succumbed to your emotional reactions in the past, try something different for a change. This involves the *reverse* of the old adage "Don't just sit there; do something!" Instead, as discussed earlier, "Just sit there; don't do anything!" You'll likely be amazed by the outcome. Remember, it takes two to make an argument! This is very difficult to start doing, especially if you happen to be stressed at the time. If it happens to be a good friend who does this to you, just remember that once words are out of our mouths, they never can be taken back.

With regard to the Tara Brach's suggestions, one approach is to try to develop a "sixth sense"—a sort of advance warning system—how you *feel* at the moment whenever faced with a challenge. You certainly know how you feel when a threat occurs, whether it's from another person, a potential accident, or a failing business venture. Obviously, these are physical threats. Physical threats may require avoidance actions: prevent a potential accident or develop a new business plan. But if the other person's behavior is just words, silence is the best avoidance.

But there also are mental threats, when you're tempted to revisit past guilt trips, "what-ifs," or lost love. Mental threats pose different kinds of challenges. You might acknowledge how you feel about the threat, recognize that it is in the past, admit that you can't change what happened then, and simply "allow" yourself to have that feeling without judging yourself unfairly.

By contrast, you might be tempted to forge into the future, trying to prevent a crisis or repair burned bridges. Once again don't consider it unusual to feel such future threats. But consider that more can likely be accomplished by postponing your mental effort to a later proper time and place, rather than by fretting about it over and over again. With mental threats, it's like my wise son advises me "Don't go there!" In other words, be alert to avoid physical and mental temptations.

## » Sensing Belief

If you were blindfolded and allowed to touch one place on a Boeing 767, how many different guesses might we find among all you readers: trying to speculate on the nature and capabilities of this marvel of technology, just by touching its outer body at one spot?

Try again, this time with all your senses open. You're looking at a laboratory Petri dish. Something is growing there. Is it the mold that introduced penicillin to the world and heralded spectacular lifesaving advances in medicine? Or is it the Ebola virus that threatened the world's populations?

Or you're at sea in a pleasure craft and suddenly you see a periscope surface. Even today, can you fully comprehend the massive size of its source and the mind-blowing capabilities of what lies beneath the water in a nuclear submarine?

It's not everyday that most of us have an experience like these. Yet we believe in all of them from what we've learned. Have you ever watched a Discovery or National Geographic program that captures the images of creatures living in the depths of the sea? Remember the fantastic abilities they have to exist under humanly intolerable conditions? Naturally, you could come back with the notion, "Why should I care? I'll never be affected by any of these." However, you certainly must marvel at these creatures' amazing abilities. Maybe their experiences will impress you with the adaptability of nature—even humans—to survive difficult circumstances, witness survivors of the Holocaust.

## » A Question of Time

So let's switch to something possibly more interesting for you. Everything we see has a beginning and an ending. Rocks may have begun and may end without our awareness. We know that plants, animals, and humans are born and die. Even episodes of weather come and go. We'd probably insist that this is part of our existence.

Many scientists claim that the "Big Bang" started it all, so far as our planet—and maybe our universe—is concerned. Sounds plausible, since it apparently happened so long ago that the only records seem to be scientists' findings in the heavens. Now some scientists are foretelling an end, maybe a reverse of the Big Bang. But we needn't be concerned about it, since it's far, far into the future. So there's no need to wonder, "What if...?"

But this poses an interesting concept for imagination: does everything *have* to have a beginning and an ending? Well, you'd say, it does while you're here on earth. I'd agree. Historians and astrologers make a living talking about the past and the future, and many people love entertaining history books. But why does the New Testament book of Revelation have such an attraction for doomsayers and a myriad of interpretations? Of course, few people take either one seriously. Why? Because most of us believe nothing of that sort is likely to happen in our lifetime!

But shake yourself loose for a moment and wonder: Is it possible for anything to exist without a beginning and an ending? Again, you could answer, "Why should I care?"

## » Eternity

This is a concept most people may have trouble with: either accepting or coping with. As mentioned elsewhere, humans see existence on earth as a time-limited aspect of life. We typically think in terms of human life spans, of the age of giant redwood trees, of fossils and radioisotope-dating, or certainly no farther back than the Big Bang.

"Eternity" is a word we've heard in places of worship, but the idea usually is reserved for Heaven. Even then, we may have difficulty believing that eternity *could* be just that: no beginning and no end.

Before I lose you in this discussion, maybe I'd better add some credibility. CNN online announced, "NASA's Hubble Space Telescope has reached back 13.2 billion years —farther than ever before in time and space—to reveal a "primordial population" of galaxies never seen before." They say Hubble has become a "powerful 'time machine'." What it now sees are galaxies as they were 600 to 800 million years *after* the Big Bang! The James Webb Space Telescope should be launched in 2014, enabling us to see even more distant galaxies.

So now we know that there are many universes and some are older than our Big Bang. Maybe eternity is for real!

## » Only One Life?

When I first got the idea for this chapter, it seemed reasonable enough to try to tackle what might be the world's greatest disbelief: *reincarnation*. It seems to rank far ahead even of skepticism about God. So I thought maybe readers might at least wonder about the possibility of reincarnation if they could consider the amount of planning that is *claimed* to be involved in reincarnation. In other words, to track what is said to be involved in the incarnation of a soul from the spirit world once it decides to reincarnate.

Obviously this idea is fraught with at least suspicion or at worst outright denial. Yet it provides the conceptual basis for how earthly influences reshape the combination of ego and soul to confront the world. After all, this is an earthly habitat the soul chooses to join to enable it to learn and grow spiritually by dealing with joys and sorrows, trials and tribulations, and successes and failures.

We adults likely will have great difficulty accepting reincarnation for two reasons. First, to humans, "taking a long view" means birth to death, but for the soul a long view is all eternity. Second, as discussed earlier in this book, the human adult typically loses touch with its soul and human nature prevails in adult behavior. Over a lifetime each of us may suffer the frailties and foibles of human existence. But it is through these experiences that our souls learn, as we humans hopefully do, the importance of spiritual lessons. To cite these challenges would take pages on end, but a few examples might suffice as reminders: jealousy, brotherhood, greed, selfishness, narcissism, hate, murder, charity, love, empathy, and compassion.

It is worth noting that reincarnation is part of the Freemasons' creed, as described in the article "Freemasonry and the Doctrine of Reincarnation" on the Masonic World Web site. Of course many of our country's founding fathers were Freemasons and thousands of Freemasons exist around the world today, which claim to be the stewards of ancient wisdom handed down through the ages.

Perhaps the newest personal account of reincarnation in the United States was the subject of Andrea and Bruce Leininger and Ken Gross's book *Soul Survivor: The Reincarnation of a World War II Fighter Pilot.* This is the story about the Leininger's son James who, around age two began having recurring nightmares involving fighter pilot James Huston's experiences during the war. Apparently young James vividly recalled some fifty different incidents. Even his father refused to accept it until he verified the details. It is a compelling case for reincarnation.

Individual cases like this surface occasionally and often make news. It seems worthwhile to review scientific research—certainly as scientific as is currently possible—that documented two thousand and five hundred cases across the world in which reincarnation appeared to be the only conceivable answer. This body of work covered forty years at the University of Virginia Department of Psychiatry. Much of this was accomplished by Ian Stevenson and is being continued by Jim B. Tucker. Both men are psychiatrists. Stevenson passed over a year or two ago, after devoting his life to this research. He wrote more than two hundred and ninety publications on the subject.

Tucker's book *Life Before Life* is one of their few lay publications.

Most are scholarly texts. All of their work focused on young children. Typical cases involved kids who spontaneously described living earlier lives. Although this usually occurred between the ages of two and four, some happened at a much earlier age. None of the children or their parents knew the persons the children claimed to have been. The previous lives usually happened hundreds of miles away, often decades earlier. The clincher is that each case was scrupulously investigated, even to visiting the site and survivors of the deceased earlier man or woman. What's more, the children not only recognized but also called surviving family members by name and gave facts about those persons. Stevenson and Tucker verified the existence of the children's claims.

There seem to be two contrasting concepts among beliefs of the world's religions. One is admission to Heaven and the other is resurrection of the dead. Timing and nature of the survivor seems to be the big difference. The first tacitly admits survival of death of the physical body by a spiritual entity without regard to timing; the second is based upon a belief in the resurrection of human bodies from the grave at the end of time. Perhaps the point of disagreement that both beliefs have with the concept of reincarnation is the opportunity to incarnate more than once on earth. Interestingly, the Catholic Church increasingly is accepting cremation.

It was called to my attention that yet another version of survival was presented by the apostle Paul in his first letter to the church at Corinth, chapter 15, verses 35-54. This seems to contradict the impression that a physical body will be resurrected from the grave at the end of time. Paul posed the question, "How are the dead raised?" He then answered "… it is raised a spiritual body."

But if you doubt the credibility of the many documented accounts of children and adults recalling past lives, you have another option, but it may be equally incredible. In Melvin Morse's book, he speculates about a universal memory field, which stores information about everything (2000). Ervin Laszlo addresses this in his book. Could young James Leininger have been accessing details about World War II fighter pilot James Huston's experiences from a universal memory field instead, as a manifestation of children's psychic experiences?

One aspect of hypnotic regression to past lives and to life-between-lives seems to disallow that subjects' testimonies could be information from a universal field. That evidence concerns the frequency with which these hypnotized patients say they recognize other persons (or souls) from their past who also are part of the subjects' present-day lives. Examples might be a child from the past who is an uncle today; a mother who is a daughter today; or another relative who is a close friend today (Newton 2000).

Newton (1994, 2000) and other researchers claim that past life (PL) regression experiences are accessed as memories stored in the subconscious mind and life-between-lives (LBL) regression experiences are memories stored in the superconscious mind. It therefore would seem that both PL and LBL regression reports from subjects under hypnotic regression are memories specific to the subject rather than information somehow randomly obtained by the subject from a universal or Akashic field.

The subjects' recognition of persons in the PL and LBL regression experiences as being people present in the subjects' current lives make it even more difficult to think that these other persons in their regression experiences could have been pulled each time from a universal field. Admittedly, young Leininger's access to details about pilot Huston's experiences may have occurred psychically, and they do not seem definitive that he was pilot Huston in a previous life.

A skeptic might say that a person from the past surely wouldn't have the same body and appearance as the person living today. True! In fact, they might even be a different gender. But the hypnotized subjects might find enough mannerisms or other clues to feel confident that the past person is the embodiment of the same soul as the person they know very well today. Newton often claimed that soul group members typically incarnate with close-knit ties (1994, 2000, 2009), although their respective soul identities probably wouldn't be evident to one another during earthly life.

This book alone obviously will not convince skeptics about reincarnation. For a historical discussion about the subject, you can search Google using the word "reincarnation" plus one of the terms "Christianity, Fifth Ecumenical Council, or church fathers" as three different search combinations. You will find that reincarnation was a popular belief among Christian leaders up until 325 AD, when the church decided the belief was counter-productive and banned it.

## » Where Did We Come From?

Babies enter this world with few demands that become evident soon after they arrive. Then, for the next couple of years, between naps, they seem to be just a lot of screams and stares. Their parents respond as best they can.

By the time they enter kindergarten, however, young children will have experienced a rite of passage that easily could be misunderstood by parents. Seldom do parents fathom the depth of significance that this journey holds for their offspring. After all, aren't babies always just babies?

Charting that passage may help the rest of us realize the nature of a young child's unconscious early introduction to life; then to recognize that the child likely will never realize or remember that passage. The child delays conscious growth and development until he or she accommodates to human needs. The memory of this earth-awareness seldom fades into oblivion as did much of his or her earlier experiences. It is the earthly influences on the human self, or ego, which subsequently control his or her future.

Conceptually, this voyage is purported to be a six-step process:

- Life planning by the soul before its incarnation
- Merger of the soul with the fetus's central nervous system
- Psychic ability and soul memory in the young child
- Implicit memory of fetal, newborn, and early child environment
- Fading of all except conscious (explicit) memory
- Development of one's self

Admittedly, all evidence of these stages except the last one is experiential, not scientific. Yet that evidence is a product of rather consistent reports from multiple, respected researchers. Our conscious self continues to be molded by later influences of childhood and adolescence, and it is even susceptible to much later experiences in our adult lives.

## » Fulfilling Our Heritage

The purpose of this exploration is to release us from the absolute necessity of explicit and orthodox beliefs that we live only once on this earth and that we have limited potential by:

- Understanding the events that presage our ego dominance
- Strengthening our belief in ourselves and in others
- Helping us recognize the unity of our joint heritage as sparks of God
- Instilling in each of us a strength of caring and compassion
- Inspiring conduct to make us worthy of our common heritage

This book charts the undercurrents of potential experiences from which newcomers mold their view of the world. Some of these are so seemingly insignificant to parents that they overlook or ignore them. But nature considers lost opportunities as wasted time.

As babies become young children, they add to and build upon these self-constructed foundations to prepare each one's readiness to shape his or her individual self-identity. It is this "self" that serves as a compass to steer each one carefully through the turbulent waves of life ahead.

The early outcomes are hidden even from the child, as unconscious imprints of behavioral and emotional responses within his or her subconscious mind. Only as the youngster reaches the stage of self-awareness and conscious memory will he or she actively begin to fit the conscious pieces of the puzzle together.

As discussed earlier, researchers have uncovered fascinating details about the part of this journey before the onset of a child's self-consciousness. Thereafter, new dimensions of his or her personality continue to emerge as this new self-identity responds to later potential influences of the world at large.

## » Death is Not the End

Barbara Barnum's book *Spirituality in Nursing: From Traditional to New Age* sheds credible light on this topic. Barnum holds an RN and a PhD in nursing. She is a former editor of the *Nursing Leadership Forum* and *Nursing & Health Care* and is presently a writer/consultant. Before retiring, her positions at Columbia University included holding the directorships of the Division of Health Services Sciences and Education at Teachers College, where she also held the Stewart Chair in the Department of Nursing Education.

Her chapter "Spirituality and the Patient" discusses "illness, dying, and death as transitional states in self-development, growth that will go on after one leaves the body." The chapter cites many references concerning pre-death encounters (with previously deceased relatives, friends, or spiritual entities) as well as near-death experiences (wherein the patient survives cardiac arrest and typically describes having visited a heavenly realm). Barnum concludes, "Medical practitioners who ignored these phenomena under the older scientific model [now] have begun to accept and study these events."

One of the most compelling personal testimonies about survival of bodily death came from the near-death experience (NDE) of Texas Baptist minister Don Piper. It originally became public in his first book *Ninety Minutes in Heaven*. His story was mentioned in one of my earlier books (2008). But so many people seem to think and even try to prove that near-death experiences (NDEs) are simply products of the mind that I'd like to update Piper's account from his newest book *Heaven is Real*. An eighteen-wheeler ran over his Ford head-on. Nine wheels crushed his car and pushed it into a bridge railing.

Teams of emergency medical technicians (EMTs) declared Piper dead and they covered the crushed car, him inside, with a tarp. They refused to let a driver of another car see Piper, "it's an ugly sight" they insisted. That driver happened to be a fellow minister, but he didn't know the "dead" man was Piper. Yet that driver lay down on the pavement blocking departing ambulances until he was allowed to crawl under the tarp. He prayed and then started singing, "What a Friend We Have in Jesus." Weakly, somehow, Piper joined in the singing. The other minister made such a scene demanding the EMTs' attention that one checked Piper again and yelled, "He *is* alive!"

Piper insists that his was a *death* experience. He said it lacked some of the core characteristics of NDEs, but he insisted, "I was in heaven, filled with utter joy, and more alive than I'd ever been before." He saw his grandmother and a dear younger friend who died earlier in a car crash.

He and both of them seemed in good health. Apparently the crash had stopped Piper's heart instantly and prevented gushing of blood from his injuries. He eventually had thirty-four major operations, spent a year in the hospital, and had two additional years in rehabilitation. Piper since has testified to his belief to thousands of people across the world.

Kenneth Ring and Sharon Cooper's book about blind near-death survivors "seeing" during their NDE was sure to meet with much skepticism. After all, among the greatest skeptics were physicians who first heard about NDEs from their patients after they were resuscitated from cardiac arrest. But most of those physicians now are converts even though medicine has not yet been able to explain the mystery of NDEs.

Ring and Cooper may have provided a step in the right direction of better understanding NDEs as they analyzed the results of their studies with the blind. Patients with normal vision reported "visual images or visual-like images." Persons who never had experienced vision "could only use metaphors or characterizations of the phenomena such as knowing the chair was there without having to touch it." In an attempt to better describe what apparently was happening in NDEs generally, in both blind and sighted patients, the authors adopted the term "transcendental awareness." This does seem to better define the NDE as "a distinctive state of consciousness and mode of knowing in its own right." These and other witness reports have had a tremendous impact on our thinking and our confidence in our survival of physical death.

The next chapter takes us back to the beginning of life on earth.

# CHAPTER TWENTY-TWO

# CONTROVERSIAL BEGINNINGS

---

*"Creation is too grand, complex, and mysterious
to be captured in a narrow creed."*

William Schulz

---

Many of us seldom give any thought to the different concepts that concern the origin of life on earth. But a great number of people do, particularly in the fields of science and education. The controversy has not remained among scientists but has spread to whether and what about these concepts should be taught in our public schools. Advocates for each of the three theories wage untiring battles on behalf of their beliefs.

To try to address these beliefs may seem a far stretch for this book. But the fact that they do create chasms between some people may recommend that a brief definition of each would be worthwhile here. Please note that this chapter does not intend to change anyone's convictions. But it is important to include both seeming strengths and weaknesses in each theory. Use of the term "theory" does not relegate any of the three concepts to a lesser status than the others.

Before discussing concepts about the origin of life on earth, it seems worthwhile to inject the subject of Lucy and Ardi. Both are humanoid skeletal archeological discoveries in Ethiopia. Lucy is said to be 3.2 million years old and Ardi 4.4 million, or 100,000 generations apart. The skeleton of a child estimated at three years of age was more recently found in the vicinity where Lucy was uncovered. It is estimated to be 3.3 million years old.

In the context of "controversial beginnings," it seems worthwhile to examine the indefinable theological term "eternity." Most of us likely would dismiss thinking about it as having no relevance to us. But it might if we coupled eternity with the possibility of a non-physical state of existence of a higher power and the eternal home of souls. This becomes more believable when we realize that astrophysicists now discuss the existence of the multiverse in *both* directions—past and future—in terms of *billions* of earth-years.

Scientists long have searched for a common ancestor of modern man. Some think our physical bodies might have shared that life form with chimpanzees and/or gorillas. With the advent of finding Lucy and Ardi it seemed that the humanoid ancestral path diverged from both of those earlier primates. However, new research capabilities have enabled scientists to track DNA changes more precisely over time. A public television Nova program quoted researchers as now believing that the supposedly common ancestor of humans and chimpanzees existed even earlier than Lucy or Ardi, perhaps as long ago as six million years.

A major reason for this is that the humanoid skeletons found thus far walked upright (bipedalism). Chimpanzees can walk upright for short distances if carrying something in their hands. But studies comparing human and chimp consumption of walking energy show that chimps consume about four times what humans do. So walking upright was a major achievement for humanoids. Yet from the waist up these ancestors were more like chimpanzees.

The area where these skeletons were discovered is today very dry and inhospitable to life. Yet the bones of a variety of animals found there suggest that it was more like a rain forest when those humanoids lived there. While chimpanzees live largely in trees, humanoids' development of bipedalism enabled them to conserve energy and reach into overhead branches for fruit. This may have become especially important as the habitat began to change.

## » First Creature on Land

The fossilized footprints of what is believed to be the first four-legged creature crawling from water onto land was found in the Holy

Cross Mountains in southeastern Poland. The creature measured approximately ten inches broad by seven and one-half feet long. The fossil is estimated at 395 million years old. The tracks have distinctive "hand" and "foot" prints and there is no evidence of a dragging body. Per Ahlberg, Professor of Evolutionary Organismal Biology, Uppsala University, Sweden, and his co-authors from the Polish Geological Institute in Warsaw report finding several tracks of different sizes and characteristics.

## » Creationism

This was the original belief that God created humankind, the earth, and the universe as it is described in the book of Genesis in the Hebrew Old Testament. The scripture specifies that this was done in six days. To my knowledge no evidence has become available to equate those "six days" with a measure of present-day earth time. In spite of the evidence, many traditional Christians and Jews interpret the days in Genesis as eons of time in order to make sense between the Old Testament story and science.

## » Evolution

About one hundred and fifty years ago an English naturalist named Charles Darwin published a treatise based on changes in life forms that he claimed resulted from characteristics in organisms and their environment, a process called "evolution." This theory lent itself to a scientific hypothesis that life on earth originated from natural forces and did not require action by God. It seemed to support atheism.

In 1953 a young University of Illinois graduate student named Stanley Miller published the results of an experiment in which he showed that amino acids could be produced in a spark chamber. Since amino acids are the precursors to proteins, this led scientists to believe that the creation of life itself was within their grasp. Although scientists continued trying to produce life in a test tube, no one has succeeded.

DNA has been an essential part of life forms from the dawn of creation. The DNA evidence suggests that these basic mechanisms controlling biological form became established before or during the evolution of multicellular organisms and have been conserved with little modification ever since. Adding to science's dilemma for producing test tube life, therefore, was the question of how these first genes developed.

In case DNA's small size might appear insignificant as a major barrier to the creation of life by scientists, some details about DNA may help us realize the enormity of intelligence incorporated in DNA. Scientists found that DNA contains an exquisite "language" composed of some three billion genetic letters. Lee Strobel's book *The Case for a Creator* contains a statement by Stephen Meyer, director of the Center for Science and Culture at the Discovery Institute in Seattle, WA, "One of the most extraordinary discoveries of the twentieth century was that DNA actually stores information—the detailed instructions for assembling proteins—in the form of a four-character digital code." Meyer elaborated on this in his book *Signature in the Cell: DNA and the Evidence for Intelligent Design.*

It is hard to fathom, but the amount of information in human DNA is roughly equivalent to twelve sets of the *Encyclopedia Britannica*—an incredible three hundred and eighty-four volumes' worth of detailed information that would fill forty-eight feet of library shelves! Molecular biologist Michael Denton's book *Evolution: A Theory in Crisis* said, "In their actual size—which is only two millionths of a millimeter thick—a teaspoon of DNA could contain all the information needed to build the proteins for all the species of organisms that have ever lived on the earth, and there would still be enough room left for all the information in every book ever written."

Even if science ever solves the dilemma of how DNA originated in life forms on earth, there remains the inevitable and inexplicable question: Where did all this information come from?

## » Intelligent Design

This concept presently involves two beliefs. One is that life originated on earth through the action of a superhuman power that is yet to be authenticated by classic scientific methods. This power is referred to as an "intelligent designer." In this regard, intelligent design shares a commonality with creationism. Creationism refers to this power as God. The other belief held by some scientists is that certain organisms possess "irreducible complexity" in their makeup. Proponents of this belief dispute that this complexity could have been achieved by evolution.

It seems conceivable that the information provided in DNA was part of the creation of life forms. Werner Gitt's seminal book *In the Beginning was Information: A Scientist Explains the Incredible Design in Nature* stresses that there is "a unique coding system ... of biological information ... in each genome." Further, Gitt quotes the conclusion of the seventh International Conference on the Origins of Life held in Mainz, Germany: "There is no known law of nature, no known process, and no known sequence of events which can cause information to originate by itself in nature."

Several characteristics about this biological information illustrate Gitt's claim: "The coding system used for living beings is optimal from an engineering standpoint." First, it can be described as three different forms: "constructional/creative, operational, and communication." Also, the information can be distinguished as "copied, reproduced, or creative." Qualitatively, the information ranges from "extremely important" to "trivial" or "harmful." Quantitatively, it varies according to "semantic quality, relevance, timeliness, accessibility, existence, and comprehensibility. This strengthens the argument that it was a case of purposeful design rather that a [lucky] chance."

In Michael Newton's most recent book *Memories of the Afterlife: Life Between Lives Stories of Personal Transformation* he said, "I believe the forces of intelligent creation go far beyond the religious concept of an anthropomorphic God. These spiritual forces ... indicate that creation of intelligent energy is so vast in our universe as to be incomprehensible to the human mind." According to the online *Merriam-Webster Dictionary,* anthropomorphic means "described or thought of as having a human form or human attributes."

## » Big Bang

There are twenty known fundamental forces and particles that, in various permutations and combinations, account for everything around us: light, magnetism, gravity and all forms of matter. But none of the fundamental particles created during the Big Bang had mass—the characteristic that constitutes atoms, molecules, rocks, trees, humans, and the entire universe. Otherwise, everything was just energy. The Higgs boson is an elusive particle that theoretically also was created during the Big Bang. It was given the name the "God particle" because physicists hope it finally will make clear how the universe works at the most basic level.

The Higgs boson also is believed to be associated with a quantum field. That Higgs field effect theoretically gave mass or weight to some particles that now exist but not to others. This was felt to explain how we now have both kinds of particles, some with mass and some without. Eben Harrell explained this is his article "Higgs Boson: A Ghost in the Machine" in the online *Time*. Even though the Higgs boson is theoretical, there is experimental evidence suggesting its existence.

Therefore, supercolliders were built to try to recreate conditions moments after the Big Bang. The idea behind these was to finally prove the theory of the Higgs boson. This effort intended to accelerate and smash protons together at 99.99 per cent of the speed of light. Large detectors were installed to observe the elusive Higgs boson. To improve experimental conditions, a massive twenty-seven kilometer tunnel was constructed under the countryside bordering France and Switzerland. So far, technical problems have interfered with fulfilling this unique experiment.

While there are many new scientific discoveries mentioned in this book, there still are some very significant scientific fields for which scientists are not yet finding the answers they seek.

The next part focuses our attention on caring for others.

## PART FIVE

# Why Do Unto Others?

CHAPTER TWENTY-THREE

# WHAT IS THE PURPOSE OF HUMANKIND?

---

*"Only a life lived for others is a life worthwhile."*

Albert Einstein

---

The title of this part of the book poses something of a dilemma each of us personally may need to resolve. It not only poses a moral challenge, but also a humanitarian issue. For each of us, the answer may lie deep within our ego. Perhaps it is time, once again, for personal reflection, another "What if...?" What if any of these discussions have a special meaning for you and your family and for many others whom you may never even meet?

This chapter naturally shrouds the conceivability of reincarnation. Both success and failure are focused on the human condition and the conviction of only one life. This life then seems to be the crux of the standoff between ego and soul in humankind.

In his book, Michael Newton says that each incarnating soul attempts to blend its unique personality with that of the fetus to create a body-soul partnership that provides a single cooperative and complementary unit (2000). Some blends apparently are more successful than others, and the degree of maturity of the soul seems to facilitate a more compatible bond.

But, as suggested earlier, the human host typically loses touch with his or her soul and any memory of the divine as environmental influences shape life on earth. One of the most significant of these is the child's development of self or ego. The human host then seems more susceptible to pursuing opportunities not in keeping with spiritual growth.

For example, Bart Ehrman offers his single-life belief as an acceptable approach to suffering. In his book *God's Problem: How the Bible Fails to Answer Our Most Important Question—Why We Suffer*, Ehrman draws from the Old Testament Book of Ecclesiastes "The solution to life is to enjoy it while we can ... we won't live forever ... so enjoy life to the fullest." Doing so, Ehrman seems to acknowledge, "a lot of bad things happen ... but life also brings good things." He agreed that we have some responsibility for helping others, "This means working to alleviate suffering and bringing hope to a world devoid of hope." But Ehrman feels that while God does not guarantee our freedom from hardship, God does offer us "peace and strength" to confront adversity.

Followers of many of the world's religions seem to agree with this premise. It provides some sustenance in times of trouble for the faithful. For the reincarnationist, however, such acceptance of the vicissitudes of life without meaning is insufficient. Many researchers have uncovered empirical evidence of multiple lifetimes. They stress that the soul's passionate *eternal* goal is spiritual growth, and that each life *has* that purpose through lessons the soul learns from all the problems and joys its body encounters.

Consequently, the trials and tribulations we face are steps that allow spiritual growth. The concept of reincarnation agrees with the idea that God provides peace and strength (grace) to facilitate such growth. To grant freedom from life's adversities would thwart opportunities for spiritual growth. But spiritual growth seems to center on the belief that our real purpose in life is to care for other persons, as conceptualized in the belief that all life is interconnected and that "we are our brothers' keepers."

Remember Maslow's theory of "self-actualization," the idea of developing or achieving one's full potential, mentioned early in this book? Interestingly, Maslow revised his theory significantly toward the end of his life, according to Mark Shaw. Maslow had believed that the highest level of human fulfillment was self-actualization, a point of total development achieved by meeting basic physical, social, mental, and spiritual needs. In his last years Maslow realized that *self-transcendence*, not self-actualization, is the highest human experience.

Living for others is a more satisfying spiritual state than merely "feeling good about oneself" from a materialistic viewpoint.

## » Spiritual Growth

If reincarnation exists and if the last statement is true, the implications are enormous. First and foremost is our ego's attitude toward caring for others. Each new incarnation brings a new human self. We certainly don't have to look far to observe the multiple variations of ego among our fellow beings. This may sound simply philosophical. But it has a practical side too.

Consider that spiritual growth—caring for, not serving, others—is our soul's passion. The term "not serving" is used intentionally. The word "serve" carries negative implications, perhaps as a consequence of colonial use of slaves in America and apparent use of slaves today in parts of the world. In the mind of the servant as in the mind of some observers, "serving" others may reek of immorality and bondage.

The phrase "caring for others" provides an expanded dimension to our thinking. We naturally are concerned about ourselves. It's an evolutionary survival instinct, shared with wild animals. Typically we also are concerned about our family members, best exemplified in a mother or father's love. Again, that's instinctive but seems all too easily ruptured in today's world. Even Ehrman stressed, "Enjoy life to the fullest." Although some people tacitly acknowledge the possibility of living multiple lives, our learned attitude is, "Look out for yourself today."

I hope that the rest of this chapter and the next one will offer sufficient reasons for all of us to be concerned about others for both practical and spiritual purposes.

## » Practical Considerations

Obviously, some people have doubts about the nature and extent to which we should care for one another. Even persons we care for might question our motives, resent perceived intrusions, or—at the opposite extreme—come to expect and depend on us rather than do for themselves. Remember "entitlement"? Mention of this last condition may seem harsh or flippant. But remember the old adage, "Give someone a fish and you feed him for a day. Teach someone to fish and you feed him for a lifetime."

Enterprises are blossoming around the world to enable individual benevolences to provide distant support for many much less fortunate people who are starving and dying from miserable living conditions. Some of these outfits loan money at little or no interest to indigenous entrepreneurs who have a skill in capitalism, of all things, but have insufficient funds to fully implement or expand their operations. Seamstresses, clay potters, and livestock herders are just three examples. Remarkably, the repayment of these loans is consistently encouraging. This has led to the term "microfinancing."

According to an online report by iNS/news/net, one such example is Terrafina, the joint microfinancing program of ICCO, Oikocredit and the Rabobank Foundation. It has already invested two million euros in just over a year to support young African microfinancing institutions (MFIs). This has in turn helped enable these MFIs to provide microcredits to approximately 200,000 African farmers and other small business owners in rural areas. Terrafina concentrates its activities on poor rural regions or "difficult" countries such as Mali, Burkina Faso, Rwanda, Ethiopia, and Congo. Terrafina will expand the scope of its activities this year to include Burundi and Senegal. Terrafina is the first Dutch public or private partnership to focus on the bottom of the African market by providing support to young, local credit organizations. Terrafina invests in local MFIs in order to bring about lasting results. Now there are about 10,000 MFIs worldwide.

Perhaps one of the largest and oldest in the United States is FINCA International, with their headquarters in Washington, DC. Started a quarter-century ago, FINCA concluded 2008 with 744,714 clients in twenty-one different countries. They have helped nearly 3.7 million children and adults in some of the poorest countries in the world.

I, for one, object to contributing to fund-raising "middle-men," i.e., organizations which solicit donations in the name of a charity but charge a share of the contribution for themselves. I think most donors would prefer to have their dollars maximized to care for the intended recipients. This seems to put a practical spin on "caring for others."

Lest you think this discussion has become too pragmatic, consider the thousands, perhaps millions, of dollars that well-meaning people have poured into the pockets of fraudulent "charities." This brings us back to the reality of truly caring for others.

A hint for evaluating charities was contained in FINCA's most recent letter to me. This involved FINCA's being given a four star rating by Charity Navigator for a seventh year in a row. This puts FINCA in the top one per cent of charities rated by Charity Navigator. Charity Navigator can be consulted online at charitynavigator.org if you have a question about any charity.

## » Benefiting Ourselves

Chaplain Sam Oliver takes a critical look at this subject in his online ezine article "Caring About Others." Oliver stresses, "When you focus on caring for others, something profound happens to you. Your attention will shift. You will move from self-centered awareness to life-centered awareness. When you begin to realize that you are part of a much greater awareness, some of your personal challenges seem smaller."

Helping others, even through small acts of kindness, seems to remind us that we all are in some indefinable way connected. This can be amazingly contagious as the book and movie *Pay It Forward* revealed. It's hard to imagine going through life *never* having something or somebody tug at your heartstrings. If you've missed this opportunity, you're missing a key reason for living.

We all are naturally most concerned about the welfare of our self, our family, and our other loved ones. At the end of each day, we likely count the day well spent or wasted in terms of how we have benefited or what we have lost. We passed countless hundreds of other people. What kind of person did we seem to each of them? Many didn't even notice us but some did. How many chances did we miss to "pay it forward"?

The true measure of spirituality seems to be a selfless willingness, often exemplified in small acts of kindness rather than in ego-satisfying possibly selfish offers of help. The measure may be how much one actually "spends" in concern, empathy, time, and energy with no apparent reward.

Our human emotions literally control our wellbeing, from the smallest cell to the extracellar matrix that unites our being. One key target of emotions is, of course, our immune systems. We truly benefit almost as much as those we care for. This alone is a powerful stimulus for reaching out to comfort others in disappointing times: to help share their grief and shore up their emotions, and even to offer more than psychological support.

An online article "Seven Principles of Spirituality in the Workplace" from the Institute for Management Excellence in Lacey, Washington, offers some interesting non-theological opportunities for interpersonal relationships that might foster spiritual growth. They are:

- Respect others
- Express positive energy
- Understand yourself better
- Work *with* others
- Be more creative
- See beyond the obvious
- Be more flexible

As you may have seen me emphasize in an earlier book, there are mechanical and genuine expressions of kindness. I'm foolish enough to believe that repeated mechanical expressions sooner or later will give you a perceptible satisfaction or boost that may become addictive, then eventually may become genuine. Ever heard, "Try it. You'll like it"?

## » Humankind's Responsibility

Ervin Laszlo, Stanislav Grof, and Peter Russell edited the book *The Consciousness Revolution* from excerpts of their two-day extensive discussion about the state of the world and its inhabitants. Imagine being able to listen in as three of the world's leading thinkers consider the paramount problems and potential solutions to what ails us all.

Another leading thinker, Ken Wilber, wrote a foreword to their book, in which he seemed to capture the essence of their challenge. It must not be the case of "we have to change others." Rather, each of us must play his or her part in "the same groundswell ... to make more sense of our lives, and to lead happier, healthier, and more caring lives." Only as we all pull together can we achieve our dream. As we each play a part, no matter how seemingly insignificant, can all the pieces come together "leading to a breakthrough or spiritual awakening." Wilbur is a leading edge philosopher with an eye on new age thinking.

Vaclav Havel, president of the Czech Republic made a very insightful speech at Philadelphia's Independence Hall entitled "The Need for Transcendence in a Postmodern World." Among the points he stressed were:

- "Human rights and freedoms must be an integral part of any meaningful world order;
- "From the countless possible courses of its evolution the universe took the only one that enabled life to emerge;
- "The Anthropic Cosmological Principle [says] we are not at all just an accidental anomaly … we are mysteriously connected to the entire universe;
- "Man can realize that [right to] liberty only if he does not forget the One who endowed him with it."

The next chapter examines the force behind caring for others: the energy of love.

# CHAPTER TWENTY-FOUR

# ENERGY OF LOVE

---

*"The power of love to change bodies is legendary.
Throughout history, 'tender loving care' has uniformly
been recognized as a valuable element in healing."*

Larry Dossey

---

Love has always been considered a significant source of energy and
emotion by bards and poets. Now science has proved this to be fact
rather than wishful thinking.

## » Magic or Science?

Incredibly, love can change water into the most beautiful ice crystals.
A Japanese scientist, Masaro Emoto, made a marvelous contribution to
the world of energy. Bradley Nelson's book described Emoto's research
into the crystalline structure of water, i.e., crystalline structures formed
by frozen water droplets. It was detailed in Emoto's book *The Hidden
Messages in Water.*

Emoto found that water would form various patterns of "snowflakes"
when exposed to different influences. Acid rock music, for example,
would result in a very disrupted crystal. A Mozart symphony would
provide a beautifully formed crystal. The most "intensely beautiful
ice crystals" emerged after water's overnight exposure to the phrase
"Love and Gratitude." This could be done by the effort of writing the
words on a piece of paper and taping them to the container. Writing

and attaching "I hate you" produced an "asymmetrical and disrupted crystal."

In another experiment, Emoto sealed cooked rice in three jars. He then entrusted each jar to a separate group of school children. For the first jar children were told to say pleasant words to it. For the second jar kids were to say harsh words to it. Children were requested to ignore the third jar. Checking all three jars a few weeks later, Emoto found the rice in the first jar as fresh as the day it had been sealed. Rice in the second jar had some mold. But the rice in the third jar was completely rotten.

## » Intention (Energy) Perception

As incredible as Emoto's results were, there seemed to be strikingly similar results reported in Lynne McTaggart's book (2007). In her book, she described a lengthy series of experiments conducted by Cleve Backster, this country's leading lie-detector expert.

Lie detectors are sensitive to the slightest change in electrical conductivity of skin, as well as blood pressure, respiration, and pulse rates. For thirty years, Backster experimented in measuring humanly imperceptible changes in plants by connecting them to lie-detector devices and registering plant changes on that equipment. His results defied explanation for the longest time, during which he endured ridicule by conventional scientists.

Initially, he found that plants exhibited their response according to their perception of his intentions: showing a pair of cutters produced a threat response; a perceived supportive intention produced opposite results. He even found that plants would respond to perceived threats to other life forms. Pouring boiling water into a sink drain surprised him with their negative response until he discovered living microbes in the sink drainpipe. Dumping brine shrimp into boiling water could elicit a negative response from the plants even if the act was committed in a distant room.

A clincher occurred when Backster and his partner set up an ingenious time-switch device whereby the shrimp could be dumped into the boiling water later, after the two humans left the premises and were unaware of the act at the time it happened. The plants reflected the threat at the time it occurred.

Rupert Sheldrakes' research showed that dogs could register anticipation of their owners' intentions to take them for a walk. Sheldrake described this in his book *The Sense of Being Stared At and Other Unexplained Powers of the Human Mind*. This occurred with the dogs in separate enclosures, being videotaped with a hidden camera, and with the owners simply *thinking* about walking them.

## » Pre-Birth Communications

This subject likely will stretch people's imagination or provoke outright disbelief. To some extent it falls into the same genre as pre-life planning, reincarnation, and psychic and mystical experiences that were explored elsewhere in this book. The closest subjective experience is precognition, having a vision of future events. Pre-birth visions or sensations about yet-to-be-born children apparently are not uncommon.

Underlying all of the personal accounts from parents-to-be about pre-birth communications is a common theme: the energy of love. If love is indeed a spiritual energy, it must have been the force that facilitated these case reports. One of the best collections of such first-hand stories is Sarah Hinze's book *We Lived in Heaven: Spiritual Accounts of Souls Coming to Earth*.

Author Elisabeth Hallett wrote about this in her online article "The Mystery of Pre-Birth Communication." Although many prospective parents are having these experiences, most seem reluctant to mention them. Both parents-to-be may have the same dream. But if one spouse does and the other doesn't, it could introduce a suspicion of disbelief.

Hallett said that these experiences might be only subtle feelings or vivid life-like dreams. Typically, the feelings actually may occur before conception, while the dreams seem more likely during pregnancy. These communications occasionally seem to take the form of messages, particularly when the prospective mother may be worried about the safety of her fetus. Even though such pre-birth revelations naturally surprise any parent-to-be, the sensation is said to represent such a warm expression of love and bonding that it becomes a great reassurance to future parents.

Hallett also wrote *Soul Trek: Meeting Our Children on the Way to Birth* and *In the Newborn Year: Our Changing Awareness After*

*Childbirth.* Another book related to this subject is Eliot Jay Rosen's *Experiencing the Soul: Before Birth, During Life, After Death.*

David Larsen examined such reports in his Latter Day Saint (LDS) weblog "Heavenly Ascent." He quoted John Denver's and Richard Dreyfuss's testimonies regarding their experiences with pre-birth communications. Larsen also claims, "Over 800 references to the pre-earth existence of mankind have been identified in Jewish and Christian sources from the time of Christ until the sixth century AD. Early Hellenistic (Greek) writings also referred to belief in a pre-earth life." The LDS.net blog also has personal posts on "What Kids Remember About the Pre-Existence."

There are a number of online first-hand accounts from prospective parents about their pre-birth communication experiences. One is Theresa Danna's "Pre-Birth Communication: The Link Of Love." For readers interested in books on this subject, go to http://www.light-hearts.com/treasury.htm. For letters from parents describing their pre-birth communications, go to http://www.light-hearts.com/letters.htm. For articles, try http://www.light-hearts.com/articles.htm.

## » From Case Files

John James's book tells of a case from the files of Massachusetts General Hospital. A well-known photo entitled "The Rescuing Hug" supports it. "Souls of twins," James wrote, "are known for their very close connections." The hospital staff felt that one twin would die. Each was in a separate incubator, as hospital policy required. Nurse Kasparian ignored orders and placed both in the same incubator.

Instantly the two snuggled together. The stronger one put her arm across her sister and held her close. The weaker one calmed her breathing to that of her sister's pace and both survived. James concluded, "Simply experiencing touch and sharing energies made her [the weaker twin] stronger."

## » Energy Bond

Gwendolyn Jones's book *A Cry from the Womb—Healing the Heart of the World: A Guide to Healing and Helping Souls Return to the Light After Sudden Death, Miscarriage, Stillbirth, or Abortion* is another example of the power of the energy of love. It deals more specifically with sudden death, miscarriage, stillbirth, and abortion, in regard to their effect on the soul of a fetus or baby. Like pre-birth communications, this book attests to the sensory bond between incarnating souls and host parents, particularly the mother. Jones's book suggests that the energy of love creates a parent-child bond sometimes even before conception, one that survives even death of the physical body.

## » Love Comes in All Shapes and Sizes

Karen Porter Sorensen knows what love is. She is the Brooklyn, New York, author of the book *love (luv) n.* For seven years, Sorensen ran a booth in New York City and, in exchange for a single rose, sought first-hand responses from thousands on Manhattan streets. Her questions were very personal, such as, "What is love?" "Who taught you love?" and "Has your love ever been tested?" She discovered some deep-seated needs that most people seem to have, among them a "yearning for love and connection with others."

Sorensen described her findings as stronger than emotions, more like "thirst or hunger." Her research also revealed that those suffering a health crisis especially prize love. This led to asking just how you can express love to a close friend or family member. For Sorensen, this became personal. Her brother and her mother had struggled with serious illnesses, and her grandmother died just before the author's book was published.

Her book captures the results of her efforts in a hundred sensible ways. Among them:

- Listen attentively and without a personal agenda
- Find ways to bring fond memories to the sick
- Avoid intruding on another's happiness with your own concerns
- Muster cheerfulness in the bleakest of situations
- Express sincere gratitude for another person's presence in your life

Sorensen's story was captured in CarePage's online article "One Woman Asks ... What is Love?" by Marie Suszynski and Pat Bass.

One of the nicest surprises, I've found, is to stumble across a remarkable discovery totally unexpectedly. That occurred in my research on Karen Sorensen.

It took the form of Erica Willards' blog ethang at http://ethangbaby. blogspot.com/2009/11/love-luv-n.html where I found the following by Anna Quindlen, a noted author, speaker, and *Newsweek* columnist. It is from Quindlen's article "Raising Children," which has been reproduced in full on many blogs:

> "... but the biggest mistake I made is the one that most of us make while doing this [raising children]. I did not live in the moment enough. This is particularly clear now that the moment is gone, captured only in photographs. There is one picture of the three of them sitting in the grass on a quilt in the shadow of the swing set on a summer day, ages 6, 4, and 1. And I wish I could remember what we ate and what we talked about, and how they sounded, and how they looked when they slept that night. I wish I had not been in a hurry to get on to the next things: dinner, bath, book, and bed. I wish I had treasured the doing a little more and the getting it done a little less."

The next chapter harkens back to the idea of focused intention discussed earlier in this book and expands it to the subject of synchronized group intention.

# CHAPTER TWENTY-FIVE

# The Power of Synchronized Intention

---

*"In union there is strength."*
Aesop

---

Throughout the literature on physics is the concept of "resonance." This involves vibrations of materials and the frequency with which they vibrate. Undoubtedly, you've seen where an operatic singer can cause a drinking glass to shatter, by causing the glass to vibrate at a pitch or frequency that it structurally could not withstand.

## » Theoretical Basis

In physics, waves that emanate from vibrating bodies merge to form a single amplified wave when they are vibrating at an identical frequency and are "in resonance." Biological information exchange within the human body and with other bodies can involve frequencies of vibrations. Heartbeats can have an influence on other parts of the body and one person's heart can affect the brain waves of another person when they are in close proximity. Recognize that an individual may be unaware of these kinds of resonance, even as they are happening. According to Valerie Hunt, the human energy field is linked with psychological and intellectual components through emotions.

## » Resonance in Bioenergetics

Vibrations also characterize energy represented in nature. Vibration frequencies can interfere with one another resulting in weakening of both, called "dissonance." They can match and strengthen one another, or resonate. The difference between a single isolated heart cell dying and two adjacent ones remaining alive is the resonance of heartbeats the pair establish (Pearce).

The ability of human energy to heal has been said to be the establishment of vibration frequency resonance between the thoughts of the healer and the cells of the recipient. This sort of resonance was demonstrated in the HeartMath example earlier in this book. Notably, the significance of electromagnetic resonance in bioenergetics was established some forty years ago at Oxford University by biophysicist C. W. F. McClare. Bruce Lipton's book cites McClare's research, "Resonance in Bioenergetics," that was published in the *Annals of the New York Academy of Science.*

## » Improving the Power of Intention

The power of focused intention therefore might be intensified by group effort, but not just *any* group effort. The effectiveness of intercessory prayer, for example, might necessitate having the activities of prayer group participants meet certain criteria to achieve resonance.

## » Group Resonance

Thought energy seems strengthened when multiple people concentrate their focus, as exemplified in the following example. Bradley Nelson's book cites a volunteer demonstration he used in his teaching seminars to illustrate the power of thoughts. A volunteer stands in the front of the room with his back to the audience. As a baseline test, Nelson has the person say the word "love" while holding his arm outstretched. Nelson pushes down on the volunteer's arm to demonstrate that person's resistance strength. After saying the word "hate," the volunteer's arm is noticeably less resistant to Nelson's pressure.

He then instructs the volunteer to keep his eyes closed and his mind clear. Nelson signals the audience behind the volunteer's back. He tells the audience that a thumb's up signal from him means that they all should try to send supportive, positive thoughts like "I love you!" to the volunteer. Likewise, on a thumb's down signal, they should send discouraging, negative thoughts such as "I hate you!" In each instance, Nelson's pushing down on the volunteer's arm produces the same outcome as the difference between the volunteer saying "love" or "hate." The negative thoughts from the audience make it more difficult for the volunteer to resist Nelson's pressure on the outstretched arm.

As mentioned earlier in this book, Renee Levi's doctoral dissertation "Group Magic: An Inquiry into Experiences of Collective Resonance" at San Francisco's Saybrook Graduate School and Research Center probed the existence and nature of group resonance. Her work was in a doctoral program in organizational systems. This subject obviously has far-ranging implications in organizational research, design, and management. Her work is accessible online.

## » Participants' Perceptions

Perhaps most interesting was the summary of participants' perceived experiences in Levi's experiments—what participation in the experiments felt like to participants individually. Nearly all of them said they sensed a collective resonance in their bodies. Several of the study's findings as reported by participants were:

- A bodily sensation
- An emotional component
- A collective experience
- A presence of energy
- A necessary total focus
- An ethereal feeling
- A sense of peace
- An expansion of physical limits
- A greater intuitiveness

## » Group Focus

Levi's study unearthed several commonalities among participants that may signal similar elements of harmony necessary throughout a group for the effectiveness of intercessory prayer. She felt, "as human beings become more authentic, more deeply in touch with themselves and what they believe, and display behaviors that express this, their energy fields change." Otherwise, their fields may vibrate at their own natural frequency rather than resonate with one another.

Focusing and aligning beliefs among participants seemed very important. Apparently, articulation by each participant of his or her beliefs and feelings allowed the group to compare experiences and arrive at central "truths" that helped establish closer ties as well as introspective insights. "A feeling of vulnerability, enabled by a sense of physical or emotional safety, was the most widely reported factor that shifted groups into resonance. This was expressed in many ways, including a willingness to reveal parts of self, acknowledging a need for help or answers, or feelings of fatigue or fear due to physical danger or disaster." These may "be important clues to discovering how human wavelengths become 'similar' enough to entrain."

## » Wavelengths of Fear and Love

Gregg Braden's YouTube presentation visually differentiates the wavelengths of human vibrations of fear and love, which he and other scientists believe are the two fundamental emotions of humans and other mammals. This seems pertinent to the results of Renee Levi's study in terms of aligning participant's feelings and therefore the wavelengths of their vibrations. This might well have been the "emotional component" that participants reported experiencing, as listed in this chapter.

## » Soul Love

C. S. Lewis' book *The Four Loves* named four kinds as affection, friendship, passionate or creative love, and selfless or godlike love. But I suspect Lewis and many psychologists would contend that the emotion of love couldn't be restricted to a simple definition. Nor is our emotion a single feeling but often a blend of two or more kinds of love. Perhaps this is due to our earthly use of the word "love" in connection with an object of that love. What's more, we humans freely use antonyms of love such as dislike and hate. Also, we may shift from a positive to a negative emotion about a person or thing in a moment, typically depending upon our perception of that person's emotions or behavior toward us or that thing's unusual taste or other quality.

The next three chapters share with you the beliefs und uncertainties I have about life, death, souls, and the afterlife from my personal experiences and research. I offer them simply for your consideration in the same manner as in my other books, "What if…?"

## PART SIX

# The Future

CHAPTER TWENTY-SIX

# WHAT'S AHEAD?

*"It is in giving that we receive,*
*it is in loving that we are loved,*
*it is in forgiving that we are forgiven,*
*and ultimately it is in dying that we live."*

St. Francis of Assisi

This final part of the book examines potential aspects of everyone's future: not a scientifically documented account of a life hereafter, but a possible scenario that seems so real because of some people's personal experiences. This part could be the most difficult one for you to honestly contemplate because of your learned beliefs. I respect those beliefs. But I still ask you just to imagine "What if...?" If any or all of this were true, what would it mean for you and for your loved ones?

I chose the above saying to reflect my personal misgivings about your likely reaction to this part of the book. Nevertheless, I'm prompted to share it with you. As a confirmed skeptic during much of my life, I too would have rejected much of what you'll read in the remainder of this book. Like most of you, I was reared and lived by the only "reality" I knew.

This book is intended to reflect on human free will choices we make that can affect our wellbeing. Much has been said about mind and body and little about spirit. But as an afterthought it seemed appropriate to dwell in more detail on spirit: our souls and the non-physical eternal world of souls.

This became more worthwhile as I uncovered new information from Michael Newton's book *Journey of Souls* and Joel Whitton's book *Life Between Life*. It was Newton's first book, after he closed his practice during the 1980s to concentrate on studying life-between-lives (LBL) hypnotic regression. I think Whitton's book is his only one, written during the 1980s.

Most people naturally are skeptical about the afterlife we call "Heaven." The typical attitude is "since nobody has returned to tell us, why [or what?] should we believe?" The consistency of reports from survivors of near-death experiences (NDEs) and the dramatic positive life changes they exhibit has led many people to suggest that those survivors may have had a glimpse of the afterlife.

As mentioned earlier in this book, the AWARE study is approaching the question of survival of consciousness during an NDE as a prelude to its survival of physical body death. This is best described in their own words: "One of the barriers to reconciling these dichotomous positions [comprehension of physical realities through religious thinking and the drive to understand the material universe through empirical reasoning] has been the relative lack of reliable scientific data to explain the nature of the "self" and the phenomenon of consciousness. Where, for instance, does the "self" originate? Does our consciousness have an objective reality, or is it purely an epiphenomenon of our neurobiological processes? And is it indeed plausible to speak of an atemporal, nonlocalized mind that exists independently of the physical body?"

The idea behind this part of my book is to explore what souls and Heaven apparently are really like. Hopefully this will guide us into a closer relationship with our own souls and as a preview of the afterlife. You may find it reassuring and comforting for your loved ones and yourself, as I did for my beloved Betty and me.

## » Human Beliefs

Many humans likely consider Heaven a restful, painless, and worry-free state of existence to which we *might* ascend after death of our bodies if we're "qualified". Those of us who also believe in souls probably acknowledge that these are the parts of us that make the ascent. Since most of us adults seemingly have lost touch with our souls in the press of earthly matters, we might not be certain what a soul is like.

Notice the word "adult." Remember the earlier discussion about young children's special talents that seem sort of "spiritual." Therefore, most of us may think of Heaven and souls in a sort of generic sense. However, from all the circumstantial evidence accumulated by researchers, understanding souls and Heaven is much more complex both here and in the afterlife.

We humans also believe in punishment, both on earth and in the afterlife. Victims of malevolent acts typically expect revenge. Forgiveness is not standard fare for humans. However, life-between-lives (LBL) researchers dispute the existence of hell. These researchers and psychologists affirm that individuals can literally create a "hell on earth" in their minds by fixating on a belief that they are destined to go to hell. Whether this results from religious beliefs or from parental condemnation, the impact can be the same. I personally can testify to that.

You will read later about karma, a concept given many interpretations. Karma seems a guiding principle in the spirit world for souls' spiritual growth. Souls are brutally honest about their accountability as they seek to master human frailties. Some less mature souls apparently spend many incarnations before being able to overcome certain earthly shortcomings.

Although karma is sometimes considered punishment for a soul's not preventing its host body from malevolent acts, I believe this is incorrect. As you'll also read later, the soul doesn't have total control of the human body. You'll read that it is possible for souls to be influenced by the emotions of their host bodies. So, to me, karma is a measure of a soul's achievements over multiple incarnations in not only coping with but also conquering human frailties. This seems to mean understanding human tendencies and being able to rise above them.

For me, the loss of my beloved wife was excruciatingly painful so long as my learned beliefs about the finality of death held sway over my thoughts. Most of us seem convinced that this is the only life we ever will have. Death never seemed to offer any alternative early in my life. Then, with aging, the specter loomed ever closer, and interment of the physical body seemed to cement the reality of our traditional belief.

Apparently, it is fairly uncommon for persons to witness the departure of souls from human bodies. Even those who may have done so likely are reluctant to admit it. Actual witnesses may have been uncertain what they saw. It must be unlike any known manifestation. This may add to people's disbelief about souls and the spirit world.

But my research has convinced me otherwise. I discovered evidence of beliefs in an afterlife down through the ages. I also found compelling reports from near-death survivors and from subjects of LBL hypnotic regression about a non-physical spirit world such as the one we call Heaven.

## » Hopes

Betty's human self embodied all the things for which I respected, admired, and loved her. But neither she nor I knew her soul-self, i.e., the eternal soul that I believe shared her earthly body. I now believe that Betty's soul-self departed her human body when it died and her soul returned to its eternal home in the spirit world.

But some organized religions seem to offer hope of access to heaven only for souls of those whose earthly lives conform to certain requirements. Since our Creator appears unchallenged as the epitome and source of all love, compassion, and forgiveness, I believe that all souls somehow will have access to their eternal home.

Some religions insist on hell's existence for sinners and for those who fail to comply with their admission requirements to heaven. But from his research on the life-between-lives (LBL), Michael Newton was convinced there is no such place as hell (1994, 2000, 2009). He conducted thousands of life-between-lives regressions for thirty years after he closed his private practice to study the spirit world. Even a good friend of mine, a Methodist minister, claimed that he could more likely believe in reincarnation than in hell.

You may have read about or known a survivor of a so-called "negative" near-death experience (NDE). These cases exist but occur much less frequently than positive NDEs. Survivors of negative NDEs often described their experiences as confusing, disturbing, or even "hellish." Some researchers suggested that patients' reactions might be caused by their fright, bewilderment, or religious beliefs (Chopra). At least one of these cases is well known through Howard Storm's book. In the midst of his turmoil Storm called upon Jesus and his NDE became very positive. This transitory negative aspect of these NDEs seems fairly common (Sabom).

## » Heavenly Rewards

I realize there is a risk in adding this commentary because it disagrees with expectations that some Muslims apparently have for their afterlife. (Remember that other authors who have disagreed with precepts of Islam have been threatened with death. But I believe the lives of many young Muslims can be saved from martyrdom by learning its futility.) It's difficult for me to imagine that life on earth is so difficult for these religious zealots that they devotedly martyr themselves fully believing in promised secular rewards in heaven.

With all due respect to them and their leaders, the world of souls has been characterized far differently that that. Naturally, no human being has returned from irreversible clinical death to validate the nature of the afterlife. But there seems to be an increasing acceptance of testimonies from NDE survivors about the general tenor of conditions there.

One factor that emerges from NDE reports seems to contradict any promises of rewards that resemble selfish earthly pleasures. Instead, survivors of "core," i.e., full-blown NDEs, typically have undergone an often-radical life-changing experience. The word "radical" is used here because, before their experience, some of them by their own admission were very "worldly." Their transformations left them with traits more akin to what we are told characterize souls:

- Compassion and concern for others
- Certainty of the afterlife
- More humility
- Joy of living
- Sharing of their abundance
- Honesty
- Accountability

An online article by Zulfikar Khan "The X-Rated Paradise of Islam" begins: "In this article I shall describe the Islamic Paradise or Jannat which was invented by Prophet Mohammed to bribe the Arabs into committing heinous crimes by promising them materialistic things which they couldn't obtain in the harsh desert. The paradise contains six important items: beautiful virgins, young boys, water, wine, fruits and wealth." (See Khan, Zulfikar in the bibliography.)

I found a revealing Web site article written by a Lebanese Muslim woman named Amina, "Islam and the Concept of Martyrdom." It is long but worth reading, full of quotes from the Qur'an and hadiths (traditions and sayings of the Prophet). Her article focuses on the conflict between Israelis and Palestinians but is applicable to worldwide suicide bombers. The premise of her article is "There is a need for every believing Muslim to 'strive', or engage in spiritual Jihad, to understand the word and will of God and to live accordingly. Failure to engage in that [spiritual] Jihad makes our responses in times of crises mere reflexes based on what we are told rather than the result of rational and independent thinking that is grounded in evidence from the Qur'an".

She argues, "We Muslims are 'reacting' rather than 'acting', repeating what we are told Islam is about, rather than carefully and directly examining what our religious beliefs are and should be about." Amina stresses that "repeating uncritically what some people in authority claim to be from God, however 'authoritative' they may be, will not save me from the responsibility of my acts should they be wrong." She concludes with "I truly urge well meaning Muslims not to sacrifice God's truth in the cause of [religious jihad]. This would be an unacceptable price to pay for believers in God. True, putting religion in the service of politics might entail some 'earthly rewards' and political gains, but most probably will end up depriving us of the greater, more enduring reward in heaven (8:28):

> And know that your possessions and your progeny are
> but a trial and that it is God with whom lies your
> greatest reward."

It is worth noting that suicide is forbidden in the Muslim traditions (Hadith in Arabic), the collected sayings and doings attributed to the Prophet Mohammed and traced back to him through a series of trustworthy witnesses. The phrase "throw their bodies on the Prophet to protect Him" did not mean intentional suicide (Muttaqun: Suicide).

Perhaps the martyrdom of young Muslims as suicide bombers is understandable in light of adolescents' idealism and great expectations for themselves as discussed earlier in this book. These young people likely are not mature enough to have experienced the vicissitudes of life that might enable them to doubt and question their teachers. David Davis and four fellow Yale history professors examine this in detail in their online Letter to the Editor of the online *New York Times*, entitled "Violence of Old Men vs. the Idealism of Youth"

## » Fears

It has been said that everyone's greatest fear is death. One of the most likely sources of that fear might be eternal damnation. Families and religions over the years have sought to shape children's and adults' morals and behavior. The term "Victorian" was used to describe some parents efforts to control their children's social lives. "Hell fire and brimstone" was a common promise to sinners from some preachers. Some people took those lessons so literally that it left them convinced they would spend eternity in hell.

It must be acknowledged that this threat did help control the surging hormones of adolescents and the self-seeking behavior of many adults down through the centuries since the advent of Christianity.

Another fear was expressed by my mentor about souls achieving their ultimate objective of full spiritual maturity. In his book, Michael Newton used the term "conjunction" with the Creator as the ultimate recognition of spiritual attainment. He said this seemed to be "the prime motivator of souls" (2000). Newton reported that advanced souls talked about "the time of conjunction when they will join the 'Most Sacred Ones'." My mentor was concerned about losing his personal identity in such a merger. But perhaps this indefinable "union" is a coming together not as a single mass of energy but as a group of advanced souls beyond the imagination of even the souls themselves.

I suspect too that, despite organized religion's promise of our seeing loved ones again in Heaven, some people fear that they'll never be reunited with their spouses and families. Whatever we might humanly fear about death and for our souls, I now am convinced it is like President Franklin Roosevelt said in 1932, "The only thing we have to fear is fear itself."

## » Reunion

My and maybe your greatest hope is reunion with our loved ones again, particularly with my beloved wife Betty. I now have every confidence in this happening. But I need to realize the nature of that reunion as based upon LBL testimonial evidence (Newton 2000).

Betty's and my souls will have as much individuality and independence in the eternal scheme of things as our two human bodies had on earth before we met. This characteristic carries with it a mandate, particularly for men or women who were controlling of their spouses, partners, family members, or close friends on earth (because of ego). The soul that was present in the other person on earth has an individual identity that must be respected as such.

Yet, I am reassured by understanding that souls have a creative ability unknown to and unimaginable by humans. As such, both Betty's and my souls can appear to each other in the afterlife as we were in our human bodies (although some reports suggest at about thirty years of age). In this way, reunion truly can be experienced with no strings attached.

Researchers also report that souls are genderless. Reports also say that a soul may incarnate on earth as a male or female gender, may reincarnate multiple times, and that each time the host body can have a different husband or wife. This seems in agreement with Jesus' answer to the question he was asked about a woman who married seven brothers as the brother currently her husband died: "Which one would be her husband in Heaven?" Jesus replied to the effect that there are no marriages in Heaven.

Perhaps this discussion so far has worried you—as it did me— about my soul possibly losing a close relationship with my beloved Betty's soul in the eternal expanse of the spirit world. But remember: unconditional love is the prime characteristic of souls even though love on earth comes in many shapes and sizes. Soul-love is non-dimensional, eternal, forgiving, and multi-faceted, i.e., soul-love is not specific or restricted to another particular soul. Souls in the spirit world seem to have memories of family members from previous incarnations. But your soul and your spouse's soul also will have memories of your lives on earth together and will be able to share that love. There is said to be something like a "merging" of souls that is far superior to anything on earth as a mutual sharing of love.

Newton's LBL regression subjects report that souls often reincarnate in "cluster groups" (1994, 2000). The soul of your child from the past may be the same soul of your uncle today; the soul of your earlier sister may be the soul of your daughter today; or the soul of another relative in the past may be the soul of your close friend today. But remember, after the "veil of forgetfulness" descends upon reincarnation, we humans typically won't recognize a fellow soul in a relative or friend on earth

It is recognized too that two souls' host bodies may have had a difficult relationship on earth. After returning "home," there is an opportunity for them to work out their earthly problems together. This seems related to having each other understand human factors that caused their problems. Sometimes having mutual loved ones involved as sort of mediators seems to help by offering perspective. Difficult relationships on earth may reflect the life challenges each soul chose to face when it planned its incarnation.

## » Soul Mates

Related to reunion in the spirit world is the question that seems to occasionally trouble us as humans: finding our "soul mate." The online *Merriam-Webster Dictionary* defines this as "a person suited to another in temperament" or "who strongly resembles another in attitudes or beliefs." But there seem to be people who feel that they have such an intimate relationship that they must be soul mates. Whether they believe in the world of souls or reincarnation is a moot point.

Perhaps the most thorough study I've found about soul mates is Newton's commentary in his second book (2000). He cites three types of closely related souls: primary and companion soul mates and affiliated souls. He cautions against use of the term "true soul mate" because it implies that all other soul companions are less than true.

Primary soul mates are "closely bonded partners" in life. It may be a spouse, a brother or sister, a best friend, or perhaps a parent: a soul who is an eternal partner. This is not to be confused with the term "primary" cluster group. Members of the primary soul cluster also can be called soul mates, companion soul mates, or soul companions. Affiliated souls are from secondary cluster groups, souls that have been selected to work with us. If they appear frequently over several incarnations we get to know them.

You may feel that this doesn't answer the question of finding your soul mate. True. Newton prefaces his discussion about soul mates with an exploration of love. You've read that our Creator is the epitome of love that souls emulate. But the feeling of love between souls may be different from the feeling of love between human beings. On earth, Newton said, "love is the acceptance of all the imperfections of our partners." For example, unsightly physical appearances and disagreements caused failed unions with the soul mate of some of Newton's subjects. So it seems that finding a soul mate may be more complicated than might be expected.

## » Reservations

I personally now have overcome any qualms about "going home." Now I see it as an adventure beyond any that earth offers. It represents the greatest unknown of the unknowable. Even with recognition of the incredible technologies achieved by science, mathematics, and engineering in recent times, the leap to the spirit world should seem very exciting, like a stellar blast into the future.

Naturally it is not "I" of my human physical self that makes the transition. Thus, in light of my not knowing my own soul very well personally while on earth, I naturally have some uncertainty about my soul resuming its place in the spirit world. But we're told that even those souls that have reincarnated many times have qualms immediately after death of the physical body (Whitton).

I think that my continuing effort to contemplate the soul and the life between lives instills in me not only an ever-growing awe of the Divine but also a child-like wonder about the sharp contrast between life on earth and life in the spirit world. My grandson's perceptive question when he was five about the earth not being "the real world" adds to my faith.

I must admit that I still have a residual dread of death. My dread, however, differs markedly from other people's. It is not that death is the ending of the only existence my spirit will ever have. I simply have a natural reluctance to deprive my loved ones of my care and visible love and to cause them bereavement.

Considering my faith that the soul and spirit world do exist and that they truly represent the "real" world, I also credit two other phenomena in my life with sustaining my faith and hope. One is my continuing intuition from unknown sources in my writing and even in my more mundane daily chores. Also, I credit spirit entities with anticipating the forks I needed to take in the road of my life as well as the assurance of proper timing in all plans involving both the burial arrangements and the Celebration of Life and Love honoring my beloved wife.

As acknowledged earlier, some scientists refuse to believe the existence of souls, reincarnation, and the life between lives because they can't objectively *prove* them. Although I've not personally witnessed any of these, it's *not* beyond my human imagination to conceive of such possibilities and even their likelihood.

Remember that concepts considered equally fallacious in earlier times now are an intrinsic part of our earthly lives. Are the very ideas of souls, reincarnation, and a life between lives totally awesome and without scientific proof? Yes. Impossible? No! That's what faith is all about, the unknown and the unknowable. That's also what scientific research is all about, to distinguish the two.

But I never *expect* human science, as we know it today, to be able to define the true nature of the spirit world. It is the manifestation of the ultimate eternal intelligence and power from which everything that *ever* has existed was created and is sustained. However, Tart and some other researchers argue that the large volume of consistent testimonial evidence about the spirit world constitutes empirical evidence that is by definition scientific.

I realize that my expectations will conflict with some persons on each side of the ongoing debate between science and religion. Only after we pass over will we know for certain.

Nevertheless, the next chapter carries us deeper into the world of souls.

# CHAPTER TWENTY-SEVEN
## THE HUMAN SOUL

---

*"Now we look forward with confidence to our heavenly bodies,
realizing that every moment we spend in these earthly bodies
is time spent away from our eternal home."*

Apostle Paul, Second Corinthians 5:6

---

Earlier you read that the reason some people don't believe in God may
be because they don't see physical manifestations by Him. In a similar
reasoning, some people may doubt or question that each of us has a soul
or spirit due to our inability to physically identify it. Since we tend to
lose touch with our souls as we accommodate to earth's influences, it
always has puzzled me what relationship our body has with our soul.
Apparently this is a commonly held lack of distinction. Therefore it
seems worthwhile to examine the nature of our soul and its role as
part of us. Perhaps this will help "humanize" our souls, differentiate
them from other spiritual entities, and give us a personal sense of
responsibility for them.

The mention of souls can be traced back to early Greeks. Socrates
(470-399 BC) said not only that the soul is immortal, but also that
it contemplates truths after its separation from the body at the time
of death, according to the online *Stanford Encyclopedia of Philosophy*.
James Hillman's book *The Soul's Code: In Search of Character and
Calling* quotes Plotinus (AD 205-270) that "we elected the body, the
parents, the place, and the circumstances that suited the soul [which]
suggests that the circumstances, including my body and my parents

whom I may curse … I do not understand because I have forgotten [therefore] we must attend very carefully to childhood to catch early glimpses of the [soul] in action, to grasp its intentions and not block its way."

As mentioned earlier, Michael Newton (1994, 2000) and Joel Whitton contributed much to our perception of what souls and the spirit world (Heaven) seem to be like. Michael Newton's first book provides a wealth of what might be called "first-hand" experiences of souls as revealed during life-between-lives (LBL) hypnotic regression. He offers twenty-nine case studies of personal testimonies tape-recorded from his subjects' superconscious state, which he feels may be the seat of the soul or the soul itself.

Newton stresses that none of the thousands of testimonies he's heard ever gave a complete picture of the spirit world from the ending of one incarnation to the beginning of another. But he has been able through guided questioning to explore each of the many facets of souls' experiences in the spirit world. He selected these twenty-nine cases to provide a general overview from death of the physical body to rebirth in a subsequent incarnation. This is covered in fifteen chapters that deal not only with different aspects of the spirit world but also illustrate individual traits and needs of the various subjects' souls (1994).

Using reports from his thousands of LBL regression subjects during the decade of the 1980s, Newton was "formulating a working model of the world between lives" (1994, 2000). He established that two kinds of cluster groups exist in the "life between lives." There are primary and secondary cluster groups. He claimed, "[members of a] primary cluster group began their existence together and remain closely associated through hundreds of incarnations. The integrity of a soul's original cluster group remains intact in a timeless way. Secondary cluster groups around our primary group can total one thousand souls or more." He calls the members of these secondary groups "affiliated souls." Selected members of these latter groups may work with us so that we get to know them over many incarnations.

Newton found that souls do not bring all of their energy to an incarnation (2000). Some of his subjects apparently indicated that, if they did, it would blow out the fetus' neural circuits. So a part of each soul's energy remains in the spirit world. Newton referred to this as soul "duality" with each part having that soul's unique identity. This seems to mean that, if your beloved spouse passes over before you do, his or her soul will be reunited with the part of your soul that remained in the spirit world. Newton's research indicates that this occurs with other loved ones too, even those still physically alive on earth.

## » Beyond Human Imagination

If, as Michael Newton suggested, souls are "intelligent light [forms of] energy," he also described them as having "a majesty beyond description" (2000). The human soul seems to be far beyond human conceivability. Newton characterized souls as having "compassion, ethics, harmony, and morality far beyond what we practice on earth."

Many people might question that each person has a soul, considering the billions of people now on earth. Where do all those souls come from? How could they be accommodated in the spirit world after death of the body? First, imagine what "finite" means. That's our earth. Then consider the words "infinite" and "eternal." We are told that neither space nor time exists in the spirit world. One apparent aspect of the spirit world is the spiritual advancement "levels" of souls. Some do not need further incarnations and fulfill many different individual roles as helpers, teachers, and counselors.

## » Nature of Souls

Newton writes about the creation of souls in the spirit world (1994, 2000). The soul has been described as a humanly inconceivable and indestructible bundle of energy. The innocent young souls are grouped into primary soul groups numbering around five to twelve, which they'll retain forever. They become well acquainted with one another in their early training together. These souls are considered immature until they've incarnated on earth several times.

Newton categorizes souls into six stages of development: beginner, lower intermediate, intermediate, upper intermediate, advanced, and highly advanced. "Development" means spiritual growth and mastery of human frailties through many incarnations. These stages correspond to levels I - VI. One of the means that distinguishes souls is the color they emanate, different according to their level, from white through dark bluish-purple. Newton said that around three-quarters of his clients are at level two, still relatively immature (1994). He suggests that this seems to correlate with the extent of human violence in the world today. He admits, however, that his clientele is composed of persons who recognize they have problems and seek him out.

Newton's and Whitton's books disclose that souls are a lot like humans in some ways but unlike us in many other ways. For example, souls and humans both have individual personalities. But the objective of incarnation seems to be to develop a uniform personality to present to the world. Newton's clients report that there are "subtle variations" between soul and body personalities in different incarnations. Souls are said to have egos too, but these apparently are more like self-identities. Like humans, souls seem to possess individual traits, including the following:

- Courageous
- Gentle
- Fun-loving
- Serious
- Conservative
- Adventurous
- Defiant
- Persistent
- Flexible
- Reticent
- Aggressive
- Light-hearted
- Risk-prone

## » Soul Creativity

Interestingly, one of the creative skills that a soul apparently can manifest in the spirit world is to appear as its human hosts did in the immediate past or even other incarnations. As discussed earlier, it seems possible that the two souls who incarnated in my wife and me in this earthly life will be able to "see" one another in human form as we did on earth. But it's also claimed that we each will appear as we did around age thirty!

Newton also recounts some of his clients' testimonies about a capability souls have in the spirit world that is unmatched in human existence: special creativity. This is not like fine painting, sculpting, musical scores and instrument mastery, dance, or even the momentous advances in technology. To me, it is best illustrated by the performances of master illusionists. Reports include a soul being welcomed back with a "spectacular seventeenth century full dress ball" and even enjoying sporting games among souls themselves.

## » Role of Souls

We may believe that our souls are immune to our thoughts, will, and actions: the "everything" that purportedly is recorded in the Akashic records. Perhaps we see souls as possessing God-given talents that vary only in the extent to which they can control the human ego. Unfortunately, souls are individual enough to differ in their compatibility with various human egos; in their susceptibility to human emotions; and in their ability to disconnect from certain human "baggage" when they "return home." Some souls are said to even carry forward into future incarnations some imprinted human emotions, interfering with their spiritual growth.

Probably the greatest challenge each soul has in incarnating is what Newton calls "amnesia." Despite the soul's selection of a variety of characteristics for its next incarnation, e.g., family, culture, and location, the soul remembers none of this during its sojourn on earth and rarely has memories from its past lives. Therefore each soul literally starts each "life" anew in each incarnation. This handicap proves especially difficult for immature souls.

Newton refers to a "soul-mind connection." He feels that souls both gain and offer "mental gifts" from and to their host bodies through a "symbiosis of human brain cells and intelligent energy." Despite the soul's selection of the body for its incarnation, the soul doesn't have total control of that body. A tug-of-war can exist particularly "if the soul and host are incompatible; if the host is psychologically unstable; or if the host's ego is disposed to malevolence" (1994, 2000).

The fear, anger, and survival instincts that characterized our ancient ancestors still exist in rudimentary forms among humans today. They give birth to emotions and drives that may lead to rampant violence in our society today. This is a shock to immature souls who were created in a matrix of love and wisdom. Incarnating mature souls are more capable in accepting human frailties, knowing that it is the soul's responsibility to learn how to cope with human nature. Human traits that souls don't *naturally* possess include:

- Selfishness
- Jealousy
- Envy
- Hate
- Narcissism
- Malevolence
- Lust
- Anger

## » Returning "Home"

Numerous authors have described the hallmark characteristics of both near-death experiences (NDEs) and life-between-lives (LBL) regressions. Survivors of NDEs tell of ineffable sights and sounds they perceived during cardiac arrest, which are similar to experiences that subjects described during LBL regressions. However, NDE survivors often mention a barrier beyond which they are not permitted to go. Whitton feels that this could be a sort of "peek around the corner" of life-between-lives existence.

From Whitton's, Schwartz's (2006), and Newton's books (1994, 2000, and 2009), enough circumstantial evidence seems available to reasonably construct what might be stages of the soul's transition of consciousness upon death of the physical body. The following therefore is a composite account of what souls might typically experience in "returning home." However, the human concepts of timing and sequence are not applicable in the spirit world, even though they may seem represented in this composite.

Whitton stressed that a soul's initial reaction to departing at death of the physical body usually is the same regardless of the number of its reincarnations. Upon exiting the "tunnel," one or more souls of previously departed friends and relatives may be waiting at the "Gateway" to welcome each arriving soul. There is nothing haphazard about these friends or relatives knowing exactly when souls are due and where to meet them in the spirit world.

After departing the physical body, the soul-consciousness (or soul):

- Is temporarily bewildered, but has no pain or anxiety
- May see its host's body lying separate and motionless
- Becomes peaceful and relaxed, sensing it still is alive
- May be met, welcomed, and accompanied by a spirit guide, as felt necessary by the guide
- Senses rapid travel, through a sort of high cylindrical passageway, possibly lighted
- Is counseled by its guide to assess and help relieve the soul's negative baggage
- Is transported to either a de-contamination or healing center if baggage is overwhelming
- May elect a lengthy period of solitude to contemplate or may immediate reincarnate into a body subject to the same kind of atrocities its host body committed, if contaminated by atrocious acts of its host
- Otherwise, is caught up in a white light of unearthly brilliance, not hot, infused with total love, warmth, and caring
- Is greeted by a spirit entity or departed friends or relatives
- Is rapidly overcome with awe, wonder, and amazement
- Undergoes an expansion of self-awareness to renew its eternal consciousness of soul-self and the spirit world reality
- Is transported to a primary or appropriate cluster of fellow souls
- Meets with the Council of Elders to assess in a frank way its successes and failures of the life just past
- Views a rapid panoramic "visual" replay of its total life experiences from its most recent incarnation
- Participates in counseling, learning, service, recreation, and socializing in the spirit world
- Makes a decision about, and plans for, its next incarnation and karmic script
- Departs for earth

Whitton said that souls typically leave behind any animal instincts affecting them when they depart the human body: "anger, sensual pleasure, lust, sadness, and jealousy." Yet both Whitton and Newton acknowledge that some souls may become so engrossed with their human hosts' life styles and emotions that those souls risk becoming contaminated. For example, a soul who is aggressive, risk-prone, and defiant might become intimately involved with a host body whose self-esteem feeds on aggressive power struggles for material gain without concern for others. Whitton found one LBL case where "his soul's anger at being betrayed was so incorrigible during the afterlife that Gary has carried his negativity back into this incarnation [and] he has difficulty trusting even those who are close to him."

Newton found that "some souls do carry the negative baggage of a difficult past life longer than others" (2000). He and Whitton both stressed that soul adjustment to the spirit world depends upon "the soul's level of spiritual growth; its attachment to memories left from this life on earth; and the nature and timing of death." Newton discovered that anger might remain toward a young life cut short without recognition that it may have been planned by the soul before incarnation. At the gateway to the spirit world, the baggage starts to diminish. The soul soon recognizes the "carefully directed order and harmony" of the world it left before its incarnation just past. Also, there is "an overwhelming impact" on the soul upon seeing previously departed people whom the returning soul may have doubted ever seeing again.

As mentioned earlier, souls each have unique features that enable recognition of each other, including the color of their aura. Souls can take on the body image they were in the previous or earlier incarnations. They also can appear as an amorphous shape. Souls recognize other souls whom they've known in previous incarnations and in the spirit world. Souls communicate unlike humans. We use our five physical senses, verbal language, and nonverbal behavior. Communication in the spirit world occurs telepathically. Newton explained, "telepathy … is so comprehensive as far as total perception is concerned [whereas] verbal communication [on earth] often leads to misunderstandings." Souls are fully integrated by thought. Unless blocked by a soul (as with its intimate discussions with its Council), souls can understand each other's thoughts.

## » Spirit Guides

Angels have been a part of religious lore forever. Many persons tell of life-threatening circumstances from which they were rescued by unseen forces or excruciating times through which they were consoled. Spirit guides are assigned to each incarnating soul. The one possible common denominator for all such sources of help might best be called "spirit entities." Reports from Newton's clients account for spirit entities in a variety of roles (1994). These more advanced entities seem able to help souls in special ways:

- Watching over incarnated souls
- Escorting returning souls through the "tunnel" or meeting and comforting them at what Newton calls the "Gateway"
- Reorienting returning souls to the spirit world
- Joining souls in their appearance before their Council
- Counseling souls in need of help
- Assisting souls in planning for reincarnation

"Advanced" typically means souls who likely have achieved optimal spiritual growth, no longer need to incarnate, and have participated in special training. One of Newton's clients said "we are always protected, supported, and directed within the system by master souls."

## » Transition and Placement

Newton's first book spent two chapters on these aspects of souls returning home (1994). This involves gathering and movement of returning souls to specific groups in the spirit world. Large numbers of returning souls are conveyed in a spiritual form of mass transit to their proper destinations.

Newton stresses several principles that apply in the spirit world (1994). First, space there is infinite, something we can't even imagine. Second, despite the population of billions of souls, there is a "structure and order to the spirit world also beyond human imagination." Third, having read about subtle energy earlier, you might accept that the spirit world has unlimited access to energy forces designed to perform various operations more effectively and efficiently than anything that engineers could design on earth.

Newton says "everyone has a designated place in the spirit world." Yet there is no hierarchy as we know it. Each soul has the same value as every other one. Several life-between-lives (LBL) testimonies spoke of souls' "universal bond." Newton comments that an outstanding characteristic of the spirit world is "a continuous feeling of a powerful mental force facilitating everything in uncanny harmony." His clients call the spirit world "a place of pure thought."

Perhaps it's obvious by now that the spirit world can address the needs of souls individually and in mass. That seems to reflect the overarching unconditional love of our Creator that also characterizes each soul. Newton's description about the spiritual care of each returning soul begins at the Gateway. Although some of Newton's clients may not have perceptible spirit entities in certain stages of spirit world "operations," he stresses that invisible forces always are at work attending to each soul's specific needs. Souls in the spirit world work with peers who are at the same level of spiritual development in a planned and ordered self-development process.

## » Destinations

At the intended destinations souls debark the spiritual mass transit into the space reserved for their colony, composed of a specific group of entities at their own maturity level. Souls in these cluster groups are intimate old friends from previous incarnations who have about same awareness level, and who have direct and frequent contact. But not all of the people close to us in our earthly lives are on same developmental level.

## » Life Planning

Schwartz, Newton, and Whitton stress that souls plan their reincarnations, as discussed earlier. Family choice, culture, geographical location, environment, and spiritual growth all are part of the selection process. It therefore seems small wonder that people may complain later about family mistreatment on earth. They forget that their souls made the selection. What's more, those experiences may be part of his or her soul's spiritual growth. Newton's clients claim, "the real lessons of life are learned by recognizing and coming to terms with being human."

## » Karma

Karma is one of the topics that are addressed in meetings with the Council, with guides, with other souls in the primary cluster, and during the planning of the next incarnation. Various human interpretations have been given to karma, even to the extreme of "an eye for an eye." Newton believes that eventually balancing the karmic scorecard is necessary for ultimate spiritual growth. But both he and Whitton say that several karmic credits can be achieved in a single lifetime.

Whitton's LBL regressed subjects provided two different aspects of the soul's accountability (karma). One is its purpose. Whitton's participants say that essentially karma is learning, as ordained by our Creator. Obviously, this learning results from a variety of life experiences, some of them naturally painful. We tread the uncertain paths of life on earth, seemingly out of touch with our souls in exerting free will choices. No wonder, as I mentioned earlier, that the absence of divine interventions cause some people to disbelieve in God or to feel that God is dead. At the time of a calamity our human focus is on "Why?" However, the soul takes the long view and measures its spiritual growth over many lifetimes.

The other aspect offered by Whitton's LBL regression subjects is each soul's confrontation of its karmic balance sheet following each incarnation. This naturally is part of the returning soul's meeting with its Council and the panoramic "full-screen" life review. This review has been described as involving everything that happened, including viewpoints from others affected, real life-like sensations, and outcomes of alternative choices that might have been made. Yet, all of this is said to occur in what seems like an extremely short time by earth standards.

The Council is portrayed as forgiving, loving, compassionate, and supportive. The soul apparently is most incriminating of itself. Soul remorse is remarkable, especially if its host body committed atrocious acts like murder. Apparently the soul is well aware that its primary goal is conquering fear of the human condition; this seems necessary in order to grow spiritually by overcoming negative emotions through perseverance over many lifetimes. But this results in souls often returning home bruised and hurt.

Newton (1994 and 2000) pictures souls as honest and loving far beyond any human comparison. It seems in this context that souls fully realize that the nature of spiritual growth involves mastering human frailties. But they recognize too that they are fully subject to human free will choices in each incarnation that could negatively shape their soul energy and create karmic debts.

Whitton stresses that service is fundamental to karma. So the Council also emphasizes commendable actions that provide karmic credit. One report involved the Council asking a soul about the "bus-stop incident." The soul apparently didn't remember, so the Council described it: "You stepped off a bus, late and in a hurry. You noticed a woman sitting on a bench in the rain, crying and looking forlorn. So you sat beside her and put your arm around her, trying to comfort her."

Souls take this very seriously. With doors locked on making amends in the life just past, souls are especially attentive to what awaits them upon their return home. Whitton stresses that spiritual growth requires momentum. So the soul's karmic record for its immediate past life likely will contribute to the karmic script for its next incarnation.

Interestingly, Whitton's research revealed that some souls established life plans that were very commendable. Yet the early environments of their hosts drastically altered those plans, sentencing the host egos to lifelong reactive-negative behavior as a result. Unfortunately, in certain instances this was caused by one of the parents.

The terms "enlightenment" or "transcendence" were mentioned earlier to signify a search for enhanced knowledge about the mystery of life. The emphasis there seemed to be on the goal and the accomplishment rather than the meaning for the individual. Instead, it would seem to be a much more worthwhile undertaking to enhance our personal relationship with our souls. Certain rare individual opportunities like cosmic consciousness, NDEs, and LBL regressions help provide that "missing" link and move our souls closer to balancing their karma. Another chance for improving access to our souls might be intuition or what might be called "soul-talk."

## » Free Will

The question of free will has been exhaustively argued in nearly all of the settings of human endeavor. Courts, universities, and churches all have seen endless debates over this basic aspect of human behavior: how freely do we choose our actions and how fully should we be held accountable?

Philosophically and theologically this matter was discussed earlier in this book as it seems related to another question: "Why doesn't God intervene?" We also examined the concept of life planning by the soul as a prelude to reincarnation. In another part of this book we considered two different aspects of free will: how much control does the soul have over it's host body's behavior and to what extent might the host body's nature of neurological and emotional development be responsible for its conduct.

From the standpoint of the existence of free will, any one of us probably could cite examples where his or her life changed dramatically because of a decision or action for which he or she would admit being solely responsible. Mitigating or encouraging circumstances obviously may have been involved, but the outcome resulted in a significant change in that person's—and perhaps other people's—way of life.

This, in turn, seems to argue against predestination. Also, it perhaps challenges the extent to which each soul is able to plan its new life on earth. But clues came from Newton's (1994, 2000) clients who described their life-planning experiences while under life-between-lives (LBL) hypnotic regression.

Some authors say that the genetic nature of future parents is available in the soul's life planning. Yet souls apparently are not permitted to view more than the present circumstances of potential parents. In other words, the spirit entities that control the viewing process seem to prevent the soul from knowing its future life beyond its moment of birth.

If true, this should add substance to the idea of free will: each of us accounts for his or her behavior. The influences on our behavior begin while we still are fetuses and these factors continue in a constellation of life experiences. Included are the biological state of a human's neurological development as well as those conditions that affect it. Obviously, in addition to the presence or absence of neurological deficits or disorders, all of the variables that have been discussed in this book are involved. To recount them all seems an endless task. Suffice it to say that we each seem to be a product of free will plus all our life experiences.

## » Soul-Talk

You read earlier that our memory of the spirit world diminishes as we develop our human identity and accommodate to earthly pursuits. As our egos develop, they literally create our drives, fuel our intentions, and motivate our behavior. Of course, our souls joined us to learn through participation in our human thoughts, will, and actions. If souls did not take part in helping shape our lives, it seems that they would learn very little. So I've long wondered just how souls participate in human endeavors. Now I'm beginning to believe that our souls' guidance comes to us through subtle influences like what we call intuition.

Perhaps the following example will illustrate the significance that following such subtle cues can have on our lives. The occasion was Amateur Night at the Harlem Opera House many years ago. A skinny, awkward sixteen-year-old girl prepares to go fearfully on stage. She is announced to the crowd as a dancer. Then, moments before she appears, the announcer says she has decided to sing instead. Three encores and the first prize later, Ella Fitzgerald was history (Hillman).

We occasionally use terms such as "hunches" and "gut reactions" in place of intuition. So it might be difficult to isolate a specific kind of conscious feeling that comes from our souls. If it is true that our souls do use a kind of messaging like intuition to communicate with us, maybe we could contemplate what characteristics it might have. First, let's examine what researchers are saying about other, better defined, sources of intuition, gut reactions, and hunches.

Research has shown that we all have a subconscious (unconscious) storehouse of memory which has been credited with our "knowing without knowing," termed implicit memory. The online article from Science Centric "That Gut Feeling May Actually Reflect a Reliable Memory" described findings at Northwestern University by Ken Paller and Joel Voss. Their study "Electrophysiological Signature of Unconscious Recognition Memory" appeared in the journal *Nature Neuroscience*. An abstract appears online. The authors told of "implicit recognition" of "valid memories" and "surprising accuracy of memories that can't be consciously accessed" in two groups of twenty-four people each. As was discussed earlier, one function of implicit memory is to subconsciously imprint emotionally based events that occur before a child develops cognition and explicit memory. It now appears that implicit memories also can be subconsciously recorded later in life.

Some scientists believe that our brains store much more information than we can be aware of. An example is so-called "procedural" memory. As discussed earlier, this involves skills and tasks we learn to perform automatically, like driving cars, milking cows, and turning light switches off or on. Imagine the complex skills that baseball pitchers, football quarterbacks, and master chess players acquire and employ without consciously thinking through them for each move. Malcolm Gladwell's bestseller *Blink: The Power of Thinking Without Thinking* was based on the work of Professor Gerd Gigerenzer, director of the Max Planck Institute for Human Development in Berlin.

More recently Gigerenzer wrote his own book *Gut Feelings: The Intelligence of the Unconscious*. Tian Dayton captured the essence of his work in her online article "How We're Wired for Gut Reactions." Gigerenzer uses the term "unconscious" in the title of his book, but he is quoted in Dayton's article as defining gut reactions as "a judgment that is fast and comes quickly into a person's consciousness." Gigerenzer attributes evolutionary development and personal experience as a rich storehouse of information that the brain can call upon both unconsciously and consciously.

So what kinds of characteristics might we assign to "soul-talk?" Like intuition, soul-talk:

- Occurs spontaneously, unexpectedly, sporadically, and without conscious intent
- May be described as an "ah-ha" moment, most often appearing to offer help as a subtle suggestion or urge
- Invariably seems in our best interests of safety, task fulfillment, and spiritual growth
- Is not subject to negotiation or discussion
- Never pursues self-serving purposes
- Is patient and persistent
- Never requires obedience, simply acknowledgement and respect

We are told that intuition is accessible to everyone and that we can improve our receptiveness with practice. Yet some people still disavow, disregard, or fail to recognize its occurrence. Nancy Rosanoff's classic book *Intuition Workout: A Practical Guide to Discovering and Developing Your Inner Knowing* provides a series of exercises to make people more comfortable and effective in developing their intuition. She has conducted training classes for corporations, universities, and other groups for many years.

Rosanoff stresses that intuition can't be forced. However, we can learn to focus our concerns, questions, and decisions in such a way that they invite intuition. Perhaps the same holds true with "soul-talk." Some of you may have had the following experience: you are in your car, waiting at a red stoplight; it turns green; but you feel an urge to pause; a speeding car runs the light across your path. Question: was it intuition or soul-talk? Or are they the same?

Whether you'd like to be more attuned to intuition or to soul-talk, here are some parameters you might like to try about either:

- It comes when you're in the present moment, not when you're worrying about yesterday or tomorrow;
- Trust your feelings—a nagging or uncomfortable feeling may suggest you're about to make a misstep, suggesting you "look before you leap;"
- Think back to similar decisions you made in the past and try to take a neutral position now to see if you get an intuitive or soul "message;"
- Emotional needs, fears, desires, and expectations can interfere with intuition and soul-talk on personal relationships and money matters;
- Impulsivity is counterproductive to intuition and soul-talk.

The source of our intuition seems indefinable, although some people who seem more familiar with it claim that it emanates from our sub- or superconscious minds. Still, many people apparently doubt their intuition and may disregard it. One of the key requirements to intuition, I'm told, is respecting the intent in which it seems to be offered: it should never be sought or used for strictly self-serving purposes.

Some time after I wrote this part of the book, I felt moved to scan Amazon's book pages. Like other times, I entered a search word related to this book. But today was the first time I saw a particular book on Amazon, despite often using this same search term —"soul." I've credited synchronicity with favorable events. Maybe this was at work again.

My discovery was Janet Conner's *Writing Down Your Soul: How to Activate and Listen to the Extraordinary Voice Within.* Her book complements my book's discussion on "soul talk." You may want to read hers. *Writing Down Your Soul* doesn't approach the subject from a scholarly standpoint. By contrast, Conner tells how her initiation into writing "morning pages" happened in the depths of a painful divorce. It's been said that soul-talk, intuition, or soul consciousness often comes to us in crisis situations. Hers were also accompanied by several seeming miracles.

Conner's Web site (www.writingdownyoursoul.com) contains the preface and sample first chapter of her book. That chapter is notably entitled "How I Discovered the Voice—or Rather, How the Voice Discovered Me." Conner included a quotation she recalled from Julia Cameron's *The Artist's Way*: "Anyone who faithfully writes morning pages will be led to a connection with a source of wisdom within." That chapter also contained Conner's Covenant, springing from her deepest feelings:

- Pray always
- Seek truth
- Surrender, there is no path but God's
- Come from love
- Honor myself
- Live in partnership
- Unite to create good

Her idea of journaling soul talk or intuition offers several benefits, among them visibly acknowledging and retaining messages from our "inner voice."

The next and last chapter fulfills what I think many people want to know—whether they ask or not—what my personal conclusions are about life, physical death, souls, and the spirit world?

CHAPTER TWENTY-EIGHT

# Personal Conclusions

---

*"The most beautiful experience is to meet the mysterious.*
*This is the source of all true art and scholarly pursuit.*
*He who has never had this experience, is not capable of rapture,*
*and cannot stand motionless with amazement,*
*is as good as dead. His eyes are closed."*

Albert Einstein

---

It's become obvious to me in researching this book that the thing people increasingly are searching for is a closer relationship with their higher consciousness. Some may call this seeking transcendence or enlightenment. A statement from Michael Newton's first book included a term I seldom hear today: conscience. He said, "The human brain doesn't have an innate moral sense of ethics, so conscience is the soul's responsibility." Unfortunately, as the individual begins to accommodate environmental influences, he or she adopts a mindset that can significantly shape his or her conscience.

Environmental influences seem to start even before birth, witness the mother's impact on her fetus. Her words and actions imprint a reservoir of implicit memory in the young child that unconsciously shapes the youngster's feelings about himself, others, and life itself. Trust—or lack of it—is a big factor there. As adolescence approaches, there are added influences: siblings, other family members, teachers, preachers, and peers. Role modeling becomes important, as the child observes how he's taught versus how others actually behave. Ethics likely is rarely discussed, but is evident (or the lack of it) in the lives of others.

My thoughts may sound harsh, but so is life. By the time our children become adults, their consciences may be consumed by their egos. Then, their souls may have stiff competition in guiding the adults' thoughts, intentions, and free will actions. Once adults encounter hardships, they have long forgotten that their souls chose their bodies and their lives for incarnation and spiritual growth.

I am convinced that the achievement of human potential resides in the individual himself or herself. No doubt significant others can help facilitate or discourage this. It is part of the environment into which each of us is born. But those who are motivated can garner support despite the worst of times and situations. Role models exist in all races, creeds, and countries. Blaming our birth state is the worst excuse. Witness the remarkable contributions of Mattie Stepanek and Patrick Henry Hughes, whose lives were described earlier in this book.

Personally, I credited synchronicity for the favorable changes that somehow occurred in my life path. Part of this was the inexplicable entrance into my life of other persons who shaped my life positively. Also, much of it occurred as a result of choices that somehow became available to me. As I look back, I often have tried to imagine where each alternative path might have led me. I can cite more than two dozen people and decisions involved. So I'm left with a conviction that "someone" was helping me somehow.

Probably one of the most profound things I think I'm beginning to appreciate is the importance of subtlety, the least conspicuous parts of our experiences. In other words, it is not the fanfare but the inconspicuous that means most in life. There is a subtlety in intuitions, visions, and other mystical experiences; in human energy fields, healing energy, and biological energy; in synchronicity, cellular behavior, and non-locality in quantum mechanics; and in just about every other thing apart from day-to-day reality.

Perhaps that is why mindful awareness is emphasized so much, from the Buddhist monk to quiet meditation to the beauty of a flower blossom. We get so caught up in the crush and rush of everyday living, that the subtle, *but true,* meaning of life may escape us.

## » Love

I also am convinced that love is the essential ingredient that unites us all. Unfortunately, it is all too frequently absent in our interpersonal relationships. Our Creator is the essence of love, reflected in our souls as the handiwork of His creation. Love is necessary for a meaningful life: love of God, love of self, and love of others. The first of these is obvious. The second is reflected in our self-esteem. The third is demonstrated in selfless and unconditional compassion and empathy. In all three, we can become dysfunctional in the absence of love.

Perhaps it is only in our latter years that each of us may begin reflecting about our lifetime on earth. If we are honest with ourselves, this may be the easiest time for forgiveness of others—and maybe forgiving ourselves too. In a sense, this could be the time for us to make peace with the world and ourselves. But most of the people who played a significant positive role in my live already have passed over without hearing a "Thank you!" from me. I now try to practice gratitude, compassion, empathy, and humility with everyone I encounter.

Consider, instead, if each of us were able to "live in the now," something I did not do. The raging river of my consciousness constantly harassed me to "take care of business" in both my professional and personal life. Like eating, I performed each and every function, but I often failed to savor the moment. I would like to say I have changed, but I still have difficulty "remaining in the now."

Sometimes I wonder what forces within us prejudice us against the love of others. In a sense, our instinctive selfishness may be the cause. Animals, other than a mother and occasionally a father, demonstrate this in their need for survival. But, as human beings, it seems sensible that we could overcome this. For couples, it may mean each unilaterally risking a personal unqualified commitment. For others, it may be difficult to offer a part of our selves unconditionally and without judgment.

I think this bothers me most about my married life. Perhaps guilt accompanies the loss of a beloved spouse, as it does even now for my loving wife, Betty. How many occasions did I miss for expressing my love to her? Women thrive on attention from husbands or boy friends. Men don't seem similarly affected. Sincerity, or the lack of it, must seem apparent. Fortunately, I have five wonderful family members with whom I try to make amends for any past failings.

## » Remembering Our Spiritual Selves

Caroline Reynolds provides a thoughtful contemplation about life in her online article "Eternal Youth & the Power of Idealism." Her words struck a resonant chord within me. Remember the earlier discussion "Great Expectations" focusing on youthful idealism. Reynolds first described how those feelings matched her youth. She said, "Youth's idealistic belief in possibility and innocence triumphs over many of the cynical and entrenched negative behaviors of the older generation."

She laments, "So where is that voice of youth taking us today? What happens to that voice within us all—does it die with time? Do we put away wonder and hope at a certain age? And how do we continue to honor and keep the voice of idealism alive, in ourselves and others?" She answers, "We live in a world that deals in the currency of fear. From early childhood, we are all systematically trained in the language of fear and the closing of our hearts. We start off as openhearted and indiscriminately loving beings. Most toddlers lovingly hug every person they meet. They open our hearts back up, lower our guard, and create real and intimate heart connections."

Reynolds reminds us, "Yet we forget we were once like that too. There was a time when you loved everyone indiscriminately. So what happened? When did it change? And why should we spend the rest of our lives feeling the pain of artificially closing our hearts when in fact keeping them open and becoming ever bigger channels and receptacles for love is the very reason we are on the planet. If we're truly to experience the beauty of being alive and help our world evolve into a genuinely peaceful and loving place, we must reclaim idealism as a powerful, ongoing, and necessary life condition and stop dismissing it as the naïve prerogative of youth in much the same way as we once dismissed the universally powerful resource of intuition as being merely a 'woman's' quality. Idealism, hope, and the desire to keep our hearts open and love indiscriminately are essential components in our evolution."

She continues, "As the 20th century took us outwards to look at civil rights, the 21st century calls us within to examine spiritual rights. We must see people from the inside out and honor our universal commonality. From the Middle East to the Midwest, we all want to love and be loved, to feel tenderness, trust, innocence, and hope. We all need to sense a purpose to our lives and we all want to believe in something. We need to acknowledge there are as many versions of

God as there are people and that individual spiritual connection is far more important than communal packaged religion. By perceiving reality with our hearts instead of our minds we can change the entire complexion of our civilization."

Reynolds proposes an initial charter for a Spiritual Rights Movement:

- "All human souls must have equal rights and freedom to grow, discover, and express their divine mission on earth;
- "All societal institutions, e.g., workplace, schools, marriage, must honor spiritual development as their primary concern;
- "Status and achievements must be valued by their capacity to bring more goodness into the world;
- "Developing emotional intelligence, working with metaphysical energy, and operating in various dimensions of reality are essential skills for all;
- "Peace, love, vision, and compassion are required components in every situation;
- "Understanding and respect are goals in every interaction;
- "Faith, humility and reverence are vital elements of real power."

"Implementing these concepts," Reynolds stresses, "means, for example, that schools teach children to stay connected to source and deal in the currency of love; prisons become places of redemption instead of punishment; old people are revered instead of neglected; healthcare is a responsibility shared by all; and communication incorporates the extrasensory. Unimaginable as this may seem, who a century ago could possibly have predicted our world today? We must make a start knowing our willingness to evolve will allow a truth far beyond our imaginings to emerge. The soul of the 21st century is still waiting to claim its identity."

She concludes, "We must move boldly from the Age of Information to the Age of Intuition and begin the steady creation of a world where we focus on developing our inner capacity for love, tenderness, trust, compassion, and vision. In this brand new and as yet uncharted millennium, it is our moral duty to keep our hearts open and practice idealism as an essential component of our human survival and evolution."

These excerpts are provided with Caroline Reynolds' permission. You will find more of Caroline Reynolds' wisdom in her book *Spiritual Fitness—How To Live In Truth and Trust.*

## » Without God?

A movement is underway to help people achieve more meaningful lives. Some news media has addressed this using terms "spiritual" and "spirituality." Some critics of teachers in this movement have denigrated it with remarks like "the antichrist" (*USA Today*). I suspect that some of the opposition believes that the methodology employed is designed simply as a "makeover" of participants' selves and lives.

I applaud peoples' efforts to find practical approaches for more meaningful lives. I have to assume that this movement, its teachers, and its disciples do include God in their efforts. I say this in the context discussed earlier in this book that God is being left out and even excluded by design in our country today. Any truly effective effort to achieve a more meaningful life does require introspection and effort, but I believe that it also must include God.

## » Our Eternal Soul

I can't deny the mind-boggling nature of souls and the spirit world. I've been unable to achieve a life-between-lives (LBL) hypnotic regression. Also, I've had no experiences that I recognized as paranormal or metaphysical: except perhaps intuition or soul-talk, to which all of us have access. If anyone asks whether I believe in souls, reincarnation, and the spirit world, I'd have to defer to the tenor of my thoughts in this book. Remember, the word "faith" is in the subtitle to this book. Albert Einstein seems to have captured the essence of faith in his words at the beginning of this chapter.

I'm reminded that it took some of the researchers in LBL regression multiple attempts before they were successful in achieving their own regression, so I intend to keep trying. Near-death experience (NDE) survivors, LBL participants, and even some spontaneous experiences called "cosmic consciousness" seem to literally transform those people. Some of them reflect about learning their "purpose in life." Some forego materialism afterwards to care for others. And all lose any fear of death and become convinced of God and the afterlife.

Every time I recite the Twenty-Third Psalm from the Judeo-Christian Old Testament, the fourth verse continues to remind me that King David seems to have been very perceptive: "Even though I walk through the valley of the shadow of death, I shall fear no evil." He used the phrase "valley of the shadow." Obviously, a shadow is not real and poses no threat. A valley can be depressing if it is in sharp contrast to towering peaks surrounding it. I believe David somehow realized that death is a false threat and that life continues in the spirit world.

Before a personal example from my past completes this book, perhaps it's appropriate to again consider the title and subtitle of this book, *Mind, Body, and Spirit: Challengess of Science and Faith.* I trust that you have found this book worthwhile reading. Perhaps you came across some discussions that will encourage you to consider ways in which you might improve life, health, and wellbeing for you and for your loved ones.

## » Angel Unaware

One personal experience lingers in my mind from my early years as a skeptic. At that time I simply was so grateful that I didn't wonder about it. My mother had been hospitalized twice and eventually was unable to care for herself. I went home to see what could be done. Hopelessly mired in doubt and worry, I heard a knock on her apartment door. There stood a huge middle-aged woman with a suitcase in her hand. She said simply, "I'm here to care for your mother." Awestruck, I must have welcomed her.

For the next year or so, this woman took over all responsibilities for Mama. She slept on a futon, cashed Mama's Social Security checks, paid the rent and utility bills, and shopped, cleaned and cooked for my mother. She had a rather gruff way about her but never seemed to need anything from Betty and me. She refused to be paid.

Mama was taken to the hospital a year later and we were told she would need care in a nursing home. So I rushed home to close the apartment, move her furniture, and make necessary arrangements. The woman had disappeared without saying anything to anyone. To this day, no one knows who she was, where she came from, or where she went. I now believe she was an angel.

I recently recalled a prayer I learned as a small child at the First Baptist Church in Farmville, Virginia. I'll use it as a close to this book, along with my very best wishes to you in your search for true meaning in your life.

Now I lay me down to sleep.
I pray the Lord my soul to keep.
If I should die before I wake,
I pray the Lord my soul to take.

# BIBLIOGRAPHY

Ahlberg, Per, et al. 2010. "Scientists Discover Oldest Footprints on Earth." CNN online. http://www.cnn.com/2010/WORLD/europe/01/07/tetrapods.poland.evolution.discovery/index.html?eref=igoogle_cnn.

Albrecht, Karl. *Practical Intelligence: The Art and Science of Common Sense.* Hoboken, NJ: Pfeiffer, 2009.

American Academy of Family Physicians. 2009. "Mind-Body Connection: How Your Emotions Can Affect Your Health." http://familydoctor.org/online/famdocen/home/healthy/mental/782.html.

American Bar Association. "The Power of Intention in Mediation and Peacemaking." *Dispute Resolution Magazine.* Fall 2007.

*American Heritage College Dictionary*, Fourth Edition. New York, NY: Houghton Mifflin, 2007.

Amina. 2004. "Islam and the Concept of Martyrdom." Mideast Web Opinion Forum. http://www.mideastweb.org/islam_martyrdom.htm.

Amir, On. "Tough Choices: How Making Decisions Tires Your Brain." *Scientific American*, July 22, 2009. www.scientificamerican.com/article.cfm?id=tough-choices-how-making.

Antinoro, Linda. 2009. "Defending Against Disease With an Anti-Inflammation Lifestyle." *Aetna Intelihealth.* http://www. intelihealth.com/IH/ihtIH/EMIHC267/35320/35327/412005. html?d=dmtHMSContent.

Ariely, Dan. *Predictably Irrational: The Hidden Forces That Shape Our Decisions.* New York, NY: HarperCollins, 2008.

———. 2009. "Predictably Irrational." http://www. predictablyirrational.com/.

Atwater, P. M. H. 2006. "Indigo Children: About the movie 'Indigo'." http://www.experiencefestival.com/a/Indigo_Children/ id/222816.

AWARE Study. 2009. http://www.mindbodysymposium.com/Human-Consciousness-Project/the-AWARE-study.html.

Barnum, Barbara Stevens. *Spirituality in Nursing: From Traditional to New Age.* New York, NY: Springer, 2003.

Barret, Feldman, P. M. Niedenthal, and P. Winlielman, Eds. *Emotion and Consciousness.* New York, NY: Guilford Press, 2005.

Baumeister, Roy and Aaron Beck. *Evil: Inside Human Violence and Cruelty.* New York, NY: Barnes and Noble Books, 2001.

Begley, Sharon. 2009. "The 'Voodoo' Science of Brain Imaging." *Newsweek* Lab Notes. blog.newsweek.com/blogs/labnotes/ archive/2009/01/09/the-voodoo-science- of-brain-imaging.aspx.

———. 2009. "Born to Be Big: Early Exposure to Common Chemicals May Be Programming Kids to be Fat." http://www.newsweek. com/id/215179.

———. "It's in Our Genes. So What? DNA Takes You Only So Far." *Newsweek.* December 7, 2009.

Benor, Daniel J. *Consciousness, Bioenergy, and Healing: Self-Healing and Energy Medicine for the 21st Century.* Medford, NJ: Wholistic Healing Publications, 2004.

Benson, Herbert and Miriam Klipper. *The Relaxation Response.* New York, NY: HarperPaperbacks, 2000.

Berg, Yahuda. *God Does Not Create Miracles: You Do!* Los Angeles, CA: Kabbalah Publishing, 2005.

Berk, Lee and Stanley Tan. 2009. "Laughter Remains Good Medicine." Science News. Science Daily. http://www.sciencedaily.com/releases/2009/04/090417084115.htm.

"Biological magnets in the human brain-could magnetite mediate health effects of electromagnetic fields?" 1992. Power Engineering Review 12:8, 13-14. http://ieeexplore.ieee.org/Xplore/login.jsp?url=http%3A%2F%2Fieeexplore.ieee.org%2Fiel1%2F39%2F3953%2F00149651.pdf%3Fisnumber%3D3953%26prod%3DJNL%26arnumber%3D149651%26arSt%3D13%26ared%3D14%26arAuthor%3D&authDecision=-203.

Blackmore, Susan. 2002. "The Grand Illusion: Why consciousness exists only when you look for it." http://www.susanblackmore.co.uk/journalism/ns02.htm.

Bloom , Howard. *The Lucifer Principle*. Boston, MA: Atlantic Monthly Press, 1997.

Bos, Rogier. 2002. "The Meaning of Transcendence in the Postmodern World." Open Source Theology. http://www.opensourcetheology.net/node/158.

Bowman, Carol. *Return from Heaven: Beloved Relatives Reincarnated Within Your Family*. New York, NY: HarperTorch, 2003.

Boyle, Patricia. 2009. "Have a Purpose in Life? You Might Live Longer." Health.com. http://news.health.com/2009/06/16/have-purpose-life-you-might-live-longer/

"Boys and Temperament." 2009. http://www.cyberparent.com/boys/boys-temperament.htm.

Brach, Tara. *Radical Acceptance: Embracing Your Life With the Heart of a Buddha*. New York, NY: Bantam, 2004.

Braden, Gregg. 2009. "The Phantom DNA Effect." World of Perspective. YouTube. http://world-of-perspective.blogspot.com/2009/08/perspective-dna-phantom-effect.html.

Brafman, Ori and Rom. *Sway: The Irresistible Pull of Irrational Behavior*. New York: Broadway Business, 2009.

Brauser, Deborah. 2010. "GAD Patients Less Able to Regulate Response to Negative Emotions." Medscape Medical News, *Medscape Family Medicine*. http://www.medscape.com/viewarticle/717028?src=rss.

Brians, Paul. 2000. "The Enlightenment." http://wsu.edu/~brians/ hum_303/enlightenment.html.

Briggs, John. *Fractals: The Patterns of Chaos: Discovering a New Aesthetic of Art, Science, and Nature.* New York, NY: Simon & Schuster, 1992.

Bringle, Mary Louise. 1996. "I Just Can't Stop Thinking About It: Depression, Rumination, and Forgiveness." *Word & World* 16/3. http://www.luthersem.edu/word&world/Archives/16-3_ Forgiveness/16-3_Bringle.pdf.

Brody, Harold and Daralyn Brody. *The Placebo Response: How You Can Release the Body's Inner Pharmacy for Better Health.* New York, NY: Harper Perennial, 2001.

Browne, Sylvia and Lindsay Harrison. *Psychic Children: Revealing the Intuitive Gifts and Hidden Abilities of Boys and Girls.* New York, NY: NAL Trade, (2008).

Buchachenko, A. L., D. A. Kuznetsov, and V. L. Berdinsky. 2006. "New mechanisms of biological effects of electromagnetic fields." *Biophysics* 51:3, 489-496. http://www.springerlink.com/content/ lhm8451754608w66/.

Buffington et al. 2009. "Developmental Influences on Medically Unexplained Symptoms." *Psychotherapy and Psychosomatics*, 2009; 78 (3): 139. http://www.sciencedaily.com/ releases/2009/06/090616080139.htm.

Burns, Littany. *The Sixth Sense of Children: Nurturing Your Child's Intuitive Abilities.* New York, NY: NAL Trade, 2004.

Burt, Cyril. *The Gifted Child.* New York, NY: Wiley, 1975.

Cacioppo, John, Louis Tassinary, and Gary Berntson. *Handbook of Psychophysiology.* West Nyack, NY: Cambridge University Press, 2007.

Cadge, Wendy. 2009. "The Healing Power of Prayer." Science Daily. http://www.sciencedaily.com/releases/2009/06/090617154401. htm.

Cameron, Julia. *The Artist's Way*: New York, NY: Tarcher, 2002.

Canadian Press. 2010. "Specialized Social Networking Site Aims to Connect Teens Living with Cancer." *Aetna InteliHealth.* http://www.intelihealth.com/IH/ihtIH/EMIHC267/333/8895/1355961. html?d=dmtICNNews.

Capo, Danielle. 2004. "The Fractal Nature of the Architectural Orders." *Nexus Network Journal* 6:1.

Carey, Benedict. 2009. "When the Imp in Your Brain Gets Out." *New York Times.* http://www.nytimes.com/2009/07/07/health/07mind. html?_r=1&emc=eta1.

———. 2009. "Some Protect the Ego by Working on Their Excuses Early." *New York Times.* http://www.nytimes.com/2009/01/06/ health/06mind.html.

———. 2009. "Studying Young Minds and How to Teach Them." *New York Times.* http://www.nytimes.com/2009/12/21/health/ research/21brain.html?pagewanted=1&_r=1&emc=eta1.

Carter, Chris. 2009. "Does Consciousness Depend on the Brain?" www. parapsychologyandtheskeptics.com/Does-consciousness.pdf.

Chafee, John. *The Thinker's Way: Eight Steps to a Richer Life: Think Critically, Live Creatively, and Choose Freely.* Boston, MA: Bay Back Books, 2000.

Chamberlain, Linda. "Crisis and Transcendence: When the Worst That Can Happen Becomes the Path to Growth." http://www. slideworld.com/slideshows.aspx/Crisis-and-Transcendence-When-the-Worst-that-can-H-206330.

Chen, Pauline. 2010. "Discovering Teenagers' 'Risky Game' Too Late." *New York Times* online Health. http://www.nytimes. com/2010/02/25/health/25chen.html?em.

Chess, Stella and Alexander Thomas. 2009. "Boys and Temperament". http://www.cyberparent.com/boys/boys-temperament.htm.

Childre, Doc and Deborah Rozman. *Transforming Stress: The Heartmath Solution for Relieving Worry, Fatigue, and Tension.* Oakland CA: New Harbinger Publications, 2005.

Childre, Doc, Deborah Rozman, and Doc Lew Childre. *Transforming Anxiety: The Heartmath Solution to Overcoming Fear and Worry and Creating Serenity.* Oakland CA: New Harbinger Publications, 2006.

Childre, Doc, Deborah Rozman, and Frank Lewis. *Transforming Depression: The Heartmath Solution to Feeling Overwhelmed, Sad, and Stressed.* Oakland CA: New Harbinger Publications, 2007.

Chopra, Deepak. *Life After Death: The Burden of Proof.* New York, NY: Crown, 2006.

Cleveland Clinic. http://my.clevelandclinic.org/services/energy_ healing/hic_energy_healing.aspx.

Cline, Austin. 2009. "Religion vs. Spirituality: Distinguishing Between Religion and Spirituality." http://atheism.about.com/od/ religionnonreligion/a/spirituality_2.htm.

Cloud, John. "Why Your Memory May Not Be So Bad After All: New Data on How Internalizing Stereotypes Affects Boomers." *Time*, June 1, 2009.

Cohen, Andrew. 2002. Quote of the Week. *EnlightenmentNext.*

Combs-Ramirez, Gia. 2007. "Emotions as Energetic Messengers." The Science of Energy Healing. http://scienceofenergyhealing.com/ emotions-as-energetic-messengers/.

Connective Tissue Overview. www.geocities.com/kamz_intro_to_ phys/63.pdf.

Connective Tissue Study Guide. http://www.siumed.edu/~dking2/ intro/ct.htm.

Conner, Janet. *Writing Down Your Soul: How to Activate and Listen to the Extraordinary Voice Within.* San Francisco, CA: Conari Press, 2009.

Cousins, Norman. *Anatomy of An Illness as Perceived By the Patient: Reflections on Healing and Regeneration.* New York, NY: W. W. Norton, 1979.

Cornell, B. A., et al. *Nature* 387, 580-583 (5 June 1997) | doi:10.1038/42432; Received 14 November 1996; Accepted 14 April 1997.

Crawford, Glenda. *Brain-Based Teaching and Adolescent Learning in Mind.* Thousand Oaks, CA: Corwin Press, 2007.

Dale, Cyndi. *The Subtle Energy Body: An Encyclopedia of Your Energetic Anatomy.* Louisville, CO: Sounds True, Inc, 2009.

Danna, Theresa. "Pre-Birth Communication: The Link of Love." Global Oneness. http://www.experiencefestival.com/a/Pre-BirthCommunication/id/21857.

Davis, David, et al. 1989. "Violence of Old Men vs. the Idealism of Youth." online *New York Times.* http://www.nytimes.com/1989/06/07/opinion/l-violence-of-old-men-vs-the-idealism-of-youth-029889.html?pagewanted=1.

Dawkins, Richard. *The God Delusion.* Boston, MA: Houghton Mifflin, 2008.

Denton, Michael. *Evolution: A Theory in Crisis.* Chevy Chase, MD: Adler & Adler, 1996.

Desaulniers, Mary. 2008. "Schumann Resonance: Healing through Alpha Brain Waves, Meditation and Dolphin Contact." http://alternativespirituality.suite101.com/article.cfm/healing_properties_of_the_schumann_resonance.

Dilenschneider, Geoffrey. *Between Two Junes is a Forest.* Beverly Hills, CA: New Millennium, 2003.

"DNA Evolution versus Creation: Find Out More." Evolution-vs-creation.net. www.evolution-vs-creation.net/dna-evolution.html.

Dossey, Larry. 2004. "The Unsolved Mystery of Healing: Distant Healing, Healing Mediated By Nonlocal Mind." Shift #05: The Science of Fields. http://www.shiftinaction.com/node/112.

Eagleton, Terry. *Reason, Faith, and Revolution.* New Haven, CT: Yale University Press, 2009.

Ehrman, Bart. *God's Problem: How the Bible Fails to Answer Our Most Important Question—Why We Suffer.* New York, NY: HarperOne, 2008.

Electromagnetic Effects and Functional Water. http://www. aquatechnology.net/electromag.html.

Emoto, Masaro. *The Hidden Messages in Water*. New York, NY: Atria, 2005.

Engdahl, Sylvia. *Stewards of the Flame* .Seattle, WA: Book Surge, 2007.

———. 2007. "The Mind's Influence on Health." Toward Tomorrow. towardtomorrow.blogspot.com/2007/09/minds-influence-on-health.html.

Epstein, Richard. *Workbook for Critical Thinking*. Belmont, CA: Wadsworth, 1999.

"Exploring Fractals and Chaos." 2008. http://cybermax.tripod.com/ Exploring.html.

"Extraordinary Cats: Homing Instincts." *Nature*. www.pbs.org/wnet/ nature/episodes/extraordinary-cats/homing-instinct/2170/.

Feynman, Richard. *The Meaning of It All: Thoughts of a Citizen-Scientist*. New York, NY: Basic, 1998.

Fin, Al. 2009. "Pin-Point Precision: Nano-Cell Biology."

http://alfin2100.blogspot.com/2009/05/pin-point-precision-nano-cell-biology.html.

Fish, Stanley. 2009. "God Talk." *New York Times*. fish.blogs.nytimes. com/2009/05/03/god-talk/.

Fisher, Sophia. 2008. "Dionysius's Brutal Sense of Entitlement: Plato's Contribution to Criminogenic Needs." *Psychology, Crime, and Law*.

Flagg, Marianne. 2009. "Anxiety: Using Positive Thinking." *Health*. http://www.health.com/health/library/topic/0,,uf9897_uf9899,00.html.

Flannery, Michael. *Alfred Russel Wallace's Theory of Intelligent Evolution: How Wallace's World of Life Challenged Darwinism*. United Kingdom: Erasmus Press, 2009.

Forman, Vicki. *This Lovely Life.*. Wilmington, MA: Mariner Books, 2009.

Fowler, James, and Nicholas Christakis. "Dynamic Spread of Happiness in a Large Social Network: Lognitudinal Analysis Over Twenty Years in the

Framingham Heart Study." *British Medical Journal* 2008:337:a2338. www.bmj.com/cgi/content/full/337/dec04_2/a2338.

Fox News. 2007. "Report: Man With Almost No Brain Has Led Normal Life." www.foxnews.com/story/0,2933,290610,00.html.

Gardner, Howard. *Frames of Mind: The Theory of Multiple Intelligences.* New York, NY: Basic Books, 1993.

Gibbs, Nancy. "The Age of Arrogance." *Time.* November 9, 2009.

Gigerenzer, Gerd. *Gut Feelings: The Intelligence of the Unconscious.* Old Saybrook, CT: Tantor Media, 2007.

Gitt, Werner. *In the Beginning Was Information: A Scientist Explains the Incredible Design in Nature.* Green Forest, AR: Master Books, 2006.

Gladwell, Malcolm. *Blink: The Power of Thinking Without Thinking.* New York, NY: Little, Brown and Company, 2005.

Global College of Natural Medicine. http://www.gcnm.com/.

Glynn, Patrick. *God the Evidence: The Reconciliation of Faith and Reason in a Postsecular World.* New York, NY: Three Rivers Press, 1999.

Goldberg, Burton. *Alternative Medicine: The Definitive Guide.* New York, NY: Ten Speed Press, 2002.

Goldberg, Elkhonon. *The Executive Brain: Frontal Lobes and the Civilized Mind.* Oxford, UK: Oxford University Press, 2009.

"Golden Oldie Gene: It Trebles Your Chances of Living to 100 and Cuts the Risk of Alzheimer's by 70%." 2010. *Aetna InteliHealth Health News.* http://www.intelihealth.com/IH/ihtIH/ EMIHC270/333/20774/1355647.html?d=dmtICNNews.

Gowin, Joshua. 2009. "Rethinking the Bad Seed: Are Psychopaths Born or Made?" *Psychology Today.*

Greene, Brian. *The Elegant Universe: Superstrings, Hidden Dimensions, and the Quest for the Ultimate Theory.* New York, NY: W. W. Norton and Company, 1999.

Greyson, Bruce. 2003. "Incidence and correlates of near-death experiences in a cardiac care unit." *General Hospital Psychiatry* 25:269-276.

Grierson, Bruce. 2009. "Weathering the Storm." *Psychology Today* 42:3.

Grossman, Lisa. 2010. "Earth's Magnetic Field Is 3.5 Billion Years Old." Wired Science. http://www.wired.com/wiredscience/2010/03/earths-magnetic-field-is-35-billion-years-old/?utm_source=feedburner&utm_medium=feed&utm_campaign=Feed%3A+wired%2Findex+%28Wired%3A+Index+3+%28Top+Stories+2%29%29&utm_content=Google+Feedfetcher.

Gunaratana, Bhante Henepoia. *Mindfulness in Plain English*. Somerville, MA: Wisdom Publications, 2002.

Hagerty, Barbara. 2009. "Can Positive Thoughts Help Heal Another Person?" NPR www.npr.org/templates/story/story.php?storyId=104351710.

———. Fingerprints of God: The Search for the Science of Spirituality. New York, NY: Riverhead Books, 2009.

Haidt, Jonathan. *Happiness Hypothesis: Finding Modern Truth in Ancient Wisdom*. Jackson, TN: Basic Books, 2006.

Hallett, Elizabeth. *In the Newborn Year: Our Changing Awareness After Childbirth*. Summertown, TN: Book Publishing Company, 1992.

———. *Soul Trek: Meeting Our Children on the Way to Birth*. Hamilton, MT: Light Hearts Publishing, 1995.

———. 2009. "The Mystery of Pre-Birth Communication." www.thelaboroflove.com/forum/elisabeth/prebirth.html.

Halperin, C., et al. 2004. "Piezoelectric Effect in Human Bones Studied in Nanometer Scale." *Nano Letters* 4 (7) 1253–1256. http://pubs.acs.org/doi/abs/10.1021/nl049453i.

Hameroff, Stuart. 1997. "Consciousness, Microtubules and The Quantum World." *Alternative Therapies* 3(3):70-79. www.quantumconsciousness.org/interviews/alternative.html.

Harrell, Eben. "Higgs Boson: A Ghost in the Machine." *Time* online: April 9, 2008. http://www.time.com/time/health/article/0,8599,1729139,00.html.

Harrington, Anne. *The Cure Within: The History of Mind-Body Medicine.* New York, NY: W. W. Norton and Company, 2008.

Harris, Thomas. *I'm OK; You're OK.* New York, NY: Avon, 1976.

Hart, Tobin. *The Secret Spiritual World of Children: The Breakthrough Discovery that Profoundly Alters Our Conventional View of Children's Mystical Experiences.* Novato, CA: New World Library, 2003.

Haruyama, Tetsuya, et al. 2005. "Bio-, nano-technology for cellular biosensing." *Current Applied Physics* 5 (2) 108-111. http://www.sciencedirect.com/science?_ob=ArticleURL&_udi=B6W7T-4CVX0XW-1&_user=10&_rdoc=1&_fmt=&_orig=search&_sort=d&_docanchor=&view=c&_searchStrId=993859405&_rerunOrigin=google&_acct=C000050221&_version=1&_urlVersion=0&_userid=10&md5=8ee633c958bf475480bd3e9807b1a290.

Hauser, Marc. *Moral Minds: How Nature Designed Our Universal Sense of Right and Wrong.* New York, NY: HarperCollins, 2006.

Havel, Vaclav. 1994. "The Need for Transcendence in the Postmodern World." http://www.worldtrans.org/whole/havelspeech.html.

HeartMath Institute. Boulder Creek, CO. http://www.heartmath.com/About-Us/Overview.html.

HeartMath Institute. 2004. "A Brief Look At Coherence." Boulder Creek, CO. http://www.heartrelease.com/coherence-1.html.

HeartMath Store. 2009. http://www.HeartMathStore.com/?mtcSRCID=1690.

Henig, Robin. 2009. "Understanding the Anxious Mind." *New York Times* online: September 29.

Henry, Laura. 2009 "The Fourth Chakra: Anahata" suite101.com http://chakrayoga.suite101.com/article.cfm/the_fourth_chakra_anahata.

Hillman, James. *The Soul's Code: In Search of Character and Calling.* New York, NY: Random House, 1996.

Hinze, Sarah. *We Lived in Heaven: Spiritual Accounts of Souls Coming to Earth*. Provo, UT: Spring Creek Book Company, 2006.

Hitchens, Christopher. *God Is Not Great: How Religion Poisons Everything*. Boston, MA: Twelve, 2009.

Hodge, David. 2007. "Does God Answer Prayer? Researcher Says 'Yes'." *Science Daily*. http://www.sciencedaily.com/releases/2007/03/070314195638.htm.

"Hubble peers back 13.2 billion years, finds 'primordial' galaxies." 2010. CNN Tech. http://www.cnn.com/2010/TECH/space/01/05/hubble.new.galaxies/index.html?eref=igoogle_cnn.

Hughes, Patrick Henry. *I AM Potential: Eight Lessons on Living, Loving, and Reaching Your Dreams*. Cambridge, MA: Da Capo Lifelong Books, 2008.

———. 2009. YouTube. http://www.youtube.com/watch?v=-qTiYA1WiY8.

Human Consciousness Project. http://www.mindbodysymposium.com/Human-Consciousness-Project/the-AWARE-study.html.

Hunt, Valerie V. *Infinite Mind: Science of the Human Vibrations of Consciousness*. Malibu, CA: Malibu Publishing, 2000.

Ibotrain, Christopher. 2009. "Does Magnetite Increase Your Psychic Ability?" http://www.associatedcontent.com/article/1634147/does_magnetite_increase_your_psychic.html?cat=58.

Impaired Consciousness Research Group. 2007. http://www.wbic.cam.ac.uk/~mrc30/index.html.

Inhen, Anne and Carolyn Flynn. *The Complete Idiot's Guide to Mindfulness*. New York, NY: Alpha, 2008.

Ironson, G., R. Stuetzle, and M. A. Fletcher. 2006. "An Increase in Religiousness/Spirituality Occurs After HIV Diagnosis and Predicts Slower Disease Progression Over Four Years in People with HIV." *Journal of General Internal Medicine*. 21: S62-68.

James, John. *The Great Field: Soul at Play in a Conscious Universe*. Fulton, CA: Elite Books, 2007.

Jana, Bhanu. *Methods in Nano Cell Biology*. Amsterdam, The Netherlands: Elsevier, 2008.

Janew, Claus. 2007. "How Consciousness Creates Reality." http://free-will.de/reality.pdf.

Jerman, Igor et al. 2005. "Electrical Transfer of Molecule Information into Water, Its Storage, and Bioeffects on Plants and Bacteria." *Electromagnetic Biology and Medicine* 24:3, 341-353.

Jones, Gwendolyn. *A Cry from the Womb—Healing the Heart of the World: A Guide to Healing and Helping Souls Return to the Light After Sudden Death, Miscarriage, Stillbirth, or Abortion.* New Braunfels, TX: Angels of Light and Healing, 2004.

Judson, Olivia. 2009. "Leopard Behind You." The Wild Side. *New York Times*: October 7.

Jung, Carl. *Archetypes and the Collective Unconscious.* 2nd Ed. Princeton, NY: Princeton University Press, 1981.

Kaloski, Bruce. 2009. "The Mind-Body Connection and Its Influence on Health." www.mlmv2.com/blog/mindbody-connection-and-its-influence-health.

Keim, Brandon. 2010. "Searching for Network Laws in Slime." Wired Science. http://www.wired.com/wiredscience/2010/02/slime-molds/.

Kelley, Thomas and Steven Stack. "Thought Recognition, Locus of Control, and Adolescent Wellbeing." *Adolescence*: Fall, 2000.

Kelly, Robin. *The Human Antenna: Reading the Language of the Universe in the Songs of our Cells.* Fulton, CA: Energy Psychology Press, 2010..

Kelly, Theresa. *Children and Psychics Abilities: How to Respond as a Concerned Parent.* Kindle Edition, Amazon Digital Services, 2008.

Kenyon, Dean. *Biochemical Predestination.* New York, NY: McGraw-Hill, 1969.

Khan, Zulfikar. 2009. "The X-Rated Paradise of Islam." Satyameva Jayate, Jai Maharaj, sponsor. http://www.flex.com/~jai/satyamevajayate/heaven.html.

King, Dana. *Faith, Spirituality, and Medicine: Towards the Making of a Healing Practitioner.* London, UK: Routledge, 2000.

King, Serge Kahili. 2001. "Territoriality." http://www.huna.org/html/territor.html.

Klotter, Jule. 2005."Exercise and Osteoporosis: Townsend Letter for Doctors and Patients." BNET, Health Care Industry. http://findarticles.com/p/articles/mi_m0ISW/is_261/ai_n13471772/.

Knight, Kevin. 2009. "Mystical Theology." New Advent. http://www.newadvent.org/cathen/14621a.htm.

Kreeft, Peter. *Angels and Demons*. San Francisco, CA: Ignatius Press,1995.

Kreitzman, Leon. "Let's Hear It for the Bees." *New York Times*. May 27, 2009.

Kubler-Ross, Elizabeth. *on LIFE after DEATH*. Berkeley, CA: Ten Speed Press, 2008.

Larsen, David. "Heavenly Ascents." 2008. http://www.heavenlyascents.com/2008/08/07/we-lived-in-heaven-sarah-hinze-on-pre-birth-experiences/.

Laszlo, Ervin, Stanislav Grof, and Peter Russell. *The Consciousness Revolution*. Las Vegas, NV: Elf Rock, 2003.

Laszlo, Ervin. *Science and the Akashic Field: An Integral Theory of Everything*. Rochester, VT: Inner Traditions, 2004.

Leininger, Andrea and Bruce and Ken Gross. *Soul Survivor: The Reincarnation of a World War II Fighter Pilot*. New York, NY: Grand Central Publishing, 2009.

Levi, Renee. 2003. "Group Magic: An Inquiry into Experiences of Collective Resonance." Collective Wisdom Initiative. http://www.collectivewisdominitiative.org/papers/levi_exec_summary.htm.

Lewis, C. S. *The Four Loves*. Orlando, FL: Harcourt, 1991.

Lipton, Bruce H. *The Biology of Belief: Unleashing the Power of Consciousness, Matter and Miracles*. Fulton, CA: Mountain of Love Productions, Inc. and Elite Books, 2005.

Long, Jeffrey. *Evidence of the Afterlife*. New York, NY: HarperOne, 2010.

Maslow, A. H. "Self-actualizing people: A study of psychological health." In Monstakes, C.E. *The Self: Explorations in Personal Growth*, pp. 160-194. New York: Harper & Row, 1956.

Mason, Angie. 2009. "Domestic violence: Male entitlement mentality a factor. Anger isn't the only driving force when it comes to abuse." *York Daily Record/Daily News*.http://www.ydr.com/ci_12174618.

Masonic World. 2009. "Freemasonry and the Doctrine of Reincarnation." http://www.masonicworld.com/education/files/ artaug04/masonry_and_the_doctrine_of_reincarnation.htm.

*Mathematical Modelling of Natural Phenomena*. http://www.mmnp-journal.org/.

May, Clifford. 2010. "The War Against the Infidels: Terrorism is Only One of the Weapons" *National Review* online. http://article. nationalreview.com/?q=Njk5MjYxZjNiNDc5YWQ0OWIzMzhj ODE2Mjc2MmJkMzQ=.

May, Paul. 1997. "Adenosine Triphosphate–ATP." http://www.bris. ac.uk/Depts/Chemistry/MOTM/atp/atp1.htm.

McCaig, C. D. and A. M. Rajnicek. 1991. "Electrical Fields, Nerve Growth, and Nerve Regeneration." http://ep.physoc.org/ content/76/4/473.full.pdf.

McCraty, Rollin, R. T. Bradley, and D. Tomasino. 2004. "The Resonant Heart." Shift Issue 05: The Science of Fields, The Body's Heart Field. http://www.shiftinaction.com/node/119.

McDavid, Glenn. 2002. "The Anthropic Cosmological Principle and Related Issues" http://home.comcast.net/~gmcdavid/html_dir/ anthropic.html.

McElroy, Molly. 2003. "Model Systems in Neuroethology: Magnetic information in animal orientation." http://nelson.beckman. illinois.edu/courses/neuroethol/models/magnetoreception/ magnetoreception.html.

McTaggart, Lynne. *The Field: The Quest for the Secret Force of the Universe*. New York, NY: HarperCollins, 2002.

———. *The Intention Experiment: Using Your Thoughts to Change Your Life and the World*. New York, NY: Free Press, 2007.

Meacham, Jon. 2009. "The End of Christian America." *Newsweek*, April 7, 2009. www.newsweek.com/id/192583.

Measurement problem. "Role of the Observer." University of Oregon. http://abyss.uoregon.edu/~js/cosmo/lectures/lec08.html.

*Merriam-Webster Online Dictionary*. 2009. http://www.merriam-webster.com/dictionary.

Meyer, Stephen. 1995. "Scientific Correctness in San Francisco." Access Research Network 15:2. http://www.arn.org/docs/orpages/or152/bio101.htm.

————. *Signature in the Cell: DNA and the Evidence for Intelligent Design*. New York, NY: Harper One, 2009.

Miller, Arthur. *The Social Psychology of Good and Evil*. New York, NY: Guilford Press, 2005.

Miller, Michael Craig. 2010. "The Angry Adolescent." *Aetna Intelihealth Healthy Lifestyle*.

"Mind-Body Medicine: An Overview." 2007. National Center for Complementary and Alternative Medicine. http://nccam.nih.gov/health/whatiscam/mind-body/mindbody.htm.

Mohler, Albert. 2005. "Moralistic Therapeutic Deism--the New American Religion." *The Christian Post*. http://www.christianpost.com/article/20050418/moralistic-therapeutic-deism-the-new-american-religion/index.html.

Moody, Raymond A. *Life After Life: The Investigation of a Phenomenon—Survival of Bodily Death*. London, England: Rider/Ebury Press, Second Edition, 2001.

Morse, Melvin. *Closer to the Light: Learning from the Near Death Experiences of Children*. New York, NY: Ivy Books, 1990.

————. *Where God Lives: The Science of the Paranormal and How Our Brains Are Linked to the Universe*. New York, NY: Cliff Street Books, 2000.

Murphy, Todd. 2007. "The God Helmet." http://www.shaktitechnology.com/god_helmet.htm.

Namka, Lynne. 1997. "You Owe Me! Children of Entitlement." http://www.angriesout.com/teach9.htm.

"Nano-sized voltmeter measures electric fields deep within cells." 2007. University of Michigan News Service. http://www.ns.umich.edu/htdocs/releases/story.php?id=6208.

National Academy of Sciences, Institute of Medicine. *Science, Evolution, and Creationism*. Washington, DC: National Academies Press, 2008.

National Council for Excellence in Critical Thinking Instruction. http://www.criticalthinking.org/aboutCT/definingCT.cfm.

National Institutes of Health National Center for Complementary and Alternative Medicine. http://nccam.nih.gov/.

Nelson, Bradley. *The Emotion Code: How to Release Your Trapped Emotions for Abundant Health, Love, and Happiness*. Mesquite, NV: Wellness Unmasked, 2007.

Nelson, Roxanne. 2010. "Near-Death Experiences: Evidence of Afterlife, Says Radiation Oncologist." *Medscape* Family Medicine. http://www.medscape.com/viewarticle/717604?src=mpnews&spon=34&uac=48293HY.

New Hampshire Natural Health Clinic http://www.nhnatural.com/services/neurotransmitterbalance.html.

"New nano device detects immune system cell signaling." 2008. Biology News Net.http://www.biologynews.net/archives/2008/09/03/new_nano_device_detects_immune_system_cell_signaling.html.

Newberg, Andrew and Mark Waldman. *Born to Believe: God, Science, and the Origin of Ordinary and Extraordinary Beliefs*. New York, NY: Free Press, 2006.

Newton, Michael. *Journey of Souls: Case Studies of Life Between Lives*. St. Paul, MN: Llewellyn, 1994.

———. *Destiny of Souls: New Case Studies of Life Between Lives*. St. Paul, MN: Llewellyn, 2000.

———. *Life Between Lives: Hypnotherapy for Spiritual Regression*. St. Paul, MN: Llewellyn, 2004.

———. *Memories of the Afterlife: Life Between Lives Stories of Personal Transformation*. St. Paul, MN: Llewellyn, 2009.

Nicosia, Gregory. 2002. "Thought Energy: the Basis of a Quantum Leap in Psychotherapy." Advanced Diagnostics. http://www.thoughtenergy.com/how-it-works.

Nikon. 2009. "Electro Physiology." http://www.nikoninstruments.com/Applications/Biological/Research/Electro-Physiology.

Oliver, Sam. 2007. "Caring About Others." Ezine Articles. ezinearticles.com/?Caring-About-Others&id=822785.

*O The Oprah Magazine.* "Who Are You Meant to Be?" November 2009.

Ortiz, Martee. 2007. "Breaking Down the Definition: Intelligent Design" ArbiterOnline.com. http://media.www.arbiteronline.com/media/storage/paper890/news/2007/04/02/News/Breaking.Down.The.Definition.Intelligent.Design-2816370.shtml.

Oschman, James. *Energy Medicine: The Scientific Basis of Bioenergy Therapies.* London, England: Churchill Livingstone, 2000.

Paller, Ken and Joel Voss. "Electrophysiological Signature of Unconscious Recognition Memory." *Nature Neuroscience.* http://www.nature.com/neuro/journal/v12/n3/abs/nn.2260.html.

Pan, Jingong, et al. 2007. "Low Resonance Frequency Storage and Transfer in Structured Water Cluster." Center for Bio-Signaling and System Research, New Jersey Institute of Technology. www.aqualiv.net/research-a-news-mainmenu-2/44-frequency

Paul. New Testament. First Corinthians 15: 35–54.

Peake, Anthony. *Is There Life After Death? The Extraordinary Science of What Happens After We Die.* Edison, NJ: Chartwell Books, 2006.

Pearce, Joseph Chilton. *The Biology of Transcendence: A Blueprint of the Human Spirit.* Rochester, VT: Park Street Press, 2002.

Pearsall, Paul. *The Heart's Code: Tapping the Wisdom and Power of Our Heart Energy.* New York, NY: Random House, 1998.

Penman, Danny. 2009. "Can We Really Transplant a Human Soul?" Mail Online. http://www.dailymail.co.uk/news/article-558271/Can-really-transplant-human-soul.html.

Pert, Candace. *Molecules of Emotion: The Science Behind Mind-Body Medicine.* New York, NY: Simon & Schuster, 1997.

Pert, Candace and Nancy Marriott. *Everything You Need to Know to Feel Go(o)d.* New York, NY: Hay House, 2006.

Peterson, James. *The Secret Life of Kids: An Exploration into Their Psychic Senses.* Bloomington, IN: iUniverse, 2000.

Pillow, William. *Grave Convictions.* Vallejo, CA: Gateway Publishers, 2004.

———. *Love and Immortality: Long Journey of My Heart.* Bloomington, IN: iUniverse, 2008.

———. *Meet Yourself Again for the First Time: Hidden Forces Shape Our Lives*, Bloomington, IN: iUniverse. 2009.

Piper, Don. *Ninety Minutes in Heaven.* Grand Rapids, MI: Revell, 2004.

———. *Heaven Is Real.* New York, NY: Berkley Praise, 2009.

Pischinger, Alfred. *The Extracellular Matrix and Ground Regulation: Basis for a Holistic Biological Medicine.* Berkeley, CA: North Atlantic Books, 2007.

Poponin, Vladimir and Peter Gariaev. 2002. "The DNA Phantom Effect." http://twm.co.nz/DNAPhantom.htm.

*Power Engineering Review.* 1992. "Biological magnets in the human brain—could magnetite mediate health effects of electromagnetic fields?" http://ieeexplore.ieee.org/xpl/tocresult.jsp?isnumber=3953.

Pratt, George and Peter Lambrou. *Instant Emotional Healing: Acupressure for the Emotions.* New York, NY: Broadway, 2006.

Pullen, Stuart. *Intelligent Design or Evolution? Why the Origin of Life and the Evolution of Molecular Knowledge Imply Design.* Raleigh, NC: Intelligent Design Books, 2005.

Radin, Dean. *Entangled Minds: Extrasensory Experiences in a Quantum Reality.* New York, NY: Pocket Books, 2006.

———. *The Conscious Universe.* NewYork, NY: HarperCollins, 2009.

Raichle, et al. 2000. "A Default Mode of Brain Function." Proceedings of the National Academy of Sciences.

Raichle, Marcus and Abraham Snyder. 2007. "A Default Mode of Brain Function: A Brief History of an Evolving Idea." *NeuroImage*.

Raman. *Power of the Mind: Experiencing, Harnessing, and Utilizing the Force Within*. Allentown, PA: Star Galaxy Publishing, 2006.

Rapee, Ronald. 1997. "Perceived Threat and Perceived Control as Predictors of the Degree of Fear in Physical and Social Situations." *Journal of Anxiety Disorders* 11:5, 455-461. http://www.sciencedirect. com/science?_ob=ArticleURL&_udi=B6VDK-3SX4M5D1&_ user=10&_rdoc=1&_fmt=&_orig=search&_sort=d&view=c&_ acct=C000050221&_version=1&_urlVersion=0&_userid=10&m d5=1ce4859eba997df497dd80129a2e462a.

Ravitch, Diane. *Left Back: A Century of Battles Over School Reform*. New York, NY: Simon & Schuster, 2001.

Reynolds, Caroline. *Spiritual Fitness—How To Live In Truth and Trust*. Camarillo, CA: DeVorss and Company, 2005.

———. 2006. "Eternal Youth and the Power of Idealism." http://www. carolinereynolds.com/files/Eternal%20Youth%20and%20The%20 Power%20Of%20Idealism%20PDF.pdf.

Ricke, Hans. 2008. "Brain Physiology, Cognition, and Consciousness Forum." Nature Network. http://network.nature.com/groups/ bpcc/forum/topics/1903.

Ring, Kenneth. *Life at Death: A Scientific Investigation of the Near Death Experience*. New York, NY: Coward, McCann, and Geohegan, 1980.

Ring, Kenneth and Sharon Cooper. *Mindsight: Near-Death and Out-of-Body Experiences in the Blind*. Bloomington, IN: iUniverse, 2008.

Robinson, Anthony B. 2007. "Articles of Faith: The Unfortunate Age of Entitlement in America." Seattlepi.com. http://seattlepi.nwsource. com/local/308772_faith24.html.

Rosanoff, Nancy. *Intuition Workout: A Practical Guide to Discovering and Developing Your Inner Knowing*. Fairfield, CT: Asian Publishing, 1991.

Rosen, Eliot Jay. *Experiencing the Soul: Before Birth, During Life, After Death.* New Delhi, India: Motilal Banarsidass, 2005.

Rosenblum, Bruce and Fred Kuttner. *Quantum Enigma: Physics Encounters Consciousness.* New York, NY: Oxford University Press USA, 2008.

Russell, Peter. 2009. "Reality and Consciousness: Turning the Superparadigm Inside Out." http://twm.co.nz/prussell.htm.

Russ's Web. "Egocentricity or Sociocentricity." http://home.earthlink. net/~bmgei/educate/docs/aperson/thinking/egocentr.htm.

Sabom, Michael. *Recollections of Death: A Medical Investigation.* New York, NY: Harper and Row, 1982.

Salerno, Steve. "Self-Help Doesn't Help—And Often Hurts." *Wall Street Journal* online October 23, 2009.

Salvato, Frank. 2004. "The First Shot in the War on Political Correctness." About.com. http://christianmusic.about.com/gi/o.htm?zi=1/XJ&z Ti=1&sdn=christianmusic&cdn=entertainment&tm=266&f=20 &su=p504.3.336.ip_&tt=2&bt=0&bts=0&zu=http%3A//www. enterstageright.com/archive/articles/1204/1204firstshot.htm.

Sanders, Laura. 2010. "Slime Mold Grows Network Just Like Tokyo Rail System." *Wired Science.* http://www.wired.com/ wiredscience/2010/01/slime-mold-grows-network-just-like-tokyo-rail-system/.

Schwartz, Barry. *The Paradox of Choice: Why More is Less.* New York, NY: Harper Perennial, 2005.

Schwartz, Robert. *Courageous Souls: Do We Plan Our Life Challenges Before Birth?* Ashland, OR: Whispering Winds Press, 2006.

Science Centric. 2009. "That Gut Feeling May Actually Reflect a Reliable Memory." http://www.sciencecentric.com/news/article. php?q=09020911-that-gut-feeling-may-actually-reflect-reliable-memory.

Scott, Elizabeth. 2009. "Eustress." About.com: Stress Management. http://stress.about.com/od/stressmanagementglossary/g/Eustress. htm.

Scribd. 2009. "Intuitive Moments: Insights for the Millenia." http://www.scribd.com/doc/16598722/Intuitive-Moments-Insight-for-the-Millennia.

Segerstrom S. C., L. J. Schipper, and R. N. Greenberg. 2008. "Caregiving, repetitive thought, and immune response to vaccination in older adults." *Behavior, Brain and Immunology.* 22(5):744-52.

"Seven Principles of Spirituality in the Workplace." 2009. http://www.itstime.com/rainbow.htm.

Shaw, Mark. *10 Great Ideas from Church History: A Decision-Maker's Guide to Shaping Your Church.* Downer's Grove, IL: InterVarsity Press, 1997.

Sheldrake, Rupert. *The Sense of Being Stared At and Other Unexplained Powers of the Human Mind.* New York, NY: Three Rivers Press, 2004.

Shmerling, Robert. 2009. ""How Much of Our Brain Do We *Really* Use?" *Aetna InteliHealth.* http://www.intelihealth.com/IH/ihtIH/EMIHC267/9273/35323/536360.html?d=dmtHMSContent.

Siegel, Daniel. *The Developing Mind: Toward a Neurobiology of Interpersonal Experience.* New York, NY: Guilford Press, 1999.

————. *The Developing Mind: How Relationships and the Brain Interact to Shape Who We Are.* New York, NY: Guilford Press, 1999.

————. *The Mindful Brain: Reflection and Attunement in the Cultivation of Well-Being.* New York, NY: W. W. Norton & Company, 2007.

Sirotin, Yevgeniv and Anirudda Das. 2009. "Another shock for brain imaging research: the signal isn't always linked to neuronal activity." *British Psychological Society Research Digest.* http://bps-research-digest.blogspot.com/2009/01/another-shock-for-brain-imaging.html.

Smallwood, Beverly. "The Dangers of a Sense of Entitlement." http://www.hodu.com/entitlement.shtml.

Smith, Christian. 2005. "Moralistic Therapeutic Deism—the New American Religion." *Christian Post.*

————. 2009. "Is God Dead (Again)?" *Newsweek,* April 7, 2009. chriscarrollsmith.blogspot.com/2009/04/is-god-dead-again.html.

Smith, Kenneth. *Awakening the Energy Body: From Shamanism to Bioenergetics*. Rochester, VT: Bear & Company, 2008.

Sorensen, Karen. *love (luv) n*. Avon, MA: Adams Media, 2009.

*Stanford Encyclopedia of Philosophy*. 2009. "Ancient Theories of Soul." http://plato.stanford.edu/entries/ancient-soul/.

Stein, Dan. *Cognitive Science and the Unconscious*. Arlington, VA: American Psychiatric Publishing, 1997.

Stepanek, Jeni. *Messenger: The Legacy of Mattie. J. T. Stepanek and Heartsongs*. Boston, MA: Dutton Adult, 2009.

———. "Jeni Stepanek on Mattie Stepanek's Legacy." ABC *Good Morning America*. http://abcnews.go.com/GMA/Books/jeni-stepanek-mattie-stepanek-book-excerpt-messenger-legacy/story?id=8960089.

Stepanek, Mattie. MattieOnline.com. http://www.mattieonline.com/about.htm.

Storm, Howard. *My Descent Into Death: A Second Chance at Life*. New York, NY: Doubleday, 2005.

Stover, Lillian, Bernard Guerney, and Mary O'Connell. "Measurements of Acceptance, Allowing Self-Direction, Involvement, and Empathy in Adult-Child Interaction." *The Journal of Psychology* 77: 262-269. 1971.

Strauch, Barbara. 2009. "How to Train the Aging Brain." *New York Times*. http://www.nytimes.com/2010/01/03/education/edlife/03adult.html?emc=tnt&tntemail1=y.

Strobel, Lee. *The Case for a Creator: A Journalist Investigates Scientific Evidence that Points Toward God*. Grand Rapids, MI: Zondervan, 2005.

Strohman, R.C. 1993. "Ancient genes, wise bodies, unhealthy people: Limits of genetic thinking in biology and medicine". *Perspectives in Biology and Medicine*, 37 (I) 112-144.

Sugawara, Jun and Takashi Tarumi. 2009. "Laughter Can Boost Heart Health." *U.S. News and World Report*. http://health.usnews.com/articles/health/healthday/2009/05/29/laughter-can-boost-heart-health.html.

"Suicide." 2009. Muttaqun Online. http://muttaqun.com/suicide. html.

Suszynski, Marie and Pat Bass. 2010. "One Woman Asks ... What is Love?" Care Pages. http://cms.carepages.com/CarePages/en/ ArticlesTips/FeatureArticles/Contributors/what-is-love.html.

Sylvia, Claire and William Novak. *A Change of Heart: A Memoir.* Boston, MA: Little, Brown and Company, 1997.

Talbot, Michael. 2009. "Spirituality and Science: The Holographic Universe." http://www.experiencefestival.com/a/Holographic_ Universe/id/5864.

Tappe, Nancy Ann. *Understanding Your Life Through Color.* www.lulu. com: Lulu, 2009.

Tarkan, Laurie. "For Parents on NICU, Trauma May Last." *New York Times* Health. August 24, 2009.

Taylor, Jill Bolte. *My Stroke of Insight.* New York, NY: Viking Penguin, 2008.

Taylor, Lucy. 2009. "Can Love Survive Without the Little White Lies?" http://www.dailymail.co.uk/femail/article-1219725/Can-love-survive-little-white-lies.html.

Terrafina. www.insnet.org/ins_press.rxml?id=3244&photo=. TheWhyFiles. 2008. "Small is Beautiful: Nanotech Meets Biology." http://whyfiles.org/287nano/index.php?g=3.txtThewhyfiles.

"The Two Pathways of Fear" (advanced). 2009. Canadian Institutes of Health Research. http://thebrain.mcgill.ca/flash/a/a_04/a_04_ cr/a_04_cr_peu/a_04_cr_peu.html.

Tiller, William. 2006. "Exploring the Effects of Human Intention and Thought Energy." http://www.gem-systems.com/research/tiller. html.

"Theology: Toward A Hidden God." *Time* , April 1966. http://www. time.com/time/magazine/article/0,9171,835309,00.html.

Tolle, Eckhart. *A New Earth: Awakening to Your Life's Purpose.* New York, NY: Penguin, 2008.

Tucker, Jim B. *Life Before Life.* New York, NY: St. Martin's Press, 2005.

*USA Today*. 2010. "'Life's Purpose' Eckhart Tolle is Serene, Critics Less So." http://www.usatoday.com/news/religion/2010-04-15-tolle15_CV_N.htm.

Vajda, Peter. 2008. "Why Being Authentic Is So Difficult." http://www.spiritheart.net/media/Why_Being_Authentic_is_Difficult.pdf.

Valea, Earnest. 2009. "The Problem of Evil in World Religions." http://www.comparativereligion.com/evil.html#10.

Van Lommel, Pim. 2007. "About the Continuity of Our Consciousness." International Association for Near-Death Studies. http://www.iands.org/research/important_studies/dr._pim_van_lommel_m.d._continuity_of_consciousness.html.

Van Praagh, James. *Ghosts Among Us: Uncovering the Truth About the Other Side*. New York, NY: HarperColkins, 2008.

Van Wagner, Kendra. 2010. "What is Cognitive Psychology?" http://psychology.about.com/od/cognitivepsychology/f/cogpsych.htm.

Vul, Edward, et al. 2009. "Voodoo Correlations in Social Neuroscience." http://neurocritic.blogspot.com/2009/01/voodoo-correlations-in-social.html.

Wade, Nicholas. 2005. "Your Body is Younger Than You Think." *New York Times*. http://www.nytimes.com/2005/08/02/science/02cell.html.

Wadhwa, Pathik, et al. *Science Daily*, March 10, 1999. http://www.sciencedaily.com/releases/1999/03/990310053349.htm.

Waldman, Mark. *Why We Believe What We Believe: Uncovering Our Biological Need for Meaning, Spirituality*. Burlington, VT: Free Press, 2006.

———. *Born to Believe: God, Science and The Origin of Ordinary and Extraordinary Beliefs*. Burlington, VT: Free Press, 2007.

Warren, Rick. *The Purpose Driven Life: What on Earth Am I Here For?* Grand Rapids, MI: Zondervan, 2007.

"Water's Memory." http://www.aquatechnology.net/watermemory.html.

Webber, Rebecca. 2009. "The Wholesome Guide to Misbehaving." *Psychology Today* 42:5.

Wegner, Daniel. *The Illusion of Conscious Will.* Cambridge, MA: MIT Press, 2003.

Weiler, Nicholas and Stephen Schoonover. *Your Soul at Work: Five Steps to a More Fulfilling Career and Life.* Hidden Springs, OR: HiddenSpring Publishing, 2001.

Weiss, Brian. *Many Lives, Many Masters: The Story of a Prominent Psychiatrist, His Young Patient, and the Past-Life Therapy That Changed Both Their Lives.* New York, NY: Fireside Books, 1988.

————. *Through Time Into Healing.* New York, NY: Simon & Schuster, 1992.

————. *Messages From the Masters: Tapping Into the Power of Love.* New York, NY: Warner Books, 2000.

————. *Same Soul, Many Bodies: Discover the Healing Power of Future Lives Through Progression Therapy.* New York, NY: Free Press, 2004.

Wellsphere. 2009. "The Reality of the Brain-Computer Interface." http://stanford.wellsphere.com/brain-health-article/the-many-facets-of-addiction/656686.

Westphal, Sylvia. 2009. "High Hopes for a New Kind of Gene." *Smithsonian* 40 (4).

"What Kids Remember About Pre-Existence—LDS Mormom Forums." 2009. LDS Net. http://www.lds.net/forums/lds-gospel-discussion/13605-what-kids-remember-about-pre-existence.html#post245053.

Whitton, Joel and Joe Fisher. *Life Between Life: Scientific Explorations into the Void Separating One Incarnation from the Next.* New York, NY: Warner Books, 1986.

"Who and What is Daemon or Daimon?" Hermetic-Esoteric-Mystical Philosophies. http://www.plotinus.com/the_daemon_copy(1).htm.

Williams, Patricia. 2005. "The Evolution of Good and Evil." The Fourth R 18:1. Adapted from her book *Doing Without Adam and Eve: Sociobiology and Original Sin.* Minneapolis, MN: Fortress, 2001.

Wilson, Gary and Marnia Robinson. 2006. "Love and Fear." *Entelechy*: Mind and Culture. http://www.entelechyjournal.com/robinsonwilson.htm.

Woolger, Roger. 2002. "Past Life Therapy, Trauma Release, and the Body." http://www.rogerwoolger.com/pastlife.html.

Wyatt, Joseph. 1999. "Is Temperament Inherited?" *Behavioral Analysis Digest* 11:1. http://www.behavior.org/journals_BAD/V11n1/digest_V11n1_temperament.cfm.

Wylie, Mary. 2004. "Mindsight: Dan Siegel Offers Therapists a New Vision of the Brain." http://surrenderworks.com/library/imports/mindsight.html.

Wysong, Pippa and Natalia Sloam. 2010. "The Pursuit of Bodily Perfection: An Expert Interview With Susie Orbach." *Medscape* Family Medicine. http://www.medscape.com/viewarticle/715387.

Yapko, Michael. "Secondhand Blues." *Psychology Today*. October 2009.

Yevgeniy B. Sirotin and Das Aniruddha. 2009. "Anticipatory haemodynamic signals in sensory cortex not predicted by local neuronal activity." *Nature*, 457, 475-479. http://www.nature.com/nature/journal/v457/n7228/abs/nature07664.html.

Zimberoff, Diane and David Hartman. 2000. "The Ego in Heart-Centered Therapies: Ego Strengthening and Ego Surrender." *Journal of Heart-Centered Therapies*. Autumn. http://findarticles.com/p/articles/mi_m0FGV/is_2_3/ai_74221521/.

Zimmer, Carl. 2009. "Brain Trust." *Discover*.

# INDEX

Pratt, George, 131
prayer, 80–81, 127
    *See also* intercessory prayer
pre-birth communications,
    204–205
*Predictably Irrational* (Ariely),
    5–6
premature birth stress, 60
private time, 43–44
"Problem of Evil in World
    Religions, The" (Valea),
    66
procedural memory, 4, 240
prostate specific antigen (PSA)
    levels, 53
*Psychic Children* (Browne and
    Harrison), 109
Pullen, Stuart, 17
purpose, 30–32
*Purpose Driven Life, The*
    (Warren), 31

# Q
quantum mechanics, 99, 101,
    148–149
quantity, 5
*Quantum Enigma* (Rosenblum
    and Kuttner), 99
Quindlen, Anna, 207

# R
*Radical Acceptance* (Brach),
    176–177
Radin, Dean, 99, 175
Raman, 25

Rapee, Ronald, 8
rationalism, 167
Ravitch, Diane, 37
*Reading and the Brain* (Dehaene),
    5
reality, 99–100, 166
"Reality and Consciousness"
    (Russell), 100
*Reason, Faith, and Revolution*
    (Eagleton), 78–79
reincarnation, 55–61, 179–182,
    195–197
*Relaxation Response, The*
    (Benson), 23
religion
    doubts and, 73–81, 161–162
    fear of death and, 165–166
    transcendence and, 167–168
"Religion *vs.* Spirituality"
    (Cline), 75
religious intolerance, 76–77
"Rethinking the Bad Seed"
    (Gowin), 70
*Return from Heaven* (Bowman),
    55
Reynolds, Caroline, 246–248
Ricke, Hans, 90
Ring, Kenneth, 162, 186
Robinson, Anthony, 63–64
Robinson, Marnia, 14–15
role models, 115, 124, 243
Rosanoff, Nancy, 241
Rosen, Eliot Jay, 205
Rosenblum, Bruce, 99
rumination, 51–52
Russell, Peter, 100, 200